Praise for *Flights Across America*

There's a lot to be learned by visiting more than 1,300 breweries, and Geier communicates that in a thoughtful, approachable way. His expertise is more than just great recon on cities across America, though -- it's also how to make the most of your brewerygoing experience, no matter where you might be.

>-Chris Drosner, Executive Editor of Milwaukee Magazine and Beer Baron columnist for the Wisconsin State Journal

Joel is America's number one "collector" of breweries, and this book is his way of sharing his mind-boggling, beer-soaked adventures with beer lovers. If you've ever considered a beercation, a brewery crawl, or are looking for some prompts for talking to your local beertender, this book is for you.

>-Anne Fitten Glenn, Author of *Asheville Beer: An Intoxicating History of Mountain Brewing* and *Western North Carolina Beer: A Mountain Brew History*

Not only is this book a great travel adventure of drinking at breweries across all 50 states, but the book lets the reader plan their own adventure— a "beercation." The host of the popular Brewery Travels podcast has written something truly unique; it belongs on your bookshelf as well as in your backpack. Read, enjoy, explore!

>-Paul Kan, Author of *Hawai'i Beer: A History of Brewing in Paradise* and Editor-at-Large of The Beer Thrillers blog

Flights Across America weaves together stories of Joel's extensive travel with his vast knowledge of the nation's breweries. Not only is this book a valuable resource for anyone curious about beer tourism, it's also an inspiration for people who want to experience this great country of ours through i

>-Chris O'Leary, Editor (3,500 breweries

Flights Across America

A BREWERY LOVER'S JOURNEY

Joel Geier

atmosphere press

CONTENTS

INTRODUCTION: WHY BREWERIES?

Because I like beer: that is the obvious and simple answer, right? It's also probably why you picked up this book. While it is true that I like beer, that doesn't make for a very compelling start. So, I'll do my best to provide the reasons behind what caused my interest in craft beer to vault into an obsession that led to me visiting nearly fourteen hundred breweries across all fifty states.

Many people are inspired by their parents, and while it was certainly not the only lesson I gleaned from them, an appreciation for craft beer was something I learned early on in life. Not from my mother, mind you; she doesn't like beer whatsoever (just like my wife, more on that later). But my father had a small beer fridge that he kept stocked, and growing up in rural Wisconsin and rural Iowa in the 1990s and 2000s, it would be easy to assume it was Miller Lite, Busch Light, or some other major macro-option filling it up. Instead, his two go-tos were **Leinenkugel**'s *Creamy Dark Lager* and **Sierra Nevada**'s famous *Pale Ale*. He had the mantra that if he was going to drink a beer, he wanted to enjoy how it tasted.

I still remember the first time he let me try that **Sierra Nevada** *Pale Ale*, and I did not enjoy how it tasted. While I can't remember my exact age, it was in late elementary school, and I thought it was disgusting. Unlike many kids growing up, I did not partake in underage drinking while in high school. So, it wasn't until I got to college that I started to try out some different forms of alcohol to find out what I liked. Maybe it was because that first memory was poor, but beer was not something I dove into until around the time I turned twenty-one.

Once I could buy alcohol, my buddies and I would go to the local Hy-Vee grocery store most weekends to pick up some "necessities." While they would typically pick up a handle of rum or a case of whatever beer was on sale, I would troop over to the craft beer section just like my father. This would have been in 2013 or 2014 in rural Iowa, so while there were several options at that point, it certainly was nothing like what you can find today. But I would make the most of it, often getting a "Pick Six" to try a plethora of beers (that were stored warm and often well past their best buy date, which I had no understanding of) or just a variety pack from a larger brewery such as **Samuel Adams** or **Boulevard**.

Either way, I tried hundreds of beers during my junior and senior years of college. From having an early appreciation for wheat beers to being appalled by **Stone Brewing**'s *Arrogant Bastard*, I still think fondly of that discovery phase of my beer journey. That particular phase would continue after graduation when my new wife Rosa and I moved to Eugene, Oregon. The primary goal was to attend graduate school there, but their craft beer scene was miles ahead of what I had personally experienced at that point. Growler Guys was a place I often found myself, and thanks to my new neighbor Patrick, I was introduced to many new breweries, beers, and even styles. It was here I tried my first sour ale (*Cucumber Crush* from **10 Barrel**) and fell in love, and it was where I also learned about the styles more in-depth, thanks to the employees. I also attended my first-ever beer festival in Bend and visited most of the breweries in the Eugene area at the time.

But these were still "Pre-Brewery Travels" days. After a year of living in Oregon, we moved to Milwaukee, Wisconsin, to be closer to family and because UW-Milwaukee is one of the few schools in the country that offered both my master's program and my wife's doctoral program. Not long after we arrived in the Badger State, I realized that I had been to a nice handful of breweries (a couple dozen at that point) and decided I should start to keep track of them. What was initially a document quickly became a spreadsheet.

Growing up, I had always enjoyed collecting things. Whether it was football cards, seashells, or a book series, I was infatuated with accumulating all I could from whatever I was interested in. I think that is part of what spurred me forward initially, as I felt like I was "collecting" breweries, in a way. Each visit became a new addition to my collection, and I loved getting to add another spot to my spreadsheet after each new stop. Soon, stickers and coasters would become a more "traditional" token I would accumulate.

And then in March of 2017, I started my Twitter account, @brewerytravels. It wasn't something I did with any goals in mind, but I felt it would be a fun way to track the breweries I visited and maybe share my experiences with a few people. It wasn't long after that when I realized I needed a better way to remember the details of my visits, particularly on days I went to multiple breweries. So, at my fifty-sixth brewery, **R'Noggin Brewing** in Kenosha, WI, I first brought my trusty notepad portfolio. I've replaced the paper inside repeatedly and have taken hand-written notes at every brewery since then. From the beers I sample to the taproom and history, I try to capture a small picture of the brewery so that I can share it with those who are curious enough to follow along.

That notebook, and why I needed it, is a big part of the answer to the question, "Why breweries?" Each brewery I visit offers a unique experience, and I want to remember them all. The tap rooms are different, the people associated with them are different, the backstories are different, and, of course, so is the beer—and not just "Oh, this place specializes in sours" or "This one is known for its flagship IPA." If you go to three breweries and order a pale ale, it is going to taste different at each one, even if the differences are subtle at times.

Also, around this time, my wife was working as a nurse and ended up having a couple of co-workers who were travel nurses. For those unfamiliar, they get temporary contracts to work in understaffed hospitals or other facilities in need. Intrigued by this, Rosa brought up the possibility of pursuing a similar career. We were both in the midst of our respective school programs but decided it was our chance to see parts of the country we were not familiar with—and, in my case, visit a bunch of breweries.

Over the next year, she would take jobs in Portsmouth, New Hampshire; Nashville, Tennessee; and San Diego, California. A massive benefit to this lifestyle is that you live somewhere for multiple months, so you can explore the entire region around where you're temporarily living. We loved visiting different cities, national parks, and, of course, breweries during this time bouncing around the country. This was also when my "Brewery Travels" account gained momentum, as people liked getting snapshots into breweries and beer scenes around the country. In 2018, I would also start my Instagram account to provide a different outlet to display my visits.

We would move back home in 2018 to welcome our daughter to the world and complete our degrees. Fast forward to 2021, and our son was born, but we still had that travel itch. While it may have been a brash and somewhat crazy decision, we decided to jump back in and go back out on the road, this time with a toddler and newborn. I was a stay-at-home dad, and my wife would take travel nurse jobs in Baltimore, Maryland and Asheville, North Carolina, before getting a remote position as a psychiatric nurse practitioner. This gave us even more freedom, and we would live in Seattle, Washington; Denver, Colorado; New Orleans, Louisiana; Ormond Beach, Florida; and Newark, New Jersey, during that stretch. Overall, we lived the travel life with our children for over two more full years and loved every second of it. In total, my wife and I lived in fourteen states across four time zones before our ninth anniversary.

This is the part where I need to talk about my incredible wife. As I briefly mentioned, she doesn't like beer. To put it bluntly, she hates it. Hates the taste, hates the smell, and simply has no desire to partake in it. But she has always been supportive of this hobby (or obsession?) of mine. During the first time around traveling, we would often stop at breweries, and she would either read a book in the car or come in to sit with me. It did bum me out that I wasn't able to share my love of beer with her. But as we traveled around with two young children, it became a lifesaver that she was more content to stay back taking care of them in the afternoon or evening while I popped out to visit breweries. We would even stop at breweries in the middle of a road trip and troop inside with our kids for lunch. I truly mean it when I say Brewery Travels wouldn't exist without her.

During this second travel stint, I worked on growing my new website by writing articles and also starting a podcast. Simply called "Brewery Travels," I previously had the desire to do something along these lines but wanted to be on the road when I started it, so when that opportunity came, I went for it. The premise was to discuss the beer scenes in different cities and areas around the country and invite two local experts to provide more in-depth details than I could on my own. Part travel guide, part history lesson, part open conversation around beer, I loved sharing this information with listeners.

So, in summary, I grew an insatiable curiosity for craft breweries and an equally fierce passion for sharing what I experienced. My hope was not only to give people the opportunity to get acquainted with breweries they were unfamiliar with but to inspire them to explore craft beer on their own. I would even finish each episode of my podcast with the same quote: "Whether it's where you're visiting or where you're living, be sure to drink local everywhere." This has become true, as no matter where you are there are going to be local breweries pumping out amazing beers, and like fingerprints, all of these breweries are unique.

As for a different question, "Why a book?" I wanted to take on a new project as we were planning to return home in a more permanent manner. Sure, I will still visit new places and new breweries whenever I can, but now that my children are reaching school age, those opportunities will not be the same as they once were. Being able to record my experiences in a book such as this became a way for me to put a bow on this crazy chapter in my life. I do want to clarify that this book is not a comprehensive view of every city's beer scene. Rather, it is about my personal experiences traveling and appreciating the breweries I was able to visit.

My hope is that this book will inspire other people to either continue their own beer journey or to start one up. While the details about the overall beer scenes in different cities and factoids about individual breweries will hopefully help promote curiosity, I also wanted to include other information that could be useful.

Broken into four sections, this next chapter will flow through the process of planning and executing a "Beercation." Here, I'll outline the steps you should take, the tools available for your use, what factors to consider, and much more. Additionally, once I arrive at a brewery, there are certain things I look for and features I notice. I'll walk you through what those are and how you can identify the things that are most important to you. I'll give you some questions that you can ask during your visit, whether you're chatting with a bartender or getting to talk with the owner. After getting through that background information, we will then jump into the City Breakdowns, where I will discuss the craft beer scenes in just about every city and region around the country. Information on the breweries, beers, taprooms, neighborhoods, and more will be featured. Finally, I will include lists of some of my favorite experiences, and pictures from my travels.

But enough preparation, let's dive in!

Visiting Breweries: What I Learned

As I just stated, we will begin with some background information, both on the craft beer sector and my own experiences exploring it. First, I'll explain why you should even plan a trip centered around beer. Or, at the least, plan a vacation with breweries as a component.

BEER TOURISM: WHY YOU SHOULD PARTICIPATE

There are many concrete reasons why supporting local beer is a fabulous idea.

Let's start with some statistics. Which I realize is not the most exciting thing for some people, but I am fascinated by seeing trends and how beer has grown around the country. We can start by looking at some of the data that the Brewers Association has published over the years. This is to showcase the growth and impact the industry has nationwide. As I'm writing this, the most current statistics are from 2022. Let's take a look at a few numbers:

In total, the craft brewing industry contributed $72.2 billion to the US economy in 2022. The study also notes the industry provided approximately 460,000 jobs, with 190,000 of them being directly at breweries and brewpubs. Below are the five states with the highest economic output:

- California ($8.8 billion)

- Pennsylvania ($5.1 billion)

- Texas ($4.6 billion)

- Florida ($4.1 billion)

- New York (3.9 billion)

Meanwhile, the five states with the highest output per capita:

- Vermont ($768.31)
- Maine ($581.46)
- Montana ($574.79)
- Wisconsin ($574.79)
- Oregon ($559.54)

Now, we can compare those statistics with the numbers from a decade prior, in 2012. The overall economic impact then was $33.9 billion, which means that during the following decade, it increased by $38.3 billion, or 113 percent. In terms of jobs, the industry was sitting at 360,000, with 108,440 directly at breweries and brewpubs. The numbers for individual states are similar in showcasing growth. First, the overall impact:

- California ($4.7 billion)
- Texas ($2.3 billion)
- New York ($2.2 billion)
- Pennsylvania ($2.0 billion)
- Colorado (1.6 billion)

Followed again by the impact per capita:

- Oregon ($448.56)
- Colorado ($436.50)
- Vermont ($418.57)
- Maine ($324.36)
- Montana ($315.37)

Most of those states should not surprise anyone, as they have been at the forefront of the craft beer movement. But what intrigues me is the growth in states that, for a long time, did not have much of a craft beer scene to speak of. Just look below at some of these examples of comparing the number of breweries in 2012 vs 2022:

- South Carolina: 16→134

- Kentucky: 14→90

- Georgia: 22→171

- Mississippi: 3→20

- New Jersey: 25→152

And yes, every state has seen a large growth (California went from 319 breweries to 957 during that time). But I wanted to highlight the fact that even states that most people don't associate with craft beer now have breweries popping up all over the place! That's a big reason why I wanted to write this book: to spotlight cities and towns that don't get your average tourist's attention.

So, why did I include this in the section about why you should participate in beer tourism? While the figures above are a macro look at craft brewing and provide a birds-eye view, you need to think about how these numbers also represent local growth. Each new opening is another community or neighborhood that can see a brewery's impact. I have seen so many breweries pop up in small, rural towns that, a decade or two ago, would have never dreamed of having their own brewery. Or in a larger city, they open up in a neighborhood that normally does not see much action. Oftentimes, those breweries are not only providing jobs and helping stimulate the local economy, but are also renovating an old building. Sometimes, they may be breathing new life into a downtown that needs more foot traffic. I know that I personally have stopped in many small towns all across the country or checked out a neighborhood that I would not have visited if not for a local brewery opening.

In this same vein, the University of New Hampshire worked on a project in 2018 to find the ways that craft breweries benefited the community. Aside from the pure economic numbers and job growth, they reported several findings:

- Breweries provide a place for connection and social interaction

- Many utilize locally sourced ingredients

- Locals and visitors mix together

- They draw people into areas they may not otherwise visit

- Many craft breweries give back to the community

Another example is when I talked with Mark Lyon of **Maquoketa Brewing** in Maquoketa, Iowa (pop. 6,000). He told me that one reason he decided to open a brewery on the main drag downtown was that he read an article that listed things that thriving downtowns have, and on that list was "Have a craft brewery." They opened in 2021, resurrecting a dilapidated building (they showed me pictures from before the renovation work) that originally opened in 1919 as a department store. They are now a staple in the community and host a variety of events along with brewing up local beer.

Going back to the list from the University of New Hampshire, there are two points I want to pause on. First, the local ingredients. Breweries can often provide a window into a region. They may do this with names and decor, but my favorite is when ingredients are involved. For example, several breweries I visited in Montana featured a beer with elderberries, something the state is known for. Or it could be centered around a regional food item, such as the *King Cake Ale* from **Mudbug Brewery** in Thibodaux, Louisiana, which is brewed with ingredients found in the famous dessert associated with

Mardi Gras. Many use ingredients that are grown locally, such as **New Glarus** using Wisconsin-grown wheat and cherries in its *Belgian Red* or **Reuben's Brewing** in Seattle being one of the many Washington breweries to use local fresh hops in their IPAs. In those cases, you are supporting multiple local businesses by drinking the beer!

The other point I want to hone in on is craft breweries often give back to the community. When you visit one, you are supporting the town or neighborhood in more ways than one. Many implement a program similar to **Gathering Place Brewing**'s "$1 for Milwaukee." Each month, they work with a different nonprofit to raise awareness and support by donating a portion of their Thursday sales. There are also breweries, like **Lady Justice Brewing** in Aurora, Colorado, that focus on specific causes. **Lady Justice** is woman and LGBTQ-owned, and their profits go to a variety of nonprofits and community partners that benefit women and girls in the state of Colorado. There have also been beers that have been brewed for specific causes where the recipe was made public, and breweries all over the country could brew it and donate the proceeds. Examples of that include **Sierra Nevada**'s *Resilience IPA*, **Weather Souls Brewing**'s *Black is Beautiful*, **Bow and Arrow Brewing**'s *Native Land*, and **Eagle Park Brewing**'s *Things We Don't Say*.

If you are reading this book, you probably did not need to be convinced to visit breweries. But in the off chance that you were not sure, hopefully you now have an understanding of what supporting a local craft brewery can mean. On top of all of that, IT IS FUN! Especially if you can put together a "Beercation." Speaking of that....

PLANNING A "BEERCATION"

Below you will find some advice I have in regards to planning a trip that includes breweries. As you will find out, this process can be as lowkey or in-depth as you want to make it!

WHERE ARE YOU GOING?

This is a simple enough question, as first you have to decide where you are going. The next question plays into this, but when you are fully planning a trip centered around beer, you have the freedom to sort through different options. That decision can be based on several factors, but hopefully, information later on in this book can help!

WHY ARE YOU GOING?

If you are planning a trip fully around beer, this question matters less. But a "Beercation" can also be a trip that includes beer, even if it doesn't fully revolve around it. Is it a work trip? Are you visiting family? Are you going on an extended road trip? Any of these examples will influence your opportunities to visit breweries. Most of the time when I am traveling, it is not specifically for beer, so being efficient with my time and making a plan is key.

HOW LONG ARE YOU GOING?

Maybe you are going to be spending multiple weeks somewhere and will have ample opportunities to visit different parts of the city. But in many cases, a trip will be shorter, so being aware of how long you have (and what days of the week you'll be there) will factor into how many breweries you can plan to visit. In some cases, breweries are only open certain days of the week, so on an abbreviated trip, having a schedule of sorts will be helpful.

WHERE ARE YOU STAYING?

Sometimes, you have full control and can find a hotel or Airbnb smack in the middle of a fantastic brewery neighborhood. But if you are traveling for work or visiting family, you usually relinquish this ability. That can possibly alter the breweries that are within striking distance during your trip. Knowing where you will be ahead of time is necessary, especially if you are in a large metro area where travel may (or may not) come easily. Cross-referencing your location with where breweries (or clusters of breweries) are is a fairly straightforward process, but one that is needed to narrow down where you want to go.

ARE THERE ANY BREWERIES ALREADY ON YOUR RADAR THAT YOU WANT TO VISIT?

Are you going somewhere that is home to a nationally-known brewery that you have had on your bucket list, such as **Sierra Nevada** or **Dogfish Head**? Maybe there's a smaller brewery with loads of hype that came across your radar like **Side Project** or **Great Notion**. Or it could be something more random. Example: my dad wanted to visit **Lazarus Brewing** in Austin, Texas because the owner was previously a pastor, which is his profession. Whatever the case is, knowing what breweries you absolutely want to visit is one way to sketch out an itinerary. It may mean you are more likely to stick around a certain neighborhood or at least a side of the city, which would narrow down your list of possible targets.

ARE THERE CERTAIN STYLES YOU USUALLY WANT TO DRINK?

Do you typically stick to drinking IPAs? Maybe barrel-aged stouts are your thing. Easy-drinking lagers could be your calling card. Or maybe you are like me, and you want to just try a variety of styles. But if there are certain styles you prefer (and maybe, more importantly, don't prefer), that is something to take into account. For instance, if you are someone who is not fond of sour ales, going to a brewery that specializes in them would not be a good fit. On the flip side, if IPAs are your favorite, you will want to know which breweries in the area excel at them. Looking at online tap lists and simply asking around can help you figure out where you want to go in this regard.

HOW FLEXIBLE OR PLANNED OUT DO YOU WANT TO BE?

Are you determined to hit as many breweries as you can, or would you prefer to just go with the flow and absorb each stop at your own pace? This can be an important factor, especially if you are not traveling alone. Some people prefer to just have a general idea of what they want to do and see where the day or night takes them. Others (like me) want to have a more detailed itinerary in mind, making sure they hit specific places. If you are alone, you can go to either extreme, of course, but if you are going with someone else or a group, it's probably best to prepare for a bit of both.

ARE YOU WANTING TO DO TOURS OF ANY KIND?

Tours at a brewery can be part of this, as you may need to plan ahead and expect to arrive at a brewery at a specific time. But this can also refer to a tour via a bus, bike, or other mode of transportation to visit multiple breweries. These types of tours can be nice as they take care of the transportation factor for you and can also be informational. You will most likely learn more during these tours than you might going alone. The downside is that you may not be able to select the exact breweries you will visit, and the tours only run at certain times. You also are following someone else's schedule, not your own.

THINGS TO PAY ATTENTION TO WHILE PLANNING
<u>Hours:</u> This has happened to me a few times! You plan to visit a brewery and forget to double-check their hours or maybe glance at Friday's closing time instead of Thursday's. The doors are locked shut on your arrival, and you leave disappointed. Make sure you look at a brewery's hours on the days you will be visiting. This is especially true if you are visiting multiple breweries, as their hours may dictate the order you visit them.

<u>Events:</u> Showing up to an unexpected event can mean a couple of things. If it's something smaller like Trivia Night or live music it probably will have a minimal effect on your experience (you may even want to join in). But if you go to a brewery and it's their anniversary, you may be greeted by crowds, lines, etc. Occasionally, a brewery will host a major event or even festival, in which case tickets must be purchased (perhaps in advance), and the experience will be completely different than a normal brewery visit. The best way to avoid this is to glance at social media and the brewery's website. But in general, you are not going to stumble upon an event that will preclude you from visiting.

<u>Location/Parking:</u> I already talked about location in relation to where you are staying and what breweries you want to visit, but in this case, location refers to something else. Depending on where you are going, parking could be at a premium. If you are visiting a brewery that is in or close to the downtown of a major city, there's an increased chance that the brewery is not going to have its own parking lot. This is a situation where taking an Uber or using public transportation can be helpful,

but if you are driving (or riding while someone else drives), it can be helpful to check what the parking options are in the area ahead of time so there are no surprises.

<u>Tap Lists</u>: There are breweries that will typically have many of the same beers on tap, with a handful of seasonals or new releases available. But some breweries have a very fluid tap list, where the turnover is weekly, and they are constantly cranking out something new. If you are planning to visit a brewery regardless of their offering, it may not mean anything to you. But if you are deciding between a couple of breweries, taking a peek at what they currently are offering could make the decision easier.

<u>Food</u>: If you are planning on being out for an extended period of time, you may want to know which breweries offer food. Even if they don't have their own kitchen, it isn't uncommon for breweries to host food trucks or at least have some kind of simple bar snacks.

<u>Kid/Dog Friendly</u>: This can be viewed as important no matter who you are. For some people, it doesn't matter either way. But if you are traveling with children or a dog and want them to be included, knowing ahead of time which breweries will allow them in is important. Some breweries even have kid areas or special dog spaces, too. On the flip side, there are people who don't want to be around either when they are visiting a taproom. So, at least being aware of a brewery's rules is a smart idea.

TOOLS TO USE
<u>Google Maps</u>: This is the most basic tool, as typing "Breweries near ______" will give you a list of available options and map them out. The pros of Google are that you can quickly view a brewery's hours, plug in directions, and have a direct link to

their website. You can also sort them by rating or hours they are open, and as with looking up anything on Google, you can read reviews, find a phone number, or sort through other links. But you also have to move the map around, and not every option will pop up in a given area unless you zoom in.

<u>Craftbeer.com's Brewery Map</u>: While the mapping function of Craftbeer.com does function somewhat similarly to Google, it does something Google does not. The map vividly marks all breweries (and only the breweries) in the country, so zooming in on a city immediately shows you where they are located throughout a city or region. It's easier to see where the denser brewery areas are, and you don't have to worry about other places popping up like you would on Google. However, you must hover over or click on the circles to see what brewery it represents. There are also links to the website and directions in most cases. I've found that the website stays fairly up-to-date but may lag behind Google slightly in that regard and doesn't necessarily have every single location.

<u>Untappd</u>: I have an Untappd account but I don't use it to record or rate the beers. My qualms with that system can be shared another time, but it can be one of the tools you use. If you are unaware, anyone can rate a beer on the app, and those ratings are compiled, giving individual beers and breweries a score between one and five. Generally speaking, anything above a 4.0 is considered "good" and the average score falls somewhere around 3.7. You can look up the highest-rated beers or breweries in a specific area, but it is important to take those ratings with a grain of salt. Certain styles (such as trendy sours, bold IPAs, and barrel-aged stouts) tend to score better than others (well-made lagers and brown ales need more love, in my opinion). But it can be one way to get a look at some of the more popular places in the area you are visiting. Untappd also sometimes will have a brewery's live tap list available too.

Social Media: I usually post about an upcoming trip I will be taking and am open to anyone providing suggestions. Sometimes I ask someone directly if I know they live in the area or have spent time there, but often, recommendations can come from any number of people! Don't feel like you get enough responses on social media? Shoot me a message, and if I can't supply recommendations, chances are I know someone who can.

Brewery Websites: I mentioned websites earlier, but it is a tool that you should check out. This will, of course, be where you can find the most information about the brewery (at least in theory). Aside from essentials like address, hours, tap list, etc, you'll be able to see if they offer food, possibly learn the background of the brewery, and become more aware of what they offer.

VISITING A BREWERY

Once you're at a brewery, what should you be doing, and what should you be looking out for? Below, you will find a few ideas to keep in mind.

TRY TO KEEP EXPECTATIONS IN CHECK.
Easier said than done, right? If you are visiting a place like **Sierra Nevada** or **Allagash**, you probably have a general idea of what to expect (at least in terms of beer). But one thing I try to do is stay somewhat level with what I'm hoping to experience at a brewery. It's basically impossible to do this entirely, as I have, in most every case, done my research or received a recommendation that I am following. But it's always more fun to walk away from a brewery impressed and surprised than to leave underwhelmed, which has certainly happened to me during my travels.

This does seem contradictory to most of what I write in this book, where I stress doing your research ahead of time. But what I want people to consider is to avoid being too influenced by rankings or scores that you read on different sites. It's good to understand and be aware of them, but it's also okay if you go to a brewery and don't enjoy it as much as other people, or on the flip side, you love a beer that you had either not heard of or read negative things about. My main point: we all have different palates, likes and dislikes, and are drawn to different experiences. Don't let what other people say about a brewery completely warp your own opinion.

TAKE INTO ACCOUNT WHEN YOU ARE VISITING.
This is something that has a major impact on your experience. Visiting a brewery on an early Tuesday afternoon is going to be vastly different than if you stop in on Saturday night. The most obvious factor in this is how busy the taproom will be. While it won't be true 100 percent of the time, a weekend will usually draw in more crowds than a weekday. This can vary if certain events, such as a trivia night or live music, cause an influx of guests, but it's generally a decent assumption to make.

Which do I prefer? Selfishly, I prefer to be there when it is slower. While it is better for the brewery to have more patrons and many people also prefer a lively atmosphere, I do have a reason for this preference. In the next section, I include "Questions to Ask" on a brewery visit. As you can imagine, if a brewery is packed to the gills, you probably won't have the opportunity to ask a bartender (or anyone else) about too much aside from information on a beer or two.

Most of my brewery visits have been one-offs. Once I have visited them during my travels, I probably will not be back. That means they have one shot to make an impression on me, and the day of the week and time of day I visit can have an effect. Unless it's a brewery in the area you live or a place you frequently visit, that will likely be the case for you as well. I'm not saying to plan every visit for the same general time for the sake of comparison, but it's at least something to be aware of when you think back on what "grade" you would give them.

HOW BIG IS THE BREWERY YOU ARE VISITING?
In the next section, I will discuss one of the questions I like to ask: "What size system do you use?" But in this instance, I am also talking about the complete size of the facility you are visiting. A vast majority of breweries you visit will probably not have a massive footprint. Whether it is in a business park

or strip mall, many breweries make do with a space that does not exactly lend itself to expansion. On the other end of the spectrum, you may be visiting one of the national goliaths, such as **Stone Brewing World Bistro & Gardens** in Escondido, California, or **Boulevard Brewing**'s multi-level location in Kansas City, Missouri.

But what I am mostly talking about here is when it may be less obvious. An example is **Pecatonica Brewing** in Warren, Illinois. Walking up to their location right along the main drag downtown, it seems to be a typical small-town brewery. But walking in, you realize it is a bit more than that. Not only did it take over one former storefront, but it transformed THREE! They are now all attached by open doorways, so it still feels like you are winding through three separate spaces instead of one open area. There are also multiple levels to the building, and they turned one of the upper ones into an event space. I would not have known about the third building being part of the taproom or the upper level unless I struck up a conversation with the bartender. Which is a reminder of why it is always a sharp idea to chat with the people working at the brewery.

WHAT ARE THE DIFFERENT POUR OPTIONS?

As the book title suggests, I enjoy getting a flight, which usually consists of several four- or five-ounce pours. When I'm visiting a brewery, it is usually the one opportunity I will have to try their beer. So, getting to sample a variety of what they offer is the general approach I like to take. The flip side of that is some people prefer to only drink a beer in a pint, or at minimum, a half pour. There is certainly an argument that it is not easy to fully grasp what a beer is if you are only drinking out of a small four-ounce glass like the ones you often get on a flight. This is especially true for certain styles (such as an imperial stout) that can change significantly as it warms.

Often, you will have several options to choose from. Below, you will see the most common choices you will encounter:

- Flights (Pre-set): Some breweries have specific beers they include in a flight. Often, it's still possible to choose your own, but it is more expensive. Usually, a pre-set flight will include flagships or other beers they are best known for. While I do not often go with this option, this can be an acceptable choice if you want to get a feel for what the brewery believes are their most representative beers.

- Flights (Choose Your Own): This is what I have done at almost all of the breweries I have visited. Generally speaking, you will select four beers, although occasionally, you will see flight boards that can hold five, six, eight, twelve, or even more beers. In the next section, I'll discuss some of the questions I ask when filling out my flight board, but my general rule of thumb is to get a variety of styles; if it is a typical brewery, that means getting something light, something dark, something hoppy, and a wild card. But it's important to note what styles a brewery is best known for. If they primarily brew hazy IPAs or focus on barrel-aged stouts, that is something to keep in mind.

- Individual Small Pours: Some breweries don't offer traditional flights, but you can still buy four- or five-ounce pours individually. So, it gives you the freedom to try a couple of beers or go crazy and order them all. I do want to briefly discuss some of the downsides to small pours/flights. While you are getting a taste, you are often not getting a "full" experience of the beer. Flight glasses rarely lend themselves to showing off an aroma as well as a larger pour, and for many beers (especially dark beers), you often will not experience any changes as it slightly warms up. It is harder to get those changes if you only have four ounces after all. In terms of service, it does take a bartender longer to put together a flight of small pours than either of the next two sizes. Also, if you are looking at pricing, the small pours are going to cost the most per ounce.

- Full Pours: This is the most traditional and popular way to consume a beer. Plopping down at the bar and ordering a pint containing sixteen ounces has long been the go-to method for most people, and it makes sense. It is the best "bang for your buck," and you get to fully experience the beer you choose. It has become more common for breweries to even use "proper glassware," depending on the beer style, to help accentuate aromas and flavors. The only downside to this size of pour is that it limits the number of beers you can try. If you want to taste several different imperial stouts or double IPAs on tap, getting full pours of each one is going to be a challenge! When I'm visiting breweries around Milwaukee, this is the size I typically order. I should also note that occasionally beers will be offered in slightly smaller "full" pours. For example, a higher ABV stout may be served in ten or twelve-ounce pours instead of the full sixteen.

- Half Pours: I saved this one for last because it splits the difference between the two above it. It lets you experience the beer more than you would with an individual small pour while not setting you back as much in terms of alcohol consumption. Sometimes, the brewery will even use the same "proper glassware" as they use for the full pours. You can try a couple more options than if you only did full pours, but probably not as many as you would be doing with a flight or two. Pricing also varies from brewery to brewery. At some places, it will simply be half the cost of the full pour, which, of course, is ideal. But many will charge a little extra ($7 for a full but $4 for a half, for example).

HOW KNOWLEDGEABLE DOES THE STAFF SEEM?

I want to clarify that I am not insinuating that staff at most breweries are not knowledgeable. But it's fair to say that early on in a conversation, you can tell if you are talking to someone well-versed in not only the beer but also the brewery itself. In the next section, I will discuss different questions I like to ask during my visits, and I generally ask the person behind the bar.

You may get lucky at a smaller brewery and one of the brewers or even the owner will be pouring you your beer. In that case, you are bound to have the chance to absorb as much information as you can handle (assuming it's not too busy in the taproom). Usually, even if the person behind the bar isn't in ownership or in charge of making your beer, they can be a reliable source of information.

But there are varying degrees. It is unfair to expect every employee at every brewery to know the history of the building prior to it being a brewery or what hops are used in each IPA. In this case, there are still going to be questions you can ask that are more opinion-based, so you can still glean some answers from them.

WHAT TYPE OF EXPERIENCE DOES THE TAPROOM OFFER?

One factor I try to consider when people ask me for recommendations is the type of experience they may be looking for. The quality of beer is usually going to be the most important, but I also know the degree to which people care about it is a spectrum, not black and white. Some people want a more well-rounded experience, whether that includes food, games, events, or even just a cool atmosphere. It's not just about making recommendations for others; we all have different features in a taproom that appeal to us more or less.

Places like **Bingo Beer** in Richmond, Virginia and **Quarter Barrel** in Cedar Rapids, Iowa, not only brew beer but have massive arcades as part of their taprooms. Many breweries serve food, but that can vary from bar snacks to a typical bar and grill, up to higher-end menus. About that, I've been to breweries that feel more like restaurants that happen to make beer, breweries that feel like a basic taproom but serve excellent food, and everywhere in between. If the taproom or outdoor space prominently features a stage (like at **Gravely** in Louisville, Kentucky or **Roundhouse** in Nisswa, Minnesota), it's a good bet music plays a big role in what the brewery offers.

And speaking of outdoor spaces, that is something many people like to focus on. While it's especially true in warmer weather states, many breweries that get true winter still have an outside section. Some feature lots of games and activities, such as **Whistle Hop** in Fairview, North Carolina, where they have mini-golf, disc golf, a small soccer field, and even a slide down a hill for children. Others are more expansive and take advantage of a rural setting, such as **Lone Oak** in Olney, Maryland, or the famous farm at **Jester King** in Austin, Texas.

WHAT COULD SET THIS BREWERY APART?

One question I get asked often: what makes for a good brewery? In short, of course the beer is the biggest factor (as we just discussed). After all, that is generally the primary reason people visit breweries. But not every brewery can be in the top 10% when it comes to talking purely about the beer, so other features can come into play. My general answer is that a brewery must be memorable in some way.

This is especially true in brewery-dense neighborhoods. Places like North Park in San Diego or RiNo in Denver are swamped with local beer options. Being notable in one way or another can help draw customers to you, and more importantly, get them to come back. When you are visiting a brewery for the first time, it's a good idea to see if there is anything about the experience that is unique. I just discussed some of the possible options that could come into play: food, entertainment, outdoor spaces, events, etc. But there are other ways that a brewery can differentiate itself.

Some, like a brewery's theme or funky beer names and artwork, may seem slightly silly on the surface, but I can say with certainty that things like that can catch the eyes of possible patrons. Some themes that I have seen are sports (baseball, basketball, hockey, rugby, etc), railroads, magic, fishing, music, sci-fi, and automotive. People enjoy when other things they like are tied in with a brewery, such as baseball fans being drawn to a place like **Broken Bat Brewing** in Milwaukee. I can tell you from my travels that if two similar breweries are both fairly average, but one has a strong theme and does not simply have a cookie-cutter taproom, the themed brewery will most likely be the more memorable one. Similarly, with beer names and artwork, I know that is something that can suck people in. Artwork may play a bigger factor when someone is buying beer at a store, but in that case the customer immediately becomes more aware of that brewery. And in a taproom, eye-catching and vibrant artwork can be a real attention grabber.

One other possible influence I want to highlight: the people. Whether it is the brewery owner or the general staff, having great people working at the brewery is a massive difference maker. If you get to know the people behind the beer, that can certainly be something that draws you back regularly. I know this from personal experience, and from talking with other craft beer lovers.

TAKE YOUR TIME WITH THE BEER.
This seems simple enough, but I'm writing this in my book as a reminder to myself more than anything else. When you have

done what I have, with a goal of visiting and experiencing as many breweries as possible, that sometimes resulted in rushing through a stop. While my notebook meant I was able to record my beers and some facts about the brewery, there have been times when I did not properly give the beers or taproom the attention it deserved.

That has been one focus of mine recently. Not rushing and trying to savor and appreciate the beer I'm currently drinking and absorbing the atmosphere of the place I'm currently in. This is particularly true now that I am back home and return to breweries here in the Milwaukee area that I love. Hopefully, visiting new breweries at a slower rate and less frequently will give me a newfound appreciation for this hobby I have had for many years.

QUESTIONS TO ASK

Ok, so you are at the brewery and have been making observations—but you want to learn more. I often try to ask questions during my visit, especially if I am there when the taproom is less busy. I've compiled some of the questions I like to ask people there, whether it's a bartender, the brewery's owner, or just another person sitting at the bar.

DO YOU HAVE ANY FLAGSHIPS OR STYLES YOU ARE BEST KNOWN FOR?

This is one of the first things I ask whoever is taking my beer order, whether they are a bartender or waitstaff. It's important to know this, as a flagship is a beer that the brewery is probably best known for, or at least is a beer they always (or regularly) have available. In a way, a flagship is representative of the brewery. Oftentimes, breweries will even have multiple flagships that showcase a variety of styles.

People will usually expect to hear the name of an IPA or some kind of sessionable lager, and while many breweries will respond with that type of answer, you never know when one could surprise you. An example I like to use comes from a visit to Dallas in 2018. I stopped in at **Peticolas Brewing** where they had a wide variety of beers on tap. When I asked what I should get, they answered by suggesting *Velvet Hammer*, their flagship Imperial red ale that has taken home three US Open Beer Championship medals and clocks in at 9% ABV. Not only did I listen, but it was my favorite beer of my time in Dallas!

If a brewery has several flagships, I don't necessarily recommend getting them all in a flight if there are other beers you want to try. But in my opinion, it is a bright idea to get at least one or two beers that fall into this category, as they typically will be beers the brewery has been making for a long time and, in theory, should be the most dialed-in.

WHAT IS YOUR FAVORITE BEER THAT YOU BREW?

This is an entirely different question than what beers a brewery is best known for, and is another question you can ask anyone working there. On top of that, if I strike up a conversation with someone else drinking there and I find out they are a local, I'll even ask them this question. You'll usually get different answers if you ask multiple people, but oftentimes, they explain their choice, whether it's a style they like, based on the time of year, or something entirely different.

You will often hear something along the lines of: "It depends what I'm in the mood for." And this is a fair point to take into account. There are times when all you want is a light, clean lager and instances where big, bold stout is what you crave. But people typically can give you a beer or two they usually lean toward. I've found that in many cases, workers indulge in something seasonal or only released occasionally. If it's a beer they don't currently have on tap though, workers are also quick to point out what they find enjoyable that's available during your visit.

I like to ask this question because people who work at a brewery usually have tried most, if not all, of the beers a brewery offers. While it's important to factor in that everyone has a different palate to varying degrees, I like to know the staff's favorites. When I'm filling out my flight card and I can't decide what my last choice should be, I usually will ask the bartender what I should get, either with something they enjoy or something that will round out my card well.

WHAT OTHER BREWERIES IN THE AREA DO YOU ENJOY?
This is another question that you can ask anyone. Usually, it is going to be people working at the brewery, but hearing from other locals who are there is a dependable resource. People who work at breweries can be a bit of a mixed bag for a couple of reasons. While plenty of workers go around and visit other places, several times in my travels, I've heard, "I really just enjoy the beer here" or "I don't visit other breweries much."

This is why if I strike up a conversation with someone else drinking there and I learn they are local, I like to hear what other places they frequent. Someone local is going to be more dialed into what different breweries offer than someone visiting, no matter how much research is done ahead of time. This is especially true if the person is similarly a craft beer fanatic who visits a variety of breweries and pays attention to new releases, seasonals, etc.

As I said earlier, I have a plan in place whenever I am going to be out visiting breweries. But there have been instances where I have adjusted on the fly because of things I learned from talking with locals. Sometimes, a brewery I was planning on visiting had gone through a controversy of some kind that I was not aware of. A few times, a new brewery not on my radar had just opened and was already cranking out amazing beers. Or, based on what I was drinking at one brewery, someone would recommend checking out another place that excelled at that style. No matter what, you can learn a lot about a city's beer scene by talking to people who live and work there.

WHAT SIZE SYSTEM DO YOU USE?
What size is the brewery you are visiting? Is it a nano brewery using a one-barrel system? Or are you visiting a massive complex like the 200-barrel brewhouse at **Sierra Nevada Brewing**? While the odds are that the answer is between those two extremes, the response to this question can tell you more

about the brewery. Sometimes, a brewery will even operate multiple systems, such as having a 20-barrel production facility paired with a smaller pilot system for experimentation.

While it is certainly not the case in every instance, I've heard several times during my travels from people who brew on a small system that they prefer the flexibility it provides. The smaller system allows them to try out different recipes without having to commit to a major batch. That means if they try to make something adventurous or a style they haven't tried before, it isn't as big a loss if it doesn't turn out the way they hoped or doesn't sell well.

WHAT WAS THIS BUILDING USED FOR PREVIOUSLY?

One of my favorite questions! During the book's upcoming "City Breakdowns" section, you'll see me reference many historic buildings that have been turned into breweries. Sometimes, it can be something obvious. Walking into the historic St. Michael's Church in Baltimore, there's no question about the history of the **Ministry of Brew**'s home. But even if it's apparent what the building's past was, there's often more to the story than meets the eye. Sometimes, it's less evident. Often, if it's an older brick building in a downtown area, it could have been any number of things. A bank? A laundromat? A space to repair old railroad cars? You will only find out if you ask! That history can even make the name of the brewery make sense, such as **Textile Brewing** in Dyersville, Iowa, being in an old sewing factory or the automobile-themed **Parts and Labor Brewing** having their location in an old Cadillac dealership repair shop in Sterling, Colorado.

A big reason why I love to hear about the buildings is that they often showcase the area's history. The building could have played a key role in the community. Maybe it served as the town's movie theater for over five decades, like **Mars Theatre Brewing** in Mars Hill, North Carolina. **Burlington Beer Company** is located in the building where America's first commercial color photography lab was founded. Or a brewery could move into a place built for a different brewery long ago, such as the spaces for **Prairie Street Brewing** in Rockford, Illinois, and **Stone Arch Brewpub** in Appleton, Wisconsin. A brewery opening in a historic (or even just old) building breathes new life into it and allows people to learn about something locally significant. Many times, you may even be able to find information displayed in the taproom about this topic.

Am I telling you to walk into a new business park and ask this question? Not necessarily, although places like that may have served a different purpose too. But pay attention to where you are drinking, and if it's an interesting place, ask someone about it! It's a fun way to learn about the brewery and the area they call home.

HOW WAS THE NAME OF THE BREWERY DECIDED?
I just talked about how the name of the brewery can come from the building they call home, but of course, there are so many other inspirations a brewery owner can draw from. It may seem mundane, considering that if a brewery makes amazing beer, it doesn't matter what they call it. But I personally love learning about the background of the name because it's just another piece of the brewery's puzzle.

Similar to the building, it's common for a brewery to be named for its location. This could be a street like **King Street Brewing** in Anchorage, Alaska, or a neighborhood such as **Georgetown Brewing** in Seattle. They may even just take the town or city's name and slap "brewing" or something similar on the end, like **Hackensack Brewing** in New Jersey or **Hilo Brewing** in Hawaii. It can even be a wider area like a county (**Floyd County Brewing** in Indiana) or state (**Maine Beer Company**). Nearby landforms or tourist attractions are also used, such as **Moat Mountain Brewing** in New Hampshire or **Flathead Lake Brewing** in Montana. These names are all pretty easy to figure out.

But many times, a name can be something more personal. It could be that the owner (and sometimes owner AND brewer) proudly displays their name, such as **Servaes Brewing** in Shawnee, Kansas. **Gilla Brewing** in Gonzales, Louisiana, is called that because it was the nickname of one of the owners' late father. Some of my favorites come from stories, which is the case at **Ghost Monkey Brewing** in Mt. Pleasant, South Carolina where one of the owners was visiting Brazil and got "robbed" by a sneaky monkey!

Maybe it's even a name that refers to the type of beer you'll be able to try, such as the famous **Bierstadt Lagerhaus** in Denver. There are many more name backgrounds that I will share later on in the book, but I recommend that people visiting a new brewery do a little digging to find out why the place they are at has a specific name.

HOW ARE YOU CONNECTED TO THE LOCAL AREA?

As I just discussed, sometimes the name of the brewery is a small part of what ties it to the area. But often, breweries are happy to tell you how they are part of the neighborhood, city, or region. They probably won't come right out and say it, but one thing breweries do is keep money local. People revel in supporting a local business and giving their money to people who live there. When a neighborhood sees breweries pop up, you will often see other businesses come in, too. Before the brewery boom, places like Scott's Addition in Richmond or Ballard in Seattle were once not all like they are now.

What you will often hear about is events. Trivia nights, live music, fundraisers, festivals, and markets. I have seen just about every type of event you can host promoted at a brewery. These events get people to the brewery (and their neighborhood), and in many cases, they are raising funds for a local organization.

Those are just a few examples, as there are numerous other ways a brewery can integrate itself into the community and weave itself into its fabric. This is one question that you will get the most details by asking, but often you'll also be able to find information posted around the taproom.

DO YOU DISTRIBUTE?

This isn't one of the first questions you ask, but I enjoy asking this at smaller breweries when I get the chance to talk with the owner. This can be helpful because it lets you know whether you can find their beer elsewhere should you desire to look for it. Maybe they have a couple of local accounts with some area beer bars, maybe they self-distribute in the region, maybe they do occasional drops in other areas, or maybe you have just been missing them, and they do have beer for sale where you live. If they don't? Well, then you grab some to-go before you leave if they are making beers you want to have again. There have been a couple of times when I visited a smaller brewery in a neighboring state and did not realize that they distributed near Milwaukee until I asked!

WHAT WAS YOUR BACKGROUND BEFORE OPENING A BREWERY?

This is a question to ask the owner of the brewery, or possibly a question you could ask the brewer if they are a different person. There are many answers to this question, but some common responses will be a former homebrewer going pro, someone who was working for a different brewery who wanted to create their own, or maybe it's someone who is a fanatic of craft beer and wanted to take the plunge (usually with the assistance of an experienced brewer). No matter the answer, this can help paint the picture of the brewery and possibly connect some dots. If the beer wows you, it's possible the brewer came from a brewery you are already familiar with!

WHY DID YOU DECIDE TO OPEN A BREWERY?

While the answer may be something simple, such as appreciating craft beer or wanting to strike out on their own after working as a brewer for many years, there are plenty of creative responses that you can hear as well. If you haven't already asked, the name of the brewery could come into play, or maybe you will learn more details about their background even if you already asked about that. Like I said in the introduction, breweries are unique, like fingerprints, and a major part of that is the people in each one are different. That is why I like to learn about them as well as the beer itself.

City Breakdowns

I have been fortunate to visit most of the major cities around the country (and many of the less major ones too). In this section, I will write about my experiences with the beer scenes of the places I have had the pleasure of going to. With a few rare expectations, the breweries mentioned are limited to places I have visited. This part of the book is broken down by region, with cities I have substantial experience with getting written about more at length while some that I have less with receiving smaller blurbs.

There are some things to note. First, craft beer changes quickly and has changed fast for a while now. In most cases, I have fairly recent exposure to the breweries I am talking about, but in other cases, it has been five, six, or even seven years since I have been there in person. Because of this, I have done my best only to discuss breweries that are currently open and to discuss any new information that could be relevant (such as new taproom locations, changes to ownership, etc). While I do make notes of specific beers and mention what style(s) a brewery is best known for, it is important to realize that it is impossible to fully explain what every brewery I've been to has to offer.

Encompassing Maine, Vermont, Massachusetts, Rhode Island, Connecticut, and New York, many iconic cities and breweries exist in this area.

This was the first region we lived in once my wife started her career as a travel nurse, as we called Hampton Beach, New Hampshire home while she worked up the road in Portsmouth. We loved exploring the region, with most of our time spent in the Granite State, southern Maine, and eastern Massachusetts. We also lived just across the Hudson River from New York City in Newark, which enabled us to check out the Big Apple and parts of Connecticut.

BOSTON, MA

Many people associate craft beer with Boston, in large part due to a certain lager that bears the name of one of the Founding Fathers. Although *Sam Adams Boston Lager* (and many other beers) are now also being produced at **Boston Beer Company** locations in Ohio and Pennsylvania, you can still sip on a pint at one of two spots in Boston! Founded in 1984 by Jim Koch, **Boston Beer Company** has gone through many expansions and changes throughout the years. Their *Cherry Wheat* was one of the beers I thoroughly enjoyed during the early parts of my craft beer exploration in college. There's also another large regional brewery, **Harpoon Brewery**, that calls Beantown home. **Harpoon** got its start in 1986 and similarly has grown substantially. They now have another facility in Windsor, Vermont, and produce many well-known beers like *Harpoon IPA* and *UFO Hefeweizen*.

But what makes Boston an interesting craft beer city, is that not many breweries are located within city limits. Many of those that have put up shop are auxiliary and secondary taprooms for more established breweries from nearby suburbs. **Trillium Brewing**, **Night Shift Brewing**, and **Castle Island Brewing** are examples of suburban success translating to taprooms in the city. **Trillium**, in particular, is an incredibly popular brewery and was my personal favorite among those I visited in the state. Their ability to nail a variety of styles is what sets them apart in my eyes (their *Vanilla Pot & Kettle Oatmeal Porter* had notes of hot cocoa with partially melted marshmallows). There are actually three locations in Boston for **Trillium**: Fort Point, Fenway, and a beer garden right downtown.

Meanwhile, **Night Shift**'s Boston location is at Lovejoy Wharf, featuring great views of the Boston Harbor and a full restaurant. It's located right next to TD Garden if you are going to a basketball or hockey game. **Castle Island** opened its south Boston location in 2019 inside the former Cole Hersee building. The brewery's name is an interesting one, as it shares its moniker with a peninsula that stretches into Boston Harbor. It was a true island until it was connected to the mainland in 1928.

These additional locations certainly help visitors check out some of the area's top brewers, but outside of that, you'll mostly need to head out to the 'burbs to find more suds from the source:

- To the west, you'll find **Lamplighter Brewing**, which has transformed an old auto body shop in Cambridge into an intimate taproom. I was introduced to Brett IPAs there and was immediately a fan. They have two locations in Cambridge now. **Aeronaut Brewing** in Somerville is another in that direction and a place where you can turn a coaster into a piece of art. If you like beer gardens, they also have a seasonal one in nearby Allston.

- Look north to discover **Bone Up Brewing** and **Night Shift**'s primary location, both in Everett. Or jaunt a bit further to Malden to check out the lively taproom and classic beers from *Idle Hands Craft Ales*.

- South of the city you can visit the original locations for **Trillium** and **Castle Island**, along with several other options as well.

My Take: Boston is an important city when it comes to craft beer and currently has a nice handful of breweries. But with how the city is set up, you must be willing to venture into the suburbs if you want to do a lot of brewery hopping. If you can venture further out, places like **Treehouse** and **Vitamin Sea** need to be on your radar.

Quick Tip: Plan ahead if you want to visit some of the downtown taprooms. They can be extremely busy, especially on the weekends. If you want to explore the suburbs, stick to one side of the city, as traffic can be brutal.

PORTSMOUTH, NH

Located along the Piscataqua River right before it flows out to the Atlantic Ocean, the lovely city of Portsmouth was the first place my wife took a job as a travel nurse. Living in the area for three months allowed us to dive into exploring the area, which included all the breweries (at the time in 2017). The downtown area in particular is a delight, and we loved walking around to the numerous shops and restaurants.

One aspect of the local beer scene that I like is no matter what you are looking for, there is an option for you. Want a traditional brewpub experience? **Portsmouth Brewing** right downtown is waiting. They were established in 1991 and are deemed New Hampshire's "original brewpub." They can be more than just traditional, though, as my favorite was a red ale brewed with kelp in conjunction with the University of New Hampshire's aquaculture program. Need something even more unique like a gruit? **Earth Eagle Brewings** is a quick walk from there. They also once brewed a brown ale with beef offal (specifically heart and liver)! Big fan of IPAs? Stop by **Great Rhythm Brewing** and quaff some hoppy beers while gazing out at North Mill Pond. Are larger regional breweries more your speed? Just down the road in Hampton, you can find **Smuttynose Brewing** and their massive array of offerings. They have been around since 1994 and are one of the classics of the New England region. I quite enjoyed the *Robust Porter*.

Some others nearby are worth a visit as well. **Throwback Brewery** is located on historic Hobbs Farm in North Hampton, while **Stoneface Brewing** in Newington and **Deciduous Brewing** in Newmarket were making some of my favorite beers in the state. A *Berliner Weisse with Guava* and *Dry-hopped Gose* were my top picks, respectively, at those two. It is also just a small hop over the bridge to Maine where you can visit both **Tributary Brewing** and **Woodland Farms Brewery** in Kittery.

My Take: Portsmouth is a wonderfully quaint, small New England city with a diverse selection of breweries. That, along with the ease at which you can get around, makes for a nice Beercation if you prefer smaller cities to large metro areas.

Quick Tip: If you want to soak up the beaches during the summer months, be prepared for large crowds, particularly on the weekends. If you want to chow down on seafood, try the chowder at River House right downtown.

PORTLAND, ME

Nestled on the south shore of Casco Bay, Portland is certainly a popular city when discussing craft beer. There are many reasons why this is so, but it begins with **Allagash Brewing**. Whether you want to try *Allagash White* straight from the source or would prefer to sample some taproom exclusives, this is a stop that makes a visit to Portland worth it on its own. Founded in 1995 by Rob Tod, they are well-known for helping bring Belgian-inspired beers to the United States. Besides *Allagash White*, make sure you try the *Hoppy Table Beer* (a sessionable Belgian ale) if you get the chance.

But of course, there is so much more to the city's beer scene than famous Belgian ales. Start in the East Bayside neighborhood, where you'll find popular **Rising Tide Brewing, Lone Pine Brewing**, and **Belleflower Brewing** (which wasn't open when I was there, but I've heard amazing things). I was especially a fan of **Rising Tide**, where you can imbibe a variety of styles from IPAs to lagers to a gose inside of a large warehouse. Then take a quick ride over to Thompson's Point for a choose-your-own-adventure, as the delicious **Bissell Brothers Brewing** is in the same complex as a distillery and coffee shop (a winery was formerly there, too). The space is over a century old and was a former railway building. IPAs are a big seller here, and my favorite was their flagship *The Substance Ale*.

Back downtown, you'll find more classic choices, such as two Maine originals that offer very different experiences. **Shipyard Brewing** moved to Portland in 1994 and became one of the largest regional breweries in New England (love the *Pumpkinhead Ale!*). But if you want a true brewpub experience, head over to **Gritty McDuff's**, which was Maine's first brewpub since prohibition. They have additional locations in Freeport and Auburn if you happen to be in either of those areas. **Liquid Riot Bottling Company** is also smack dab in the middle of downtown near the water. If you are looking for more than just beer, they are also a distillery and have a variety of whiskeys and rums available. The sours at that stop were a highlight for me, including *Raspy Trouble*, which was aged on over 100 pounds of local raspberries.

I do want to step a little outside of Portland to highlight one other brewery. A short drive to the north, you'll find Freeport's **Maine Beer Company**. They underwent a huge taproom renovation shortly after I visited, and you can sip on their uber-popular *Lunch IPA* or *Dinner Double IPA*. My personal favorite, though? *Peeper Pale Ale*. Founded in 2009, they have the motto "Do what's right," and they are not just talking about brewing good beer. They are a member of 1% for the Planet, donating 1 percent of gross annual sales to environmental nonprofits, and are also known for implementing a variety of sustainable practices.

My Take: Obviously, Portland is worthy of a Beercation, and while I did say **Allagash** alone makes the journey worth it, there's a plethora of other local options that will delight every beer drinker, no matter what styles or experiences you are looking for!

My Tip: If you need help getting around (or just want to learn more about the breweries while you tour the area), check out Maine Brews Cruise, as they offer bus, bicycle, and walking tours. Also, while I did not get to them during my time in Portland, there are numerous breweries right by **Allagash: Definitive, Battery Steele, Austin Street,** and **Foundation.**

BURLINGTON, VT

Vermont. A state that beer lovers have a deep affection for. I'll get this out of the way: I was a huge fan of **The Alchemist,** located up in Stowe. I personally felt *The Crusher Double IPA* out-punched the famous *Heady Topper*. However, I want to focus on the scene in gorgeous Burlington. Situated on Lake Champlain, this is a lovely place to visit, even aside from the beer.

The highlight of my visit was **Foam Brewers**. A stone's throw from the lake inside a quirky taproom, they offer a variety of IPAs while also serving up unique sours, stouts, and lagers. I had a *Smoked Apple Gose* that was not only one of the more memorable brews from my time in Vermont but also one of the best. This is one place I wish I could have spent an entire evening just working my way through the tap list. When I say "quirky" taproom, I do mean that. It has a whimsi-cal and eclectic feel that features plenty of artwork and some cool lit-up inlays around the bar. Not too far from here is **The Vermont Pub & Brewery**, located in the middle of downtown. This was the state's first brewpub when Greg Noonan opened the doors in 1988. If you like the vibes of a traditional brew-pub, this is the place for you!

From there I'd recommend heading south of downtown, as that is where much of the action is. There are four brewer-ies within less than a mile of each other, making for an ideal brewery-hopping experience in the South End. If your palate likes to focus on traditional European styles, I'd suggest start-ing at **Queen City Brewery**, which was established back in 2014. Make sure to check out the décor, too; I enjoyed look-ing at all the old beer serving trays and cans. **Zero Gravity Brewing** is conveniently located across the street, and right off the bat, I was a fan of their hummingbird logo. I'd rec-ommend the *Green State Lager*, and not just because it's a good beer. One dollar from each *Green State Lager* sold goes to a dif-ferent environmental organization each month.

Just a few blocks away is **Switchback Brewing**. They actu-ally opened up a new tap house and beer garden attached to their former space in the summer of 2024. Founded in 2002, they are a Burlington staple. My favorite was the flagship

Switchback Ale, a "reddish-amber ale," according to their website. I also loved their Vermont-shaped flight boards! Right next door is **Burlington Beer Company**. Now, when I visited them back in 2017, they were located to the east in neighboring Williston. But a few years later, they made a move to Burlington, opening up inside the historic Lumiere Building. Interestingly, this is where America's first commercial color photography lab was founded in 1904. I had a very nice coffee porter called *Barista* during my stop there, for what it's worth.

My Take: Although they lost local icon **Magic Hat Brewing** in 2020, Burlington remains a truly exceptional place to base a Beercation. One wonderful thing about it is that you are also able to visit many of the more rural breweries scattered across Northern Vermont while you are there. Some of the names to keep in mind are **von Trapp Brewery** (Stowe), **Lawson's Finest Liquids** (Waitsfield), **Frost Beer Works** (Hinesburg), **Hill Farmstead Brewery** (Greensboro Bend), and **Rock Art Brewery** (Morristown).

Quick Tip: If you are looking for a non-beer activity, it's only about thirty minutes to get to the home of Ben & Jerry's! You can take a tour, try different ice creams, and check out their "Flavor Graveyard" to see what's been discontinued.

NEW YORK, NY

The Big Apple. The City That Never Sleeps. While the largest city in the county goes by many names and is known for a plethora of things, you should be adding its beer scene to that list. You most likely will be visiting to see the Statue of Liberty, Central Park, the Empire State Building, or one of the numerous museums, but I highly recommend taking the time to visit some of the local breweries as well. I was able to visit at least one brewery in each of the five boroughs, although, as you are about to read, they are not all on the same level when it comes to craft beer.

A major reason why New York City took home my Best Beer City (Large) award in 2023 was because of the options in Brooklyn. This is where you will find a majority of the breweries and where we will focus most of our attention. The first neighborhood (and probably my favorite) is Gowanus, just south of downtown. Within a few blocks, you will find some incredible breweries. **Threes Brewing** has its flagship location here, and along with awesome beers like *Short Fuse* (a foeder-fermented smoked helles), you can also get food, coffee, and cocktails. Around the corner is my favorite brewery in NYC, **Wild East Brewing**. *Patience & Gratitude 2023*, their foeder-lagered Czech pilsner, won my Best Lighter-style Beer in 2023! Their website describes it as a "triple-decocted Czech-style pilsner, with additional lagering in our oak foeder." **Finback Brewery** opened an additional location in a former warehouse a block away in 2020, and their *Whale Watching DIPA* was divine. **Strong Rope Brewing** and **Other Half Brewing** also have spaces in this neighborhood.

The other breweries in Brooklyn I want to highlight are further north in Williamsburg and Bushwick. One of them has been a stalwart since its first sale in 1988, **Brooklyn Brewery**. They opened in Williamsburg in 1996, and many are now familiar with their brewmaster, Garrett Oliver. Their *Post Road Pumpkin Ale* is one of the best examples of that style I've had. Moving east, **Talea Beer Company** has four sites scattered around Brooklyn and Manhattan, but their flagship location in Williamsburg opened in 2021. The *Weekender Masala Chai Lager* was my favorite at this spot, which had a cool vibe.

One of my other favorites from the city was **Grimm Artisanal Ales**. They were named New York State Brewery of the Year in 2021 and 2022, thanks partly to beers like *Super Spruce*. This dry-hopped gose with spruce tips won my Best Sour in 2023, and it is delicious. You get a nice melding of the ingredients on your senses: piney, light citrus, acidity, and a salty touch that I always love when I find a high-caliber example of this style. Oh, and they also have a rooftop terrace! Finally, **Kings County Brewers Collective** in Bushwick opened up in 2016 inside a former auto body shop. I dug the massive mural by the in-house artist! This also happens to be the home base brewery for my friend and fellow brewery traveler extraordinaire Chris O'Leary.

I only made it to one brewery in both Queens and the Bronx. Part of the reason is that there are far fewer options in these two boroughs, but I did have nice visits at the pair I was able to get to. **Alewife Brewing** is the only all-immigrant-run brewery in New York City! They are in the Sunnyside neighborhood of Queens and moved into this larger facility in 2020 after originally opening in 2011 in Long Island City. The *Plzen Czech Pilsner* was my top selection there. Flip up to the Bronx, and you will find **Gun Hill Brewery**, named for the local landmark where colonial residents stored guns and ammunition during the Revolutionary War. *Void of Light*, their export-style stout, was a nominee for my Best Dark Beer in 2023! When they opened up, they were the first brewery to brew in the Bronx in nearly five decades.

Often the "Forgotten Borough," Staten Island has only two breweries, but one of them will soon be opening another location, and that is **Kills Boro Brewing**! The name is a reference to the local tidal straits, and they are located inside an old engine mechanic shop. They had an array of lagers and IPAs on tap during my visit, and by the time you are reading this their location nearby in Snug Harbor may be opened. Back by their first location in the Tompkinsville neighborhood, **Flagship Brewery** is right around the corner. They opened in a former car dealership in 2014, and the *Hawk City Pilsner* was the beer I would order again.

Finally, we arrive at the borough most people think of when picturing New York City: Manhattan. While the bright lights of Times Square, the lush greenery of Central Park, or one of the many skyscrapers are what draw in tourists from all around the world, there are some options for local craft beer as well! In terms of pure breweries that are brewing in Manhattan, your first stop should be **Torch & Crown Brewing** in SoHo. Their modern space opened up in 2020 and turned an empty lot next door into a beer garden. The logo and branding are a perfect fit for NYC, and I enjoyed the *Almost Famous Hazy IPA*.

Several other breweries now have taprooms in the ever-expensive borough as well: **Talea**, **Other Half**, and **Bronx Brewery** all set up shop. **Other Half**'s Manhattan location is right next to the Rockefeller Center, and they are best known for their IPAs such as *Broccoli*, *All Citra Everything*, and *Green City*. Many people will tell you that what sets Manhattan apart is the numerous beer bars. Places like Blind Tiger and Beer Culture provide visitors with a chance to try beers from all over in one sitting.

My Take: New York City is home to a rich array of high-quality breweries. While the majority of them can be found in Brooklyn, you will be able to find local beer in any area you are visiting. There's a reason I named them my Best Beer City (Large) in 2023, after all!

Quick Tip: More so than any other city, make sure you are well-versed in public transportation. My preferred method of getting around was the subway and trains, but buses, taxis, and yes, even walking are all options depending on where you are.

OTHER CITIES AND AREAS

<u>Northeast Massachusetts:</u> In between Boston and Portsmouth there's a variety of communities with their own brewery. In Newburyport, you'll find **Newburyport Brewing**, a music-inspired joint with a flavorsome pale ale. A towering smokestack in Amesbury marks **Brewery Silvaticus** inside the former boiler room of a manufacturing plant. Such a cool taproom. If you want a water view, visit **The Tap Brewing Company** along the Merrimack River in Haverhill. A bit further south in Salem, you'll find some of the best lagers and session beers anywhere at **Notch Brewery**. Their taproom is located on water, specifically an inlet of the Salem Harbor. They also now have a location in Brighton, which is closer to Boston if that is where you are located.

<u>Plymouth, MA:</u> **Mayflower Brewing** has one of the most epic stories you can imagine when it comes to the founder. John Alden was a beer barrel cooper on board the real Mayflower when it came to America. Centuries later, one of his tenth-great-grandsons founded a brewery in Plymouth. I'd love to hear a story that can top that. Quick history lesson: back then, a barrel cooper tended to the wooden barrels that held the beer. Sailors aboard the Mayflower were given one gallon of brew for a daily ration! I was a fan of their *John Barleycorn Cream Ale*, which I enjoyed on nitro.

<u>Concord, NH:</u> The capital of the Granite State actually has a brewery that is themed around being the capital, **Concord Craft Brewing**! It features beer names such as *Kapitöl Kölsch* and *The Gov'nah*, an Imperial IPA. The city is also home to the music-inspired **Lithermans Limited**, and they made an awesome sour ale with orange, passionfruit, and nutmeg called *Throne of Gods*. They also now have a location in downtown Portsmouth, just a few blocks from both **Portsmouth Brewery**

and **Earth Eagle Brewings**. A bit west of Concord, in the backwoods you can find **Henniker Brewing** along with their impressive growler collection.

Manchester, NH: While I only visited two breweries in the city itself (**Stark Brewing** and **Backyard Brewery and Kitchen**), there was another brewery in a nearby town that stuck out. To the south in Derry, the Viking-themed **Kelsen Brewing** has several award-winning beers. They opened in early 2014 and also serve hand-tossed pizza. I should clarify that I also enjoyed the beers at **Backyard**, particularly the *Stone Wall Stout*.

Southern Maine Coast: I mentioned in my Portsmouth section a couple of the breweries on the Maine side. But there's also a terrific string of them from there all the way up to Portland. One of my favorite beers in this area was a *Whoopie Pie* Stout from **SoMe Brewing** in York (SoMe=Southern Maine). **Kennebunkport Brewing (Federal Jacks)** in Kennebunk is interestingly the birthplace of Portland's **Shipyard Brewing**, and further north in Saco is the intriguing **Barreled Souls Brewing**, which features plenty of imperial delights.

Acadia National Park Region (Maine): One of the many beautiful places in New England, we had a fabulous time visiting this area, and there's also some local beer to be found after you've done some hiking. **Atlantic Brewing** is the long-standing option on Mt. Desert Island. My top pick was their brown ale. Across the water in Ellsworth, I had a delicious *Cherry Chocolate Stout* at the cozy **Airline Brewing**. You'll find two hyper-local options to the southeast, **Strong's Public House & Patio** in Sedgwick and **DeepWater Brewing** in Blue Hill. **Strong's** was previously **Strong's Brewing**, but they recently went through a rebrand. They have been around since 2013 and I had a wonderful conversation with co-owner Mia Strong during my visit.

<u>Rochester, NY:</u> Rochester is a city I need to make a return trip to, as it has developed a robust beer scene. But I did love a *Cherry Sour* at **Swift Water Brewing** and also dug a Pumpkin Ale down the road at **Lock 32 Brewing** (which is located along the Erie Canal in Pittsford).

<u>Southwestern Connecticut:</u> My short but productive stop in this part of the Constitution State led me to three spots. A major highlight was **Two Roads Brewing** in Stratford, which has grown to be a huge brewery since being founded in 2012. Located in a former US Baird manufacturing building, the expansive second-floor taproom features a bar made from the original factory floor. In 2023, they also won my awards for Best Flight Board and Most Surprising Beer: *Roadsmary's Baby*, a rum-barrel-aged pumpkin ale. Not far from away in Bridgeport is **Brewport**. Housed in a building that was built in the 1940s as a distribution point for out-of-town newspapers, they've been serving up beer and pizza since 2016. Further to the southwest in Norwalk is **Spacecat Brewing** inside the former factory for J & J Mill. I loved the towering windows here, as well as the *Whistleville Pils*.

<u>Rhode Island:</u> My singular brewery visit in the state was **Revival Brewing** in Cranston, which is sadly no longer open. Rhode Island is the only state where I have only visited one brewery, which unfortunately happened due to a mix-up with another brewery's hours (remember, I told you to pay attention to that). But I have my sights set on a return trip in 2025 to hopefully check out such places as **Tilted Barn, Narragansett, Long Live Beerworks**, and **Proclamation Ale Company.**

Pennsylvania, New Jersey, Delaware, Maryland, Washington DC, Virginia, West Virginia, and North Carolina compose this section, where a variety of large and small cities offer intriguing beer scenes.

We have called this part of the country home thrice during our travels, living in Baltimore, Asheville, and Newark. The diverse group of cities was fun to visit, and a few of them are contenders for my favorite beer city! North Carolina is also the state where I visited the third most breweries, behind only California and my home state of Wisconsin.

NORTHEAST NEW JERSEY

This is one of the more interesting areas to discuss when it comes to craft beer. Across one border, you have New York, and a short drive in the other direction takes you to Pennsylvania. Those two states rank second and third, respectively, in terms of total breweries. Sandwiched between them is New Jersey, which ranks nineteenth for total breweries and is towards the bottom in terms of breweries per capita. New Jersey was slow to adapt to the craft movement, and to this day, the state is making it difficult for breweries due to a variety of regulations and laws that limit them. Whether it's restricting events, limiting food, or issues with licenses, it has continued to be a tough slog for local breweries.

Maybe it's because of those reasons, but one thing that jumps out in this region is there is not really one particular town or area that has developed a dense brewery scene. Most towns that have a brewery (including the largest city in the state, Newark) are home to just a singular option. A couple of places like Hackensack and Jersey City have two breweries, but only Hackensack's are close enough to walk between. On the positive side, many cities, suburbs, and towns in this area have a brewery, so no matter where you are, you are probably not too far from one!

As I just said, the largest city in the state, Newark, has a singular brewery. But that's where we will start since we called the city home for a spell in 2023. The one brewery there, **Newark Local Beer**, is located right downtown in the historic Walker Building. Inside, you'll find a larger-than-expected taproom, along with many beers named after the train theme. My personal favorite was *Train Wreck*, a New England IPA. If you start heading toward New York City from there, the two breweries you'll find are the pair in Jersey City. **Departed Soles** was a fun stop, where I especially liked the huge Statue of Liberty mural, skateboard flight board, and the fact that they make some excellent gluten-free beers along with their normal selection. They were also the city's first brewery since prohibition, opening in 2015. Down the road is **902 Brewing**, which has an expansive taproom and brewing facility that opened in 2020.

Now making a counterclockwise circle around the region, there are five breweries to the north of Newark. As I mentioned, Hackensack has two breweries right next to each other: **The Alementary** and **Hackensack Brewing**. The owners of the former come from a science background and have a dog-friendly taproom, while the latter had a wider array of options on tap. South of there, I had an appetizing blueberry and spruce tip gose called *Blue Christmas* at **Brix City Brewing**, and not far from there is **Bolero Snort**, where your palate will get tested by a cornucopia of interesting ingredients and combinations in their beers. **Bolero Snort**'s *Jersey Vice*, a session sour with raspberry and lime, was a finalist for my Best Sour in 2023. Rounding out this area is **Ghost Hawk Brewing**. Opened in April 2019, the name is a tribute to the owner's brother, who passed away in 2016. I admired the beer here, especially the *Sawtooth West Coast Pilsner*.

The options to the west of the main metro area are a little more spread out, but this is also where you will find my favorite stop in the state, **Autodidact Beer**. Located in Morris Plains, their name means "a person who has learned a subject without the benefit of a teacher or formal education." But they sure seem to have a strong grasp on brewing, as I loved their *Daylily Pale Ale* and *Obsidian Black Lager*. Not too far from there in Morristown is **Glenbrook Brewery**, tucked away in downtown. Many of the beers have a Revolutionary War theme due to the area's history, such as *Colonial Ale* (pale ale) and *Jacob Arnold's Porter*. I'd like to round out this area by mentioning **Twin Elephant Brewing** in Chatham, which opened in 2016 inside a former physical therapy office. This cozy, rustic space had a bunch of IPAs on tap, along with a couple of lagers and sours.

My Take: New Jersey is continuing to make progress on making their state more "brewery friendly," and while there may not be one specific location that has become a hub for craft beer, there are many options scattered throughout the area.

Quick Tip: You may not know that New Jersey is the "Diner Capital of the World" and is home to more of them than any other state. If you stop in to grab a bite to eat, I highly recommend that you check if they have disco fries, a regional diner specialty. Fries are bathed in gravy and mozzarella cheese. It's as good as it sounds! My family's favorite was Tops Diner in East Newark.

PHILADELPHIA, PA

The City of Brotherly Love was one of the first cities to host a true "Beer Week" when they founded one in 2007. Not only that, back in 1793 the city was producing the most beer in the entire country. While it may look different nowadays, there is still a lot to be excited about if you are visiting.

For starters, I highly recommend **Human Robot** if you are a fan of lagers like me. More specifically, *Czech 10°*, their Czech pale lager. Fun fact about their interesting name: it is a reference to brewing classic styles (human) while also making some using more modern techniques (rob*ot). I visited* the main spot in the Kensington neighborhood, which was originally the carriage house and stables for Theo Finkenauer Lager Beer Company dating back to the 1870s. There are also three other locations around the metro area. Not far away you'll find **Evil Genius Brewing** inside a building that also dates back to 1870 and was used to repair railroad cars. They are on the other end of the beer spectrum from **Human Robot**. *Purple Monkey Dishwasher* (Chocolate Peanut Butter Porter), *#Adulting* (guava IPA), and *Om Nom Nom* (apple cider donut ale) deliciously push the envelope with a variety of different ingredients.

Closer to downtown is a nice pocket of breweries. **Yards Brewing** is one of the mainstays of Philly, brewing in the city since 1994. A few blocks from there, you'll find a duo that utilizes some of the older buildings in the neighborhood. **Triple Bottom Brewing** is a Certified B Corp and is powered by renewable energy. The taproom is inside the former office space for a railroad company and has a relaxed, welcoming feel. Just around the corner from there, you can find **Love City Brewing** (which was my 700th brewery visit). This spot is inside a former rail parts factory and repair shop and still has a lot of the original building features such as the brick and pillars. A bit northwest of that area is another brewery I was a fan of, **Crime and Punishment Brewing**. Located in the Brewerytown neighborhood inside a former community center, they had a great blood orange gose called *Sudden Zest* and a honey and pink guava IPA named *Space Dogs: Damka.*

There's a handful of suburban breweries to have on your radar too. To the south in Aston, **2SP Brewing** features a unique name. Why? Two of the owners own the Two Stones Pub chain! They make quality beer, and I was fond of *Pony Boi*, a Golden Lager. Just over six miles away in Media, **Iron Hill Brewery & Restaurant** has one of its twenty locations. Twelve of them are in the Keystone State, and for being a chain they produce impressive award-winning beer! *Neon Vibez*, a Hazy IPA, was my favorite.

Across the Delaware River, we need to pop briefly back into New Jersey. Below are the four breweries I visited in the Philadelphia area across the state line, along with my favorite beer at each:

- **Tonewood Brewing** in Oaklyn: *Fuego* American IPA

- **Westville Brewery** in Westville: *Pineapple Habanero IPA*

- **Eight & Sand Beer Co.** in Woodbury: *Monkey & the Engineer* Hefeweizen

- **Death of the Fox Brewing** in Clarksboro: *French Toasty* Red Ale

My Take: If it wasn't obvious, there are plenty of cool taprooms in Philadelphia, especially those that utilize old buildings (particularly from the railroad days). While most people think of the Liberty Bell or Independence Hall, there are plenty of local beers to try if you are ever touring the city.

Quick Tip: If you're like me and want to visit breweries in as many states as possible, it's not too far of a drive to get into Delaware (plus New Jersey as I mentioned). Oh, and don't forget to get a Philly cheesesteak!

BALTIMORE, MD

Another city that my family was lucky enough to call home for a three-month stint, Charm City is truly an underrated spot when it comes to beer. Even though I was living there and enjoying the breweries, I didn't think to include them as a nominee for Best Beer City (Large) in 2021 when I absolutely should have. Which just goes to show you how easy it is to take an awesome beer scene for granted!

Peabody Heights Brewing, which is located on the site of Old Orioles Park north of downtown, may have had my favorite beer in the city. *Feasts of Trumpets* was a delectable honey cake porter, and their imperial black peanut butter chocolate wit called *Memphis Flash* was also delicious. Another favorite of mine was **Checkerspot Brewing** (located near M&T Bank Stadium), where the *Rye Lager* was an absolute winner. At **Suspended Brewing**, I found *Tears & Toil Porter* and *Poetry in Motion Grapes Sour Ale*, both of which had me walking away impressed. **Suspended** closed their Pigtown taproom, but are still distributing beer and are hoping to move to a new location at some point.

Another thing that stuck with me from my time in Baltimore is that many taprooms repurposed old buildings in beautiful ways. The most obvious and striking example is the **Ministry of Brew**, as they rebuilt the former St. Michael's Roman Catholic Church (constructed in 1857) into a stunning taproom and brewery. It should not be shocking that it won my Best Taproom award in 2021. This was definitely one of my favorite brewery settings. Another eye-catching building is the Crown, Cork, and Seal Factory (built in 1898), which now houses **Guilford Hall Brewery** (where they make some authentic European-style lagers). Fun fact: Crown, Cork and Seal Company was the enterprise started by William Painter when he invented the bottle cap (I learned this from Maureen O'Prey, one of my podcast guests who wrote *Brewing in Baltimore* and *Beer in Maryland: A History of Breweries Since Colonial Times*).

There are plenty of other examples: an old Sears warehouse that is now **Union Craft Brewing**, the former Westinghouse Electric Corp factory that is now **Mobtown Brewing**, and **Waverly Brewing** located in a 1918 building that was a mechanic shop. **Diamondback Brewing** has one of the more striking features, as the towering smokestack casts a shadow on the building that has housed Coca-Cola and a mattress company. One of the older breweries, **The Brewer's Art**, also falls into this category. Founded in 1996, they moved into a townhouse in the Mt. Vernon district that was built in 1906. Basically, a good chunk of breweries in Baltimore have been able to repurpose buildings throughout the city!

There is one more history lesson here in Baltimore, which is brought to light by **Wet City Brewing**. On their website, they explain why they decided to go with the name **Wet City**. Maryland was the only state that would not pass any enforcement act to support federal restrictions during prohibition. Because of this, Baltimore (and specifically Chesapeake Bay) became the nation's hub for bootleggers.

These are some of my other favorite Baltimore beers:

- *Polydribbles #8*, a sour ale with raspberry, hibiscus, and vanilla from **Nepenthe Brewing**

- *Sunny Fields*, a saison with lime and sea salt from **Monument City Brewing**

- *Guildford Lager*, a helles lager from **Guildford Hall Brewery**

My Take: Don't sleep on Baltimore! Similar to other East Coast cities, there are some spectacular taprooms in historic buildings, and more importantly good beer being served inside of them. Come for crab cakes, but be sure to grab a local pint!

Quick Tip: Venture outside of the city if you can. Sapwood Cellars Brewery in nearby Columbia has some of the best beer in the state. Their *Cheater Hops #18 Hazy IPA* won my Best IPA in 2021. But if you're sticking around Baltimore, check out the National Aquarium, especially if you are traveling with children.

MARYLAND FARM BREWERIES

Speaking of venturing outside the city, it may surprise you just how many breweries in the state of Maryland are out on rural plots of land. Within about thirty minutes of Baltimore, you will find a host of options that provide varied experiences. I always enjoy visiting a farm brewery because it is a change of pace to get out into the country and view some scenery. Often you will see animals, taste beer made with fresh ingredients grown on-site, and hear interesting backstories.

Arguably, my favorite brewery experience in the state falls under this category: **Manor Hill Brewing**. Located outside of Ellicott City (west of Baltimore), they are located on a gorgeous fifty-four-acre farm. Chickens, goats, bees, and cattle all call this place home. There's also a garden with fruits, vegetables, and herbs, a two-acre hop field, and a fourteen-acre corn field. The taproom has a rustic feel, and I savored the *Uno Altro Italian Pilsner*. Before continuing further west, we take a quick detour up north to Havre de Grace. There, a little west of town, you will find **Hopkins Farm Brewery**. This particular farm has been in the family since the 1920s, but only more recently did they build out the brewery. It is unsurprisingly surrounded by cornfields, and inside the taproom, the exposed wood beams look great.

Head back to Baltimore and then continue west, a little further out from the metro area. There are two groupings out in this direction, and I'll start with **Lone Oak Farm Brewing** in Olney. They are named for a pre-Civil War tree on the grounds that sadly fell during a storm in 2023. Thankfully, they have been able to repurpose some of the wood. They also feature fire pits, tents, an outdoor pavilion, a playground, and a sunflower field on their twenty-nine acres. Oh, and they do some of their own malting! Not far away in Brookeville is **The Brookeville Beer Farm**, home to hop yards, patches of berries and mushrooms, honey-producing bee hives, and plenty of outdoor seating. The final two part of this group (all four are within ten minutes of each other) are both in rural Gaithersburg. **Elder Pine Brewing & Blending** is a remarkable spot and a bit different than the others. There's a pine forest out behind the brewery, but they have a hop yard too. The best beer here was *Villeinage*, a dry-hopped saison. **Waredaca Brewing** is located on a farm that boards and trains horses! But don't get any ideas; they have signs up instructing you not to pet or feed any horses that may come by.

The final trio I want to highlight are all in rural Mt. Airy, forming a triangle a little east of Frederick. Again, all within ten minutes of each other, they make for a fun afternoon of brewery hopping. The coolest space belongs to **Frey's Brewing**. The taproom is located in a 200-year-old barn, and they did an outstanding job turning it into a place to consume beer. The beams are still original to the structure, and they used the old flooring for the bar top. Order the amber lager called *The Troll & The Bean* here. **Milkhouse Brewery** is right down the road and played a key role in the Maryland beer scene. One of the co-owners, Tom Barse, was a lawyer and helped get the Maryland Farm Brewery Law passed in 2012 to pave the way for breweries just like this. The open-air taproom looks out on rolling hills, and they also have a hop yard, bee hives, and a donkey named Jezebel. Finally, **Red Shedman Farm Brewery and Hop Yard** is part of a sprawling 200-plus-acre farm. It is not only home to the brewery but also a hop yard and Linganore Winecellars. With a space this large, they, of course, have an expansive outdoor area as well.

My Take: I've been to farm breweries in other parts of the country, but having so many of them close together in Maryland was a fun surprise. I was impressed with how they each had very distinct experiences and had some appetizing beers along the way.

Quick Tip: These farm breweries are fun places to take families (or large groups). Most of them have tons of room to run around, and some even have kid-specific areas to play (like a playground).

WASHINGTON, DC

The nation's capital has an interesting history with beer. I learned from my podcast guest Mike Stein, who is the president of Lost Lagers and Senior Staff Writer at DC Beer, that the city's first production brewery in 1770 was in present-day Alexandria, and it would end up selling beer to George Washington until the 1790s. But fast forward a bit, and from 1956 to 2011 there was not a brewery within the city's limit (although there were several great beer bars). Washington, DC did eventually join the craft brewery boom and now offers an array of superb options. Whether you live there or are one of the many tourists, you will find an option that pleases you.

Starting with some closest to the action (i.e., the National Mall), you'll find a pair of breweries worth checking out in the

Navy Yard near Nationals Park. While they offer an array of styles, I would highly recommend visiting **Bluejacket Brewery** for their lagers. My favorite beer in the city was *Always Wonder*, their Schankbier Lager that comes in at just 3.5% ABV. They also offer an extensive food menu for those who are hungry and have a cool taproom that was part of the ship and munitions manufacturing complex dating back to 1919. A brisk walk down the street will lead you to one of the **Atlas Brew Works** locations (which is 100 percent solar-powered). There's a baseball theme inside, probably because of its proximity to the ballpark. My favorite beer was the American IPA Tropic Thunder.

Heading north, you'll find two locations for **Right Proper Brewing**, where I was especially delighted by the sour ales and the amazing chalk mural on one wall at their Shaw Brewpub. Their production house and tasting room are further northeast in Brookland. **City-State Brewing** is in the nearby Edgewood neighborhood. With beer names and decor that celebrate DC's neighborhoods and history, the converted freight rail warehouse and depot is a fun place to drink some beer. Journey a bit further northeast, right up to the border with Maryland to discover **DC Brau**, the classic spot that ended the brewery drought for the city when it opened in 2011.

I want to mention **Aslin Beer Company**. I visited their location across the Potomac River in Alexandria, but they also have a place in the Logan Square neighborhood in D.C., as well as locations in Herdon, Virginia Beach, and Pittsburgh. They make a massive variety of beers, and my personal favorite was *How Now Brown Cow: Pumpkin Spice*, a milk stout with pumpkin pie spices and vanilla. Another brewery that set up shop in The District is **Other Half Brewing**, as the New York stalwart opened a location in the Ivy City neighborhood on the northeast side of DC. Interestingly, this is where their largest production facility is too.

My Take: While DC may have been a bit later to the party than others when it comes to opening craft breweries, they now have fantastic options that seem to produce a variety of well-made styles. But plan ahead since most of them are not very walkable from the main tourist attractions.

Quick Tip: Because of their unique Gray Laws, you can often find beers from breweries that you probably wouldn't expect floating around the city. So check out the beer bars and bottle shops to see if you can find any surprises.

RICHMOND, VA

A city that I was very excited to visit, Richmond lived up to the hype. The main focus here is the Scott's Addition neighborhood, where there are numerous breweries within walking distance, not to mention a couple of cideries and a meadery. What's great about the neighborhood is that it isn't filled with cookie-cutter breweries. They offer an assortment of different experiences, both in terms of a taproom and the beer.

The Veil Brewing is possibly the most well-known, and with the wide selection of trendy IPAs and sours that match the modern taproom, it's not hard to see why. They also have a second location in Richmond in the Forest Hill neighborhood, as well as one in Norfolk. A couple blocks down you'll find possibly my favorite beer in the city, **Väsen Brewing**. While they have plenty of different options on tap, their more traditional stuff is what caught my attention, in particular, the stunning *Hefeweizen*. It's a unique space, too, as it was formerly an industrial laundry complex. They also have their own running club and climbing club.

If lagers are more your thing, stopping at **Ardent Craft Ales** is an absolute must, as you can drink a pint of their award-winning *Pilsner*. Opened in 2014, they have a spacious beer garden alongside the taproom that essentially doubles their space. Do you want to play any type of arcade game you can think of while also being at a brewery? May I suggest **Bingo Beer Company** for the evening? It feels like an adult Chuck E. Cheese! And right by **Bingo**, you can pop over to **Three Notch'd Brewing**'s Richmond taproom as well. They are based in Charlottesville, but now have six total locations scattered across the state.

If you have a hankering for a meal with your beer, head to **The Answer Brewpub**, where the unique tap list and food have long lured people further Northwest than any other brewery in the city. Founder An Bui founded Mekong, an award-winning Vietnamese restaurant with a variety of international beers available, in 1995. Then, in 2014, An opened up **The Answer**, and since then, this has been a highly-rated destination for both beer and food. For the IPA fanatic, you can't go wrong with **Triple Crossing Beer**, which thankfully converted a former CrossFit gym downtown into something much more productive. When the weather is nice, **Hardywood Park Brewery** has possibly the best outdoor space of any brewery in the area, with fire pits, a live music stage, and a diverse selection of seating options. Finally, if you want something a bit quirky, **Garden Grove Brewing** is a brewery/cidery/winery hybrid that has the coziest taproom I visited in the city.

My Take: Richmond surged onto the craft beer scene and rapidly became a destination for those interested in breweries. Scott's Addition was one of my favorite brewery neighborhoods I visited during my travels, both for the number of options and the quality of beer they were serving.

Quick Tip: Aside from basing yourself as close to Scott's Addition as possible, my other advice would be to hike over to Belle Island, which is located in the middle of the river downtown. Aside from the skyline views, it's a top-notch place to see wildlife and learn more about the area's history.

ASHEVILLE, NC

Where to start? Asheville is another city that my family called home during our travels, and it is certainly one of my favorites when it comes to the beer. By my count, I visited twenty-seven unique breweries within the city of Asheville itself and twenty more in the surrounding area. That doesn't even include a handful of other auxiliary/secondary locations for breweries that are based elsewhere or additional taprooms for some of the local establishments.

I suppose the easiest place to begin is in the South Slope neighborhood, another of my favorite beer destinations when it comes to options and walkability. By my count, there are twelve breweries or taprooms, along with a cidery, two distilleries, a winery tasting room, and a ginger beer taproom. Just a few blocks north to downtown, you'll find four more breweries, plus another cidery taproom. It's truly astonishing how that area has exploded with beer.

One of my favorites in Asheville, **Burial Beer Company**, has its original location in the southern half of the neighborhood. The tap list is a tapestry of styles, from classic lagers to adventurous sours and stouts, and the taproom has a very intimate feel. Their other location in Asheville is on the south side of the city, plus they now have spots in Charlotte and Raleigh as well. The best I had during my first visit was a pineapple and sage mixed culture saison called *Enticed by Confounding Mirage*, but you will be pleased with whatever style you order. Within a block or so, you'll be able to find the classic **Green Man Brewery**, **Twin Leaf Brewery** inside a former photo studio, **Catawba Brewing**'s Asheville location, and if you enjoy sours, you'll find plenty of them at the **Wicked Weed Funkatorium**.

The north side of South Slope has more to offer, but sadly, another favorite of mine, **Bhramari Brewing**, has now closed. Named for the world's first word for black bee (and the Hindu Goddess of Bees), they had an interesting tap list, with my favorite being a *Czech Dark Lager rested on French oak barrels*. Not far from there, though, you can still find locations for both **Asheville Brewing** (love their pizza) and **Hi-Wire Brewing**, along with **Wicked Weed**'s brewpub and San Diego-based **White Labs Brewing**'s taproom. I'll discuss **White Labs** more in-depth in the San Diego section, but what they do with yeast is incredibly cool. **Hi-Wire** has seen some of the most explosive growth of any brewery I've visited. They now have several locations around Asheville, and also opened up taprooms in Birmingham, Charlotte, Cincinnati, Durham, Knoxville, Louisville, Nashville, and Wilmington. Some flagships include *Hi-Pitch Mosaic IPA*, *Leisure Time Lager*, and *Bed of Nails Brown Ale*. They even ship to 42 states now.

Looking elsewhere, a major highlight for me is downtown's **DSSOLVR**, which was my 800th brewery visit. Similar to **Burial**, you can find just about any kind of style you desire, from their flagship *Thank You For Existing Kolsch* to experimental options like *Wicked Engine*, the pumpkin spice cheesecake sour ale. What's impressive is that they do them all very well! One of the co-owners, Mike Semenec, made sure my visit was special, and I had a memorable time chatting with him about the brewery and trying all the beers. It's one of the few breweries I've made multiple return trips to. Plus, they have a convenient location if you are walking around to the barrage of local shops and restaurants downtown. Downtown is also home to **One World Brewing**, **Thirsty Monk**, and a taproom for **Highland Brewing** inside the S&W Market.

There are two breweries north of downtown I want to highlight, and they are nearly neighbors along Riverside Drive. **Zillicoah Beer Company** makes beautifully clean beers and has an expansive outdoor area with gorgeous views of the French Broad River. They were in my top three or four breweries in the area, and I especially doted on the *Dry-hopped Berliner Weisse*. Then just up the road is the incredibly unique and interesting **Outsider Brewing**. Co-founder Julian Arena designed and got a patent for a one-of-a-kind glass brewing system that allows people to watch the beer brewing process in a way you can't find anywhere else. I thoroughly enjoyed my chat with him and learning about the process that led him to build the system. Oh, they make good beer with it, such as their *Czech Pilsner*! Also, along this stretch you can visit **Riverside Rhapsody Beer Company** and **Ginger's Revenge**. At the latter, they specialize in ginger beer.

We can move west or south next, but the area closest to where we've already discussed lies in the former. In almost a perfect line along Haywood Road, there is a string of six breweries. **UpCountry** is the furthest west, with **Archetype** being the other bookend. The highlight of this row, in my eyes, is **Cellarest Beer Project**. All of their beer touches wood at some point in the process. Not far from there, you can also find **Wedge Brewing** and the massive **New Belgium Brewing**'s East Coast location. The latter is nestled along the eastern side of the French Broad River and offers several beers you don't normally see in distribution.

To the south and southwest, there are a number of breweries worthy of your attention. Based purely on beer quality, **New Origin Brewing** is one of the best you'll find in Asheville. My favorite was the *Zwickel Lager*, but if you want a sour, IPA, or stout, they will have a quality choice for you. Their neighbor along the Swannanoa River, **Brouwerïj Cursus Kĕmē**, uses herbs and hops grown on the property where they transformed a tractor-trailer repair facility into the brewery and taproom. A bit further west, you will find the primary location for Asheville's first brewery since prohibition, **Highland Brewing**. Their large complex was formerly Blue Ridge Motion Picture Studios and is now home to their brewery, taproom, event space, and rooftop bar. **Highland** has been around since 1994, and its beers like the *Gaelic Ale*, an amber ale, are part of the fabric of brewing in the area. Finally, if you start heading toward the famous Biltmore Mansion, you'll find **Hillman**

Beer serving a dependable brown ale with patios in both the front and back of the building located along Sweeten Creek.

While this has been one of the longer city write-ups, I also want to shout out a few of the others you can find around the area. **Mars Theatre Brewing** (formerly known as **Hickory Nut Gorge**) in Mars Hill converted the town's movie theater into an amazing brewery and taproom, **Burning Blush** in Mills River brews impeccable lagers, and **Black Mountain Brewing** in the town that bears the same name has a splendid rooftop deck and delicious small batch beers. Also in Mills River is the jaw-dropping **Sierra Nevada Brewing**. You will read more about the brewery's history later, but this facility was completed in 2015 and is one of the most impressive breweries I have visited. Complete with a restaurant, amphitheater, and huge gift shop, this stunning place became the first production brewery in the country to earn LEED Platinum Certification. **Whistle Hop** in Fairview has such a unique atmosphere, complete with a 1969 train car and 1948 box car as part of their outdoor taproom space, and not far away is **Turgua Brewing**, located on Cane Creek in a former tractor repair shop. It's named after a region in Venezuela where the owner raised his family and worked as a research ecologist studying birds! While most people visiting focus on the city of Asheville (as they should), there is a wealth of experiences and delectable beer in surrounding communities.

If you are looking for an even deeper dive into Asheville beer, I can recommend two books from Anne-Fitten Glenn, who was a guest on my podcast. She wrote both *Asheville Beer: An Intoxicating History of Mountain Brewing* and *Western North Carolina Beer: A Mountain Brew History*.

My Take: Asheville lives up to the hype. When it comes to beer scenes in smaller cities, you'll have a tough time beating it out. It's easy to get sucked into the South Slope area and just wander to all those breweries, but be sure to look around at all the options since it isn't difficult to get around the city.

Quick Tip: For some killer BBQ, visit Luella's north of downtown. If you want a quirky spot and revere arcades, visit the Asheville Pinball Museum, where admission allows you to play a slew of retro pinball games. Oh, and they serve beer.

CHARLOTTE, NC

While Asheville has long received headlines as a craft beer destination, Charlotte has seen its own brewery scene rapidly expand. I walked away very impressed after we visited the city. As with many of the cities discussed in this book, looking at different neighborhoods is the easiest way to attack the area, and in my case, I found the NoDa neighborhood to be my favorite.

Three breweries in that area deserve recognition, starting with my favorite in the city, **Salud Cerveceria**. It is located upstairs above the well-known Salud Beer Shop, and they are cranking out phenomenal beers. In fact, their *Dairelynerweisse*, a fruited sour, took home my award for Best Sour in 2021. Bold flavors of raspberry, blackberry, and pomegranate are waiting for your senses in that one. Just north of there, you can pop in at **Divine Barrel Brewing**, which features an array of wood-fermented and barrel-aged options along with your typical IPAs, fruited sours, and lagers. *Defensive Pancakes*, a porter with maple and vanilla, was truly like drinking liquified pancakes! The third stop I'd make in this neck of the woods is **Heist Brewery**. Housed in the historic Highland Park Manufacturing Company Mill No. 3, the food here is a tasty compliment to some flavorful IPAs.

Just south of NoDa there's a pair of breweries I dropped

in on, although one of them is not a "true" Charlotte brewery. **Fonta Flora Brewing** from Morgantown, North Carolina, has a devout following and opened up a small taproom inside Optimist Hall. They do magnificent work across a variety of styles, including wild ales, IPAs, and lagers. Close by is a "true" Charlotte brewery, as **Birdsong Brewing** was the third brewery in the city when it opened in 2010. Fun fact: they got the name because the head brewer sounds like a bird when he snores! I would drink more of the *Rewind Lager* if given the opportunity.

If you head just a touch southeast from **Birdsong**, you'll arrive in the Plaza Midwood neighborhood, where you'll find **Resident Culture Brewing & Blending** making some of the best beer in the city inside the home of a former printing company. *Country of Silence Helles Lager* was so good. There's also a second **Resident Culture** location on the opposite side of the city in the South End and a smaller one in Uptown at the Market at 7th Street. **Legion Brewing** is another with multiple spots, as they have FOUR of them around Charlotte, but the original can be found here in Plaza Midwood. Their flagship Berliner Weisse *Supernova* comes in two different flavors, but the one that I tried (and liked) was passionfruit orange guava (the other is cherry lemon).

Another area to consider if you are planning a Beercation here is south of the city between the York Road and Brookhill neighborhoods. There are several pockets of three or four breweries that stretch from just south of downtown out toward the suburbs. Unlike Asheville however, you probably don't want to go from one side of the city to the other, at least in one night, so be sure to make your plans before arrival.

My Take: Maybe it's because Asheville saps away attention, maybe because much of the brewery growth has been more recent, but I feel like Charlotte has been flying under the radar when we talk about good craft beer cities. There are so many options that make appetizing beers in the Queen City.

Quick Tip: I mentioned that Salud Cerveceria is situated above Salud Beer Shop. If you want to try a variety of beers from different places without doing as much traveling, stopping in there would be a smart decision. Also, for a great rooftop deck with views of downtown, HopFly Brewing is a nice destination.

RALEIGH/DURHAM, NC

The Research Triangle metro area is anchored by the cities of Raleigh and Durham. It is a fast-growing region and home to several well-known universities. I've made a couple of visits to the area thanks to one of my college roommates, Eric, calling the region home for several years, and I've been able to drop in on many breweries there. Aside from breweries in Raleigh and Durham, I also stopped by several in the nearby community of Wake Forest.

But let's begin in the state capital, Raleigh, and with the brewery named for the city, **Raleigh Brewing**. With thirty-two beers on tap, they have a ton to choose from. Not only that, but their flight board is shaped like the state of North Carolina! Now we move closer to downtown, where we first find one of the **Trophy Brewing & Pizza** locations. I visited the original nanobrewery and tried both things highlighted in their name. *The Heart Spelt* (a spelt session ale) went very well with my meat lover's pizza. Not far from there is **Crank Arm Brewing**, which features a bicycle-themed taproom. But it's more than just a theme for them. There is a Crank Arm Brewing Race Team that competes in a variety of bicycling events for men and women. But the most intriguing choice is right downtown: **Brewery Bhavana**. Not only are they a place to try craft beers, but they are also home to a Chinese restaurant, flower shop, and bookstore! It's truly a place where you can get a variety of experiences. I had a fabulous *Foeder-aged Brett Saison* during my visit.

Next up we can travel I-40 to the west toward Durham. While I did not get into the main part of the city, I did visit two breweries on the southern extreme of its boundary. Both of them left me pleased that I was able to stop by. First up, we have **Tobacco Wood Brewing**. It was the first female, veteran-owned brewery in the state when it was first established in 2018. Although they are based in Oxford, North Carolina, about a half hour or so north, they opened this location in Research Triangle Park in 2021. All the beers were well made, including *Rocket Surgery*, a juniper Kolsch. Just down the road from them is one of the locations for **The Glass Jug Beer Lab**. Located in a shopping center, it is not only home to a brewery making beers like a red wine barrel-aged Berliner Weisse called *Torque*, but also is a retail beer store and bottle shop.

Finally, we can head to Wake Forest, which is less than thirty minutes from downtown Raleigh. In downtown Wake Forest are a pair of breweries, the eldest being **White Street Brewing**. Opened in 2012 and located in the Service Chevrolet building that dates back to 1920, I was there in October 2023 during their eleventh-anniversary party. The vibes were high, and I enjoyed drinking a *Kolsch*. A quick walk will get you to **Norse Brewing**, which opened in late 2019 inside a former pizza pub. Now, it's a brewpub with a Nordic theme. The *Mango Hefeweizen* was the treat here. The other two options are not downtown, but still worth a visit. **Blackbird Brewery** is part of the Wheatfield Shopping Center and has a very spacious patio outside, and there is a location for Cary-based **Fortnight Brewery**, where you can get some of their beers on cask. A special shout out to my friend Eric (a different college roommate, yes, there were two Erics) who was with me for these visits in Wake Forest and let me use his phone for pictures since mine had broken.

My Take: I would relish returning to this area to try more of what both Raleigh and Durham have to offer. But what I have been able to sample was enjoyable, and the scene continues to grow.

Quick Tip: If you are flying in and/or out of the Raleigh-Durham airport, one of the local breweries, Lonerider Brewing, has a taproom in Terminal 2.

OTHER CITIES AND AREAS

<u>Northern Jersey Shore</u>: A trio of breweries were part of my experience the day we visited the area. The most established is **Kane Brewing**, which opened in 2011. Named for the husband-and-wife team that founded it, they developed a strong reputation in the New Jersey beer scene and backed it up with several awards. This spot in Ocean Township is best known for its IPAs, but my favorite was a Czech pale lager called *Special 13*. Closer to the ocean in Asbury Park is the delightful **Wild Air Beerworks**. They opened in 2022 and have a lovely taproom with wood ceilings, faux bookshelves, a converted van for seating, plenty of plants, river rock behind the bar, and some exquisite beers. *Fortuna*, an Italian pilsner, and *To a God Unknown*, a wild ale with elderberries, were my favorites. The final piece of this puzzle was **Birdsmouth Beer**, just a little way north in Oceanport. They specialize in making straight-forward lagers and do it quite well. The taproom is very open and spacious.

<u>Harrisburg, PA</u>: I have only been to one brewery within city limits, **Zeroday Brewing**, which had a delicious mango habanero pale ale. But there is a lot to try around the immediate

area. **Troegs Brewing** in Hershey is incredibly well-known, and the *Troegenator Doppelbock* lives up to the hype. They have an impressive facility, and the readers of USA Today voted it The Best Brewery Tour in America four times. Fun fact: **Troegs** won my "Brewery Madness" bracket that I did back in 2020 too. **Ever Grain Brewing** in Camp Hill was recommended to me and didn't disappoint. Had a great hefeweizen there. You could also check out **Pizza Boy Brewing**, where they have over 100 beers on tap, including close to 50 of their own!

Pittsburgh, PA: My goodness, I was impressed with Pittsburgh! All four breweries I visited were amazing, with **Trace Brewing** leading the way and winning my 2023 Best Brewery (Small). Not only did they win Best Beer (All Other Styles) with their *Foeder Saison*, but they also had nominees in the IPA, Dark Beer, and Best Taproom Interior categories. Located in a former brass foundry that was built in the 1900s, it's an incredible space. I also want to shout out Aadam, the head of marketing, for being a great host. **Gristhouse** and **Dancing Gnome** also had nominees that year in the Dark Beer and Best Beer (All Other Styles), respectively, for a Schwarzbier and Dunkel. Another quality option is **Cinderlands**, with its two-level taproom in the Strip District.

Frederick, MD: There's a quartet of breweries right next to each other near downtown. Two of them, **Idiom Brewing** and **Steinhardt Brewing**, are located in the Union Knitting Mills Building along Carroll Creek. Because of this, they both have excellent interiors and nice patios along the water. Right across the creek, you'll find **Smoketown Brewing** in a former textile production building and the laid-back **Attaboy Beer**.

Maryland and Delaware Eastern Shore: Dividing it by state, Maryland features a pair of solid breweries in the town of Berlin. **Burley Oak Brewing** and **Sinepuxent Brewing** had some nice beers with very different atmospheres. **Burley Oak** has a rustic, but more traditional taproom, while **Sinepuxent** is located on a farm that grows a variety of fruits that they use in their beer. Then, to the north in Delaware, I highly recommend the coastal vibes and beer at **Thompson Island Brewing** in Rehoboth Beach and delicious options at **Dewey Beer Co.** in Dewey Beach. Interestingly, **Dewey Beer Co.** now has two other sites, including one in Denver. And, of course, I have to mention **Dogfish Head Brewing**. Their original brewpub in Rehoboth Beach is still there, but the main location in Milton is incredibly impressive and worth a visit. I was a big fan of *Midas Touch*, the first beer in their Ancient Ales series. It was made with ingredients found in a 2,700-year-old drinking vessel from the tomb of King Midas and is somewhere between a beer, wine, and mead!

Wilmington, DE: Both breweries within the city limits I went to were satisfying. I especially liked **Stitch House Brewing**, which is downtown in what was once Linen Mart and Diamond Ice & Coal Co. Loved the Philly Cheesesteak there! I also visited one of the auxiliary **Bellefonte Brewing** locations, where the *Orange Street Ale* with orange blossom honey was the winner. Just south of there, be sure to visit **Midnight Oil Brewing** and **Autumn Arch Brewing**, both serving tasty beer in Newark, Delaware, along the same street.

Greensboro, NC: Some intriguing repurposed buildings here. My two favorites in terms of beer both fall under this category, as **Pig Pounder Brewery** is inside a former repair shop and covered with murals, while **Little Brother Brewing** downtown is in a building from the 1890s that was originally a livery but also served as a restaurant, pharmacy, and comedy club. **Oden Brewing** is another example, as their vintage home was a bottling plant in the 1930s and a metal manufacturer in the 1960s.

<u>Weaverville, NC:</u> Just north of Asheville, downtown Weaverville has a trio of breweries that make for a nice little beer trip. **Zebulon Artisan Ales** has been around since 2016 and has become well-known for their rotating mix of unique and traditional beers. You can sample them in two- or six-ounce pours, and you keep track of your tab on a sheet of paper. **Leveller Brewing** is in a former flower shop and is making enjoyable farmhouse IPAs and lagers, while nearby **Eluvium Brewing** is named for gold deposits (before the California gold rush, North Carolina was the country's leading gold producer).

<u>Belmont, NC:</u> Slightly west of Charlotte, I was part of a bachelor party that visited two breweries in town. Our favorite was **Primal Brewery**, and we visited their main production facility inside a former textile mill. Founded in 2013, this location opened in 2020 and produces excellent beer such as the *Lawn Boy American Lager*. A short walk away, **Jekyll & Hyde Taphouse and Grill** has one of their three locations in the heart of downtown. This steampunk-themed space in Belmont is home to the brewery, while the one in Waxhaw is home to Jekyll & Hyde Distilling Co.

<u>Charleston, WV:</u> I was quite pleased with my visit to the capital of West Virginia. They have slowly been growing their beer scene and now have three breweries within a block of each other right downtown. My favorite was **Fife Street Brewing**. Stretching along the Brawley Walkway (which was formerly Fife Street), the former shoe shop now has incredible beer inside. Their *Straight Kolsch, Homie* and *Chuck's P51 Porter* were particularly incredible. **Short Story Brewing** is based in Rivesville but opened up a taproom here in 2022. *Room to Roam IPA* was a good option, and the taproom has a very chill vibe. If you are hungry, **Bad Shepherd Beer Company** has a full food menu from Black Sheep. They are the city's longest-running brewery!

Here, we look into the growing beer scenes in South Carolina, Georgia, Florida, Alabama, Mississippi, Louisiana, Arkansas, Tennessee, and Kentucky. Many of these states got a slower start to craft beer than others around the country, but are quickly catching up.

We have lived in three very different parts of this region. First was Nashville back in 2018, and then in 2023, we lived in New Orleans and Ormond Beach, Florida. This allowed me to explore the beer scenes in three distinct areas of the Southeast.

CHARLESTON, SC

Another city where I thoroughly cherished my time (beer and otherwise). Charleston is a unique place to visit, whether you are considering culture, architecture, activities, etc. Between there, Greenville, and Columbia, the state of South Carolina has quietly developed a highly underrated beer scene. But first, let's focus on Charleston. My experience there can be broken down into three areas: the city itself, North Charleston, and Mt. Pleasant.

Starting with the actual city of Charleston, there's a trio of breweries on the northside right next to each other that offer wildly different experiences. **Edmund's Oast** has a story that includes a beer store and restaurant along with the brewery, but now they are predominantly known for their work with sours (although they do offer a variety of styles). Right next to them, you'll find **Munkle Brewing**, which lies on the other end of the spectrum with its focus on old-world Belgian and German beers. If you want a little of everything, **Brewlab Charleston** will fit the bill.

Stray south from that grouping to visit **Revelry Brewing**, which not only has a sweet rooftop bar, but also the best West Coast IPA I had in the area (it was named *Lefty Lousey*). They now also have a location in nearby Folly Beach, just steps from the ocean. The other spot within city limits I want to highlight is **Charles Towne Fermentory**, located to the southeast in a former dry-cleaning building from 1907. They offer plenty of styles, but the *Sungazer IPA* was my favorite.

Heading north to North Charleston, you'll find **Holy City Brewing**, which got its name from the local skyline full of steeples. Also located in the area are **Tideland Brewing** and **Commonhouse Aleworks. Commonhouse**, located in the Park Circle neighborhood, was my favorite of the group due in part to their *Brown Ale*. I also liked that they donate a portion of their proceeds to local community groups. **Commonhouse** also has a taproom at the Charleston airport if you are flying in or out of the city. **Tideland** is a family-friendly spot that includes a diverse tap list and food menu, along with a large, open taproom and spacious outdoor area.

You can also have a full day by zipping west to the suburb of Mt. Pleasant. There's a quartet of breweries there located in the same area. You can read about the previously mentioned "monkey event" that led to the name of **Ghost Monkey Brewery** on a plaque in the taproom, and I had an incredibly fun cotton candy sour there! If you favor barrel-aged and imperial stouts, Westbrook Brewing is definitely the move to make. **Two Blokes Brewing** and **Hobcaw Brewing** both offered a nice selection (my favorites were a pretzel gose and Helles lager, respectively).

My Take: My entire family enjoyed our visit to Charleston. It's a fun city to walk around, whether you're at the City Market, Rainbow Row, The Battery, or one of the area's beaches. But there is now also a rapidly growing beer scene that deserves your attention!

Quick Tip: Although it's a coastal city, if you like to go to a beach just know that you'll have to drive to one of the suburbs to get to one. There isn't a traditional beach in the city itself.

GREENVILLE, SC

Greenville has rapidly become a hotspot. It's one of the fastest-growing cities in the country and was named as one of the "52 Places to Go" by the *New York Times* in 2023. The award-winning downtown features trails, waterfalls, tree-lined streets, and plenty of food and drink options. In fact, they rate toward the top of the list when it comes to cities with a high number of breweries per capita.

Right downtown, you'll find a pair: **Fireforge Crafted Beer** and **Yee Haw Brewing. Yee Haw** is a Tennessee-based brewery but opened up a location here with a "sports bar" type feel. **Fireforge** was definitely a highlight, as I enjoyed a New England IPA and the huge outdoor area. They are located in a former tire warehouse and have been around since 2018. A little south of there, you can find a traditional brewpub (**The Velo Fellow**), a location for Atlanta-based **New Realm Brewing**, and the trendy **The Eighth State Brewing**. While I was not able to visit **The Eighth State**, they have garnered plenty of attention and have consistently been rated one of the top breweries in the state.

Elsewhere, you can discover **Pangea Brewing** and **Southernside Brewing** on opposite sides of Swamp Rabbit Trail along the Reedy River. The former is named for the supercontinent and also features a pizza kitchen, while the latter is named for the neighborhood and has a solid *House IPA*. Back on the other side of the city is **Tetrad Brewing**, where you can try their award-winning stout. "Tetrad" means a group or arrangement of four, in this case referring to the main four ingredients in beer: grain, hops, yeast, and water. I also want to shout out the nineties-themed **Double Stamp Brewery**, and **Liability Brewing**, where they make gluten-reduced beers.

My Take: Greenville is a fun little city! After we visited, I understood why it is such a thriving area, and as it continues to grow, I imagine the beer scene will also see more gains. Only two "out of town" breweries have opened up a spot there, but it wouldn't surprise me if other regional breweries at least explored the possibility.

Quick Tip: Aside from walking around downtown, another activity if you have kids is The Children's Museum of the Upstate. We have gone to many different children's museums, but this one stuck out to us.

NASHVILLE, TN

Another place my wife and I called home during our travels, Nashville is a thriving and trendy city, and with that comes a growing beer scene. I have had the pleasure of experiencing most of what the area has to offer when it comes to breweries. We lived there in 2018, but I was able to stop through in early 2023 to check out some of the newer spots and was blown away.

Let's start there, as **Barrique Brewing & Blending** and **Fait la Force Brewing** are two of the more recent additions to the scene and are incredible in different ways. **Barrique** is a more intimate space, with barrels creating a long wall that spans the taproom. As the name suggests, they do some blending while also offering an array of lagers and wild ales (some of which are "still" beers, meaning they are served uncarbonated). **Fait la Force** is just south of downtown, and you can see the skyline from their deck. The space itself is very modern, but it's decorated with a cornucopia of old and repurposed furniture and art. Even the tap list menu is a retro Pepsi board menu. Here, you can indulge yourself with one of their many Belgian styles or a helles lager.

One nice thing about the brewery scene here is that a lot of them are located pretty close to downtown. Two of the closest options are **TailGate Brewery**'s Music Row location and **Tennessee Brew Works**. TailGate's main brewery is outside of the city to the west, but Music Row is more convenient and you can still try their wide variety of styles (my favorites were the sours and *Peanut Butter Milk Stout*). **Tennessee Brew Works** is a music-themed spot just south of downtown with a multi-level taproom AND multi-level deck! If you jaunt just a bit south of **Tennessee Brew Works**, you'll find a pocket of breweries, including the aforementioned **Fait la Force**. They are joined by **New Heights Brewing** and **Jackalope Brewing**.

Heading north now, you'll find the popular IPA slingers, **Bearded Iris Brewing**. Their quirky taproom is where you go if you want something hoppy, such as the flagship *Homestyle IPA*. Nearby, Atlanta-based **Monday Night Brewing** opened a location, and just across the river is **Barrique**. From there, if you head east and north a bit, you'll find some other quality spots such as **Smith & Lentz Brewing**, **East Nashville Beer Works**, another **TailGate** location, and **Southern Grist Brewing**'s first home, which was my 200th brewery visit.

But **Southern Grist** also opened a larger space to the west of the city in The Nations neighborhood, which has become one of the city's most dense brewery hotbeds in the last few years. They are known for their creativity, whether it's dessert-inspired sours, unique adjuncts in stouts, or IPAs with a variation of hops. Their tap list will always be intriguing. Several other established breweries also made the move to The

Nations, including **Little Harpeth**, **Honky Tonk**, **Fat Bottom**, and **Czann's**. Add in a couple of fresher faces like **Turtle Anarchy** and **Harding House** and you have a true brewery neighborhood!

My Take: Nashville's beer scene was good when we lived there in 2018, but with the new additions it has continued to improve and is now a true destination for beer. So, while you may be visiting to take in some live music or hot chicken, be sure to carve out some time to check out the beer scene.

Quick Tip: If you want some of that hot chicken, Hattie B's is my personal favorite—go to their Melrose location just two miles south of Broadway. From our experiences, it's typically a much shorter wait than either Midtown or Lower Broadway.

KNOXVILLE, TN

Knoxville, home of the 1982 World's Fair and the University of Tennessee, may not be the first place you envision for a Beercation. But honestly, the quality and diversity of options here are worth a visit. With a location near the Great Smoky Mountains National Park, it can be easy to tie in with a trip to check out the outdoors as well.

Let's start with glassware. Why? Because of **Pretentious Beer Co.**, which is an offshoot of Pretentious Glass Co. Founded in 2012, they make some of the most unique and amazing beer glasses you'll find anywhere. I own many of their products and love each and every one. They would eventually expand into brewing and have a small taproom attached to the glass-blowing studio where you can watch the artists work.

Aside from that, there's also a traditional German-focused spot, **Schulz Brau Brewing**, with its wonderful beer garden and castle-like exterior. The trendy **Xül Beer Co** is located within an old Volkswagen showroom. The angled wall of windows makes for a unique taproom, and beers like *Betty's Blackberry Cobbler Sour Ale* will keep people coming back for more. **Next Level Brewing** (inside a triangle shaped building that was a car repair shop) is making possibly the best beer in the city in my eyes. If I had to recommend one from there, I would say *Big Boi Map*, a New England IPA.

A few other notes:

- **Hi-Wire Brewing** has a location here, complete with a rooftop bar.

- **Elst Brewing** has an interesting location, as the building they call home was previously an alleyway between two buildings.

- If you are a Green Bay Packers fan, you will feel at home at **Last Days of Autumn Brewing**, thanks to their decor.

My Take: It's easy for a city like Knoxville to fly under the radar when it comes to craft beer. But I'm here to tell you that it deserves some attention. Thanks in part to a preferable location, I would recommend adding The Marble City to your list.

Quick Tip: If you want one of the awesome beer glasses from Pretentious Glass Co., you can buy one in person. But also check their website, as aside from some of the flagships, what they offer does ebb and flow a bit.

LOUISVILLE, KY

Horse racing and bourbon. That's what you go to Kentucky for, right? Well, yes, you do. But you should also check out their craft beer scene! While other barrel-aged alcoholic beverages may be more associated with the area, I can vouch for the quality (and now quantity) of options if you are looking for something with a lower ABV than Buffalo Trace or Jim Beam. One nice thing about the beer scene here is that most of the breweries are centrally located, in particular around the East Market District near downtown.

That is certainly an acceptable place to start, as there are eight breweries within about a half-mile radius. **Against the Grain Brewery** (which is attached to Louisville Slugger Field) is one of the better-known craft breweries in the entire state and is on the western edge of this area. On the opposite side of the neighborhood, you'll find **Gravely Brewing**. This music-themed spot has a large stage in one room and features downtown skyline views from their upper balcony. Oh, and a delicious German pilsner! In between those two are several options, such as **Goodwood Brewing and Spirits** (which now has several locations around the area), **Akasha Brewing** (where I loved their gose), and an outpost for the Lexington-based **West Sixth Brewing**.

Just to the east of that area is another small cluster of breweries, including **Butchertown Brewing**, inside the Mellwood Art Center. I actually recorded a collaboration podcast episode here with David McKinney (host of Brewery Adventures) and enjoyed the sours. There's also the cozy **Apocalypse Brew Works** inside a former heating/air conditioning business, where the apocalypse-themed taproom is called the "Fallout Shelter," as well as **Gallant Fox Brewing**, where that particular mammal is the focus for the decor.

Looking back south of downtown are two of my favorites in the city in terms of beer. First is **Atrium Brewing**, where a former dive bar has been painted black and now brews along with serving up suds. I would recommend the *Neur Koln Kolsch*. Keep heading south, and you'll stumble upon **Monnik Brewing**. Aside from trying the *Eagle Skull Saison*, make sure to look behind the bar at the original cooler doors from the building's life as a bakery. In a similar vein, you can visit a former neighborhood grocery store a little to the west at **Old Louisville Brewery**. At **Old Louisville**, I had a fun peanut butter and jelly stout.

My Take: Louisville has continued to see more and more quality breweries open and thrive, and they are doing an outstanding job of working to market that fact. I interviewed Louisville Ale Trail co-founder Michael Moeller on my podcast, and you can check out their passport program if you are visiting the city!

Quick Tip: I mentioned horses in jest during the first paragraph, but if you have time, I would recommend visiting Churchill Downs. This is especially true if you are a sports fan, but even my wife (not a sports fan) had a great time doing the tour and going through the museum.

ATLANTA, GA

ATL. The largest city in Georgia and one of the largest metro areas in the country has continued to grow its craft scene year after year. This growth was expedited in 2017 when a new law was passed to finally allow breweries to sell directly to consumers in their taprooms. Since then, more and more breweries have opened, and although it still deals with similar issues to other large metro areas (it can take a long time to get around the city), it certainly has many awesome options if you want to seek out some local beer.

Let's start in the Northwest, where a nice grouping of breweries is in the Bolton/Underwood Hills neighborhoods. **Scofflaw Brewing** has been a trendy name here since it opened in 2016, in particular for its IPAs such as *POG Basement*. Places like **Second Self**, **Rightside**, and **The Bold Monk** are nearby, and if you keep working your way back toward downtown, you'll find one of **Monday Night Brewing**'s locations. With a wall covered in ties that have been hung there by visitors, it's a fun taproom, and beers like the *Drafty Kilt Scotch Ale* and *Blind Pirate IPA* have helped grow them into a regional powerhouse with locations in Birmingham, Nashville, and Charlotte.

Northeast of downtown, you used to be able to find one of my favorite spots in the city, **Orpheus Brewing**. When I visited in 2018, they took me into one of their back rooms and let me try *Stone & Flesh*, a wild ale aged in wine barrels with peaches. It was the most intense beer I had during that particular trip to Atlanta. Sadly, they closed down in 2023. **New Realm Brewing** was one of the newest breweries in the area when I visited, and aside from a nice selection of IPAs, they also had a pleasant mild ale called *Fourteen Twenty*. **New Realm** is another Atlanta brewery that has seen regional growth, as they now have locations in Virginia Beach, Charleston, Greenville, and Auburn. **Torched Hop Brewing** is another option on this side of the city, where I enjoyed a Belgian golden with chai.

On a more recent visit in 2023, I stuck around the south-side and visited the incredible **Halfway Crooks Beer**, a finalist for my Best Small Brewery that year. The eccentric taproom has the vibes of a Belgian cafe, and the lagers here are incredible. *Radix*, a German pilsner, was a nominee for my Best Lighter Style Beer in my 2023 Annual Review awards. A bit further south is **Eventide Brewing**, which opened up in 2015 after brewing its first batch the year prior. The Kolsch and relaxed taproom were a nice combination. **Elsewhere Brewing** is right next to them, but they sadly closed early the night I visited, so I was not able to indulge.

My Take: I should also mention **Sweetwater Brewing** since they are possibly the most well-known craft brewery in the state since its founding in 1997. Besides their main Atlanta taproom, they have locations in Fort Collins, the Atlanta airport, and the Denver airport. And while it may have taken Atlanta twenty more years before the craft scene could truly start to shine, it has certainly taken the steps to get there now.

Quick Tip: As I mentioned, Atlanta is a big metro area, and if you are trying to traverse it (especially on a weekday), you're better off picking a neighborhood or at least one side of the city to focus on for any given night. World of Coca-Cola is a fun stop too.

NEW ORLEANS, LA

The Big Easy. Crescent City. Birthplace of Jazz. Whatever name you think of when you picture Louisiana's largest city, you're most likely also imagining the music, food, or culture. Craft beer probably is not at the top of the list. But after we spent a short spell living here, I can tell you that there are some quality spots scattered throughout the city. So, if you can pull yourself away from the French Quarter, you'll be able to find some local beers!

But my personal favorite in the city is actually just off the outskirts of the famous "Vieux Carré," **Brieux Carré Brewing**. The French term for the French Quarter gets a little twist in its name! This hole-in-the-wall spot has a narrow taproom that leads to a courtyard-like beer garden in the rear, and they are making phenomenal beer, particularly the light lagers and sours. *Decaturade: Lemon Lime*, a gose, was one of my nominees for Best Sour in 2023. Also in the French Quarter is **Crescent City Brewhouse**. It is the oldest brewpub in Louisiana, opening in 1991. If you travel a little further west, you can find **Parleaux Beer Lab** making small-batch lagers and ales in the Bywater neighborhood. Another worthwhile outdoor space there, too.

You'll find some heavy hitters south of downtown, and **Urban South Brewing** is probably the most well-known beer maker in the city. Their huge warehouse-style taproom is often busy with people ordering a *Holy Roller Hazy IPA*, *Who Dat Golden Ale*, or *Paradise Park Lager*. A bit further downriver is **NOLA Brewing** with a first-rate mix of traditional and interesting options (I had a blonde ale with crab boil seasoning during my visit). Just blocks from there is **Miel Brewery**, whose taproom has the best outdoor-to-indoor flow. They had several interesting sours and Belgians on tap during my visit. Back closer to downtown I'd recommend **Courtyard Brewery** for those who are a fan of IPAs. **Courtyard** is one of the older breweries in New Orleans, as they started serving beer in 2014 inside their laidback taproom.

Elsewhere, you'll find **Second Line Brewing** to the north. Established in 2014 and named for the local parade tradition, this spot is women, veteran, and minority-owned. Also to the north is a newer player, **Skeeta Hawk Brewing**, where the focus is on traditional styles. Meanwhile, to the west is **Zony Mash Beer Project**. Located inside the historic Gem Theater, this impressive taproom features the old stage on one end between rows of brewing equipment. Loved the Czech lager there. And one bonus: the chain **Gordon Biersch Brewing** has a location downtown, and I was actually quite impressed with their *Golden Export Lager*.

My Take: New Orleans doesn't boast the sheer numbers of some other similar-sized cities, but there are plenty of quality options around. There's still room for growth, so hopefully, by the time you visit, there's even more to check out.

Quick Tip: As I mentioned, food is a major enticement for visitors. Whether it's beignets and café au lait at Café du Monde, some catfish at Dooky Chase Restaurant, or you want to indulge in gumbo, po'boy, or jambalaya, pencil in some time to find something to eat.

JACKSONVILLE, FL

Jacksonville is an interesting city. Like some of the other cities in Florida you are about to read about, it is large and spread out. In fact, it is the largest city by area in the contiguous United States and the second least densely populated in the country. I have visited a handful of times thanks to my college roommate Jacob living there for several years, and he graciously put up with my itch to visit many of the area's breweries. While there is some distance between many of the breweries, some are in groups that are a bit closer together.

Downtown is one of the areas where a few breweries have set up shop. Two of them are secondary or new locations for existing breweries. **Bold City Brewery** has a larger location to the west but also opened a downtown taproom. Back in 1968, Jacksonville was branded as the "Bold New City of the South," hence the name. While the space downtown is on the smaller side, you can still snatch up their beers like *Dukes Cold Nose Brown Ale*, *Killer Whale Cream Ale*, and *Mad Manatee IPA*. Right around the corner is **Ruby Beach Brewing**, which originally opened in Jacksonville Beach before relocating to a 116-year-old building downtown in 2021. It was previously a vinyl record store, and they have a nice outdoor space. The other spot downtown I liked was **Intuition Ale Works**. Founded in 2010, they opened this multi-level spot in 2016. The rooftop deck has a view of EverBank Stadium, and they have a music venue next door called Bier Hall. I enjoyed a milk stout brewed with datil peppers during my visit.

There are a few other spots near downtown, too. To the north, **Strings Sports Brewery** speaks to me on a personal level. Basketball was my favorite sport growing up and I even went on to play in college. From the logo to the taproom theme, basketball is present here. They even have an actual basketball hoop inside a netted area where you can get some shots up here! The outdoor space is nice as well, and the *Bullet*

Bob Hazy IPA was quite good. Right by **Strings Sports Brewery** is **Hyperion Brewing**, which was named after a Greek god. My favorite there was a wheat ale with orange peel. Another of my favorite local spots, **Aardwolf Brewing**, is south of downtown. They had several unique beers when I visited, including *Robo Whale*, an Imperial stout with smoked pineapple, coffee, and orange. It has a nice brick interior for the taproom inside a former tile factory in the San Marco neighborhood.

To the southeast, there are a handful of breweries, although they are spread out a bit. **Veterans United Brewery** is unsurprisingly veteran-owned, and the decor in the taproom is a variety of military pieces that are interesting to look at. **Wicked Barley Brewing** has a wide variety of beers on tap, especially in regard to sours and lagers. They also had food, and when I visited, I loved my cherry-wood-smoked ham sandwich. On my more recent visit, I made it to **Bottlenose Brewing**, and it is quite the spot. Located inside a former World of Beer location, they had thirty-eight of their own beers on tap. I had a quality sour ale called *Tom & Cherry* on my flight.

Many of the best area breweries are actually in the beach communities a short drive to the east. My favorite in Northeast Florida was **Reve Brewing**. Opened in 2018, they transformed a space in a small, unassuming strip mall into an eye-catching and memorable taproom. Leather couches, plants, taxidermy, and a pizza kitchen all funnel into the experience, and I enjoyed all aspects of my visit. My favorite beer was a pilsner, for what it's worth, but everything I tried was well-made. Just to the south in Jacksonville Beach, **Southern Swells Brewing** was a favorite from my first visit in 2018, and I loved the bright, airy taproom. They had just released a collaboration, an oatmeal stout with donuts, with the donut shop next door, too! Other spots in Jacksonville Beach include dog-friendly **Green Room Brewing** right near the beach, and **Engine 15 Brewing**, which was named for an old fire engine the owner bought.

My Take: Jacksonville's beer scene is still growing, and although it's a large, spread-out area, there are still some quality breweries to be found. The smaller towns along the coast create a great place to brewery hop with the ability to dip your toes in some sand and ocean waves.

Quick Tip: While I myself have not made it up there, there's another cluster of breweries to the north in the area between Yulee and Fernandina Beach. I've heard good things about **SJ Brewing**, and my buddy Jacob is also a fan of **Mocama Beer Company**.

ORLANDO, FL

I've been to Orlando a handful of times, but on my most recent visit in 2023, I walked away more impressed with the breweries than I expected. It's safe to say that a majority of people visiting Orange County are there to visit Disney World, Universal Studios, or any number of other theme parks and attractions. But if you venture into the actual city of Orlando, you can find some excellent breweries that offer an assortment of beers.

Orlando doesn't sport the sheer number of breweries that some cities boast, and there isn't necessarily an area that I would classify as a brewery neighborhood. But there are some rewarding options depending on where in the city you are. To the east of downtown in the Milk District is **Sideward Brewing**, inside a renovated 100-year-old warehouse. The three co-founders all grew up in Orlando and are making some delectable beer. In particular, I was impressed by an English pale ale fermented on ex-bourbon barrel staves called *Make it Dangerous*. Just to the south of there is **Hourglass Brewing** in the Hourglass District. Except, the name isn't due to the location, believe it or not. This is their second taproom, with the main spot located in the suburb of Longwood to the north. The name they chose just happened to correlate with this neighborhood. *Brown Beer Brown Beer, What Do You See?* was an unforgettable brown ale, and I also had a pleasing IPA brewed with orange blossom honey. Although it was a bit further to the northeast of downtown, **Tactical Brewing** in the Baldwin Park Village Center is a worthwhile destination as well. Opened by a former marine, the sours and IPAs were both well done. I also bought a Jurassic Park-themed tank top there!

To the west of downtown in the Paramore District is where you could find my favorite, **Deadwords Brewing**. Sadly, they are now closed, but I wanted to include them as they made some incredible beers. Their name was inspired by a 4,000-year-old beer recipe written in a dead language, and they were known for resurrecting ancient styles in small batches. Overall, they offered a variety of classic and modern beer, including the phenomenal *Bridge American Lager* that won gold at GABF in 2022. Not far from their old taproom inside the former Al's Army Store is one of the longer-standing local options, **Broken Cauldron Brewery**. Located right by Inter & Co Stadium (home to Orlando City SC), it's been around since June 2016 and is run by a third-generation brewer (after his grandfather and great-grandfather).

My Take: It's not an issue specific to Orlando in the Sunshine State, but the options are overall pretty spread out if you want to visit a few different breweries. However, even if you only get to a couple, I can say I thoroughly enjoyed many of the beers at the breweries I discussed.

Quick Tip: If you are staying down by Disney, you are a bit of a drive to get into the city. The closest option is **Half Barrel Beer Project**, a small brewery and beer bar that was about to go through an expansion when I visited in early 2023. They have an intriguing guest tap list as well as a couple of their own beers.

TAMPA, FL

As we continue through the Sunshine State, we zip across the peninsula toward the Gulf Coast and find ourselves in Tampa. In my opinion, Tampa has the strongest beer scene in the state. The number of breweries in the area is unmatched elsewhere, and the quality across the board is unlike the other major cities I'm profiling in the state. Many of the breweries are more centrally located, making for easier travel between your stops.

The largest name is **Cigar City Brewing**. Producing their first beer in 2009, they have grown into one of the most well-known breweries in the entire Southeast and now distribute to more than forty states. They are located near the airport just west of downtown, and I sampled some of their classics as well as more exclusive taproom delights. Whether it's a traditional *Maduro Brown Ale* or a *White Oak Spirals & Peach* variation of the famous *Jai Alai IPA*, there are plenty of options to choose from. They also have a taproom by Amalie Arena downtown and operate a brewpub in the airport. If festivals revolving around a specific beer are your thing, their Hunahpu's Day annual event is certainly something a stout lover would not want to miss.

But my favorite brewery in the city is just a bit north of downtown in the Tampa Heights neighborhood. **Angry Chair Brewing** was founded in 2012 and moved to a larger location in 2022, and wow, I was impressed with all the beer. Imperial stouts, such as *Approbation* featuring hazelnut, maple, cinnamon, and vanilla, are probably what they are best known for, but I also had a delightful gose and session IPA. The *Greenhouse Wheat Lager conditioned in American Oak Foudre* was special too, but in reality, many people are going there to indulge in something with a higher ABV. In fact, the aforementioned *Approbation* (a collaboration with **Side Project** that you will read about later) won my Best Dark Beer in 2023! It isn't far from there that you can stop in at **Woven Water Brewing** as you work back toward downtown. Inside a century-old storefront, fruited sours and what they call "Blurry" IPAs are the focus.

And a skosh south from there is another small grouping of breweries. Two places here really impressed me: **Magnanimous Brewing** and **Hidden Springs Ale Works.** The latter dates back to 2015, and while everything here was well done (like an excellent peanut butter milk stout), sours are the main calling card. About half of the beers on tap when I visited **Hidden Springs** were of that variety, and *Riot Juice*, their sour ale with blackberry, lime, and vanilla, is a pleasing melding of those flavors. Right by them is **Magnanimous**, located inside a former Salvation Army worship center. Again, there is a variety here, but one style takes up just over half the tap list. This time, it's IPAs. Ranging from 6% up to 11.5%, it was hard to sort through the eleven different options of that style, but I was very happy with *Death To All But Mosaic*, a DDH hazy IPA. There is another **Magnanimous** in the Seminole Heights neighborhood, as well as in Bradenton.

We can now turn our attention just east of downtown to the Historic Ybor City District. While it is well-known for many things, this is another section of Tampa that has grown into a craft beer neighborhood on top of what else it offers. The best lagers I had while in Florida can be found at **BarrieHaus Beer Co.** The *Family Tradition Vienna Lager* was probably my favorite, but I loved all four in a flight which also included a phenomenal German gold lager called *Tampa Export*. Interestingly, the founder's great-great-great-grandfather founded Peninsular Brewing in 1863 in Detroit. Another popular spot in this area is **Coppertail Brewing**, which features a gorgeous taproom. A balanced tap list features two flagships you don't always see: a Belgian Tripel and a porter. Central to this neighborhood is **Tampa Bay Brewing Company**, which was established in 1995. The *Reef Donkey Pale Ale* is a big seller here, but I've also had some killer hazy IPAs and sours from them as well. I gobbled up a calzone on my visit to the taproom too!

My Take: As I said earlier, Tampa has the best beer scene in Florida, and that's before you even look across the bay to St. Petersburg (home to places like **Cycle Brewing** and **Green Bench Brewing**) or the dense brewery areas in nearby Dunedin and Tarpon Springs. That's why this part of the state would be my first recommendation for a Beercation in Florida.

Quick Tip: My first visit to Tampa was in 2018 for the Gasparilla Pirate Festival. It was an absolute blast. It is essentially a party for the entire city, and you may want to partake in that experience. But if you don't want to deal with massive crowds, street closures, and an overall chaotic environment, be aware of when it is. The season runs from mid-January to early March and peaks with the main parade on the last Saturday of January.

MIAMI, FL

First, the bad. Miami's beer scene is widely dispersed across a large metro area that can take a long time to traverse. The one semi-walkable brewery neighborhood, Wynwood, has four breweries, but two of them are owned by big beer and one is a franchise from Argentina. But now for the good. There are some very high-quality breweries calling this city home, and while you may have to venture around a bit to hit them all, they will be worth your while.

We can start in the aforementioned Wynwood neighborhood, which is a quick hop north of downtown. Here, you will find my favorite brewery in the city, **J Wakefield Brewing**. Opened in 2015, the small taproom sports a strong Star Wars theme (think huge mural and a Han Solo carbonite table) and is certainly one of the most well-known and beloved spots in South Florida. The *Pils, Pils, Pils* and *Hop For A Teach IPA* were both very well-done. The other nearby breweries in the neighborhood include **Veza Sur Brewing**, **Temple Craft**, and **Cerveceria La Tropical**.

The rest of the places I visited were to the west and southwest, out past the airport. Two that ARE walkable distances from each other: **Lincoln's Beard Brewing** and **Unseen Creatures Brewing & Blending**. Both are making amazing beer but have very different vibes. **Lincoln's Beard** has an industrial space that is very interesting, fun, and almost chaotic. Some of the decor includes a giant skeleton, upside-down lamps, random signs, a penny-topped bar, and huge murals. The *Bratwurst Lager* and IPAs were exceptional. Meanwhile, about a block away, **Unseen Creatures** (named for the locally foraged yeast and bacteria) took their industrial space and turned it into a more mellow taproom, although there is a stage for live music on one end. The sours were delectable here, especially *Doomed Expedition*, a wild ale with banana-passionfruit and guava.

Some of the others I visited had a variety of options, but certainly are ones that I could recommend for specific styles. The uber-trendy **Tripping Animals** is in Doral, but it's closer to downtown than some others that are technically in Miami. The IPAs are a big draw here, although the sours and lagers should catch your attention, too. A little jaunt to the northeast takes you to **The Tank Brewing**, and they have an impressive facility. The lagers here are the go-to. I particularly enjoyed *Reinforcement*, the Czech dark lager. There's also a cigar bar and the flight board is a cigar box! If you venture to the far southwest side of the city, **Spanish Marie Brewery** is where I will send you if you want some crazy fruited sours! My favorite was a sour with rum and coke along with lime ice cream, but they also had some made with different flavors of cotton candy. Bonus: If you are flying in or out of Miami International

Airport, **Beat Culture Brewing** and **Prison Pals Brewing** are both nearby.

My Take: If you are not as obsessed as I was with hitting all these spots in only a couple of nights, it's probably for the best. You are better suited to hone in on a specific part of the city and absorb what those breweries have to offer. But if you have plenty of time, there are lots of praiseworthy breweries just waiting for you to visit.

Quick Tip: Everyone goes to South Florida to visit the Everglades (we did, too, honestly), but don't forget there's another national park just as close, if not closer, to downtown Miami. Biscayne National Park offers boat tours, snorkeling and scuba opportunities, and some beautiful beaches out on its keys.

OTHER CITIES AND AREAS

<u>Columbia, SC</u>: One of the biggest surprises on my travels was stumbling upon **Columbia Craft Brewing** inside an abandoned warehouse. Their *Carolinian Blonde Ale*, which won gold in 2020 at GABF, is one of the best blondes I've ever had. It opened its doors in 2017 and is located just a quick hop from downtown. This is also one of the taprooms where I had a phenomenal conversation with the bartenders.

<u>Myrtle Beach, SC</u>: I am fully aware most people are visiting Myrtle Beach for the sun and sand, not so much for the beer. But **New South Brewing**, which began life back in 1998, has a nice selection of beers. They host "Porter Palooza," where they have an array of porters available with different ingredients and recipes.

<u>Memphis, TN</u>: First of all, I highly recommend everyone visiting to take time at the National Civil Rights Museum. It

is very well done and powerful. After you finish there (and maybe check out Graceland and Beale Street), you can drink up at one of the local breweries. **WISEACRE Brewing** (dug the *Coffee Milk Stout*), **Memphis Made Brewing** (where you can play some pinball), and **Ghost River Brewing** (named for a hidden current below the Wolf River) are all decent choices.

Huntsville, AL: Home to the US Space and Rocket Center, this booming city has a growing beer scene to match. **Straight to Ale** embraces the "Rocket City" nickname with rockets hanging from the ceiling inside the space that was formerly a school. Just steps away you can also find **Yellowhammer Brewing**, named for the state bird, the Northern Flicker. Their *Smoked Scottish Ale* was my favorite beer from my time in the city.

Birmingham, AL: The largest city in the state, there are plenty of breweries located near downtown here. My favorite was **TrimTab Brewing**, which calls an expansive building formerly taken up by Motus Motorcycles home. *Paradise Now*, a raspberry Berliner Weisse, was the star of the show here. Make sure to also check out the impressive **Good People Brewing** next to Regions Field (get the *Snake Handler Double IPA*) and **Birmingham District Brewing**, where I happily put away a Schwarzbier.

Little Rock, AR: My personal favorite from my stop in Little Rock was **Flyway Brewing**. Named for the largest bird migratory route in the Americas, they not only have satisfying beers like the *Thrasher Black Lager* but were featured on Guy Fieri's show, *Diners, Drive-Ins, and Dives* for their food menu! **Lost 40 Brewing** is also worth a visit, as they won Mid-Sized Brewery of the Year at GABF in 2020, and **Diamond Bear Brewing** paved the way for all craft beer in the Natural State as Arkansas's first craft brewery in 2000.

Baton Rouge, LA: **Tin Roof Brewing** is located just south of downtown in a large warehouse, and I thoroughly enjoyed the oatmeal stout there. Then head east to Mid City and check out **Cypress Coast Brewing**, which was opened by two homebrewers. But the big winner in the area is **Gilla Brewing** in nearby Gonzales. It is named for the late father of one of the owners (whose nickname was Gilla). They had a variety of amazing beers: lagers, IPAs, sours, you name it. But the *Peanut Butter Porter* was my favorite of the bunch.

Covington/Hammond (LA): Established in 1986, **Abita Brewing** is the largest brewery in the state. Their original brewpub down the road in Abita Springs is still in business, but the main hub in Covington opened in 1994. Big fan of the lagers and Berliner Weisse here! But one of the big surprises of my travels comes from Hammond just to the west. Not one, but two excellent breweries that I was not previously aware of are located here. The skateboard-themed **Gnarly Barley** nailed everything, especially their *Milk Stout*. Meanwhile, you'll find the laid-back **Low Road Brewing** tucked behind a mobile home parts store, and I loved their *Peanut Butter Porter*.

Savannah, GA: I had a wonderful visit to Savannah, which is a beautiful and culturally unique city. My favorite was **Two Tides Brewing**, which not only makes amazing beer (like the *Rainbow Sherbet Sour*), but has a memorable taproom. The brewery is downstairs of an old house in the Starland District, and upstairs is the taproom, which is still divided into a variety of different rooms with distinct artwork, seating areas, and activities. **Service Brewing** also has some enticing beers, like their *Peach Sour* and a wide variety of IPAs. They are veteran-owned and are located in a former paper company near downtown. My other stop was a classic, as **Moon River Brewing** was founded in 1999. Their building was originally built in 1821 as the city's first hotel, and they won Best Mid-Sized Brewpub at GABF in 2017.

<u>Valdosta, GA:</u> There's only one show in town, **Georgia Beer Company**, and in fact, they are the only brewery in this part of the state. But I wanted to highlight them because they won my "Most Surprising Brewery" in 2023. I stopped there randomly on our way down to Florida and had a great experience. They are located in the city's former waterworks building and did a superb job with all their beers. This was especially true for the *Azalea City Amber* and *Pavilion Peanut Butter Porter*.

<u>Mississippi Coast:</u> I walked away delighted with my experience at **Chandeleur Island Brewing** in Gulfport. The fishing theme is strong: fishing pole tap handles (which won my Best Tap Handles award in 2023), a fishing chair, and even an actual fish tank. But the main attraction in my eyes was *Rose of the Coast*, a rosé gose brewed with Shiraz grapes and strawberries. Not too far from there is **Lazy Magnolia Brewing** in Kiln. In 2005, they became Mississippi's first packaging brewery since prohibition. Some of the state's most classic beers can be found here, such as *Southern Pecan Nut Brown Ale*.

<u>Northeast Florida Coast:</u> We called Ormond Beach home during our time living in the Sunshine State. Just north of Daytona Beach, this provided a nice base to check out what the region had to offer. In town you could find **Ormond Brewing** and **Ormond Garage**, two separate breweries that lean into the local car racing history. You'll find coastal vibes at both **Coquina Coast Brewing** in Flagler Beach and **Dunes Brewing** down in Port Orange. Port Orange is also home to one of the **Persimmon Hollow Brewing** locations, which particularly impressed me. I was fond of the blood orange wheat there. Don't overlook **Red Pig Brewing** in Holly Hill either.

<u>St. Augustine, FL:</u> North of the area I just discussed is the historic city of St. Augustine. In fact, it lays claim to being the oldest city in the country. But once you are done touring the

Castillo de San Marcos and visiting the St. Augustine Alligator Farm, you can also check out some local suds. My top pick was probably **Bog Brewing**. Located in the West King Street District inside a former pharmacy and soda shop (that would also be a pawn shop later on), they are serving up a nice variety of beer. There's also a permanent taco truck on the patio. **Old Coast Ales** was another sound option. They opened on Anastasia Island along A1A, and the gorgeous bar is 100-year-old cypress wood. For convenience, **Ancient City Brewing** has a taproom right downtown next to the Cathedral Basilica.

Sanford, FL: Located between Orlando and Daytona Beach, I had a pleasant time visiting a pair of breweries in town. My entire family went to **Dees Brothers Brewing** for lunch in downtown. The building has a neat history, as it was originally a bowling alley but later also served as a Buick dealership and paint store. I enjoyed the *Black & Blue* sour ale with blackberries and blueberries, while my children had a blast playing with the free arcade games. A couple blocks away is **Deviant Wolfe Brewing**. I loved the campfire flight board and also browsed the local art for sale on the walls.

The area of the country where I have spent the majority of my life. Wisconsin, Michigan, Ohio, Indiana, Illinois, Missouri, Iowa, and Minnesota are the focus here. Many of the beer scenes in these states don't get enough love and attention on a national level.

Growing up in Wisconsin and Iowa, I got my start loving beer here, and since 2016 we have called the Milwaukee area our true "home." Wisconsin is the state where I have visited the most breweries, and being close to Minnesota, Illinois, and Iowa has enabled me to get acquainted with the beer scenes there as well (all three are in my Top 10 for brewery visits).

MILWAUKEE, WI

Buckle up. I realize that Milwaukee may not have the most breweries of any city in the country, but it does have a very robust beer scene and also happens to be the place I call home. Because of this, it should not be a surprise that this section will be a bit longer and more in-depth than others. But really, it does make sense that "Brew City" is heavily featured. There is a strong argument that no US city has been shaped more by beer than Milwaukee. Pabst, Schlitz, Miller, Blatz; so many brewing giants emerged from this city, in particular during the mid-nineteenth century. Today, many businesses have repurposed the iconic old brewing buildings for new uses. Even the baseball team is called the Brewers. And like most other cities it has also witnessed explosive craft brewing growth.

In an attempt to move through the city in an orderly manner, we will try to mainly move from south to north, and with that, we will start in one of the trendiest neighborhoods, Bay View. It has become a hotspot for all types of businesses, and breweries are no different. In fact, two of my favorites in the entire area are located here. First, **Supermoon Beer Company** took a 1902 building that was originally a general store owned by German immigrants and transformed it into their brewery and taproom. They brew a variety of styles but are specifically known for their incredible work with farmhouse ales and mixed fermentation. *Wait Until Yesterday*, a red IPA I tried during my first visit, is one example of how they make styles you don't often see (and make them well)!

Just north of there is **1840 Brewing**, which is another of my top recommendations for Milwaukee. They originally had very limited hours when they first opened in 2017. Thankfully, that is no longer the case, and their unassuming space in Bay View is a place I have frequently visited. I love the beers here, whether it's one of their IPAs, a unique sour, or something more on the funky side. I also purchased two of their barrels to repurpose into a bar for my basement! They now have a location in West Bend, which is northwest of the metro area. **Enlightened Brewing** has made two different moves since opening in 2015 but has always been in Bay View. Their newest facility is a sprawling space that was home to the Louis Allis Company. Their *Cream City Brix* cream ale is one of my "go-to" choices for local beer.

We need to stay in Bay View for one more paragraph, but will only talk about one building. That is because the Lincoln Warehouse is what I like to call Milwaukee's "Brewery

Incubator." There are now three breweries (along with a distillery and a handful of other businesses) in this large building: **Component Brewing**, **New Barons Brewing Coop**, and **Torzala Brewing**. The space Torzala calls home is particularly interesting. It is located on the second floor of the warehouse and can be a bit tricky to find. But it has been home to three other breweries, and all three of them have gone on to be successful. You already learned about **Enlightened**, will soon read about **Component**, and later on will hear about **Eagle Park Brewing**. They all started in the humble abode. Torzala seems to be on their way to promising things too, and I quite enjoyed the *Forty-Eighter Blood Orange Hefeweizen*. Downstairs, you will find **New Barons**, which took over **Enlightened**'s second home. They were founded in 2016 and opened up the taproom in 2020. When **Component** outgrew the space upstairs, they decided to move downstairs around the corner from **New Barons**. I drank a variety of lagers here, and they also make some excellent sours.

We now leave Bay View for the nearby Walker's Point neighborhood, and here you will find some of the most unique breweries in the city! And that uniqueness is at its peak at **Mobcraft Beer**. It is here where they turn "Ideas into Beer." Since 2011, they have crowdsourced beer recipes, where anyone can submit ideas and then vote on what beer "wins" each month and is made. Sure, they still have flagships, but it's interesting to see what concoctions they put out. There's a wall in the taproom dedicated to all the previous winners, too. Sports fans will want to make a stop at **Broken Bat Brewing**. The baseball theme jumps out to visitors, featured in beer names such as *Batter's Rye IPA*, *High & Tight New England IPA*, and *Soft Toss Cream Ale*. They also have a bunch of bobbleheads on display, and did I mention they have an indoor wiffle ball field? You can rent it out, and they even host leagues there.

On the southern edge of Walker's Point is **Urban Harvest Brewing**, which has been open since 2016 inside a space that was formerly a theater. Our final stop in this neighborhood is a transplant, **Indeed Brewing**. They are based in Minneapolis but opened up a brewery and taproom in Milwaukee in 2019. The space has an "old-school supper club" feel to it, in my opinion, and they did a commendable job integrating themselves with the community by brewing beers like *Hello, Milwaukee Lager*.

Just across the Menomonie River, it's hard to miss **City Lights Brewing**. The complex was built for the Milwaukee Gas Light Company, and the massive tower rose in 1903. In terms of beer, their *Hazy IPA* won a silver at GABF in 2019, and the *Coconut Porter* is also popular. The next stop is right down the road and is one of the breweries I always include in my Milwaukee recommendations. **Third Space Brewing** is a place I will always send people to because no matter what style (or styles) you are looking for, they probably have something on tap. Their *Unite the Clans Scottish Rye Ale* is another one of my go-tos, and it has won multiple GABF medals. They offer other reputable beers as well such as *Happy Place Pale Ale*, *Frog Weiss Fruited Sour*, and *Ice Bear Baltic Porter*. They also have a location to the northwest in Menomonee Falls.

Moving more into the downtown area, **Explorium Brewpub** set up its second location in the Historic Third Ward. Located in the Pritzlaff Building that was built in 1904, they are another brewery that offers a large variety of options (plus, very good food). Their first location is in the suburb of Greendale and is oddly located inside a mall. Look for beers like *DAMN! That's Good! Double IPA* or the *Cream City Crusher Cream Ale*. The Third Ward is also home to **The Copper Turtle Brewery & Tavern** and the fun, magic-themed **Wizard Works Brewing**. **Wizard Works** also features one of my all-time favorite brewery logos!

Sticking around downtown, there is a trio of breweries near Fiserv Forum, the home of the Milwaukee Bucks. One is literally part of the Deer District, the entertainment development surrounding the arena. **Good City Brewing** has a taproom directly across from the arena, and although this is not their main location (which is in the East Side neighborhood), you can grab a *Home Lager* or *Fetch West Coast IPA* before going into the game. They also have locations in the suburbs of Wauwatosa and Mequon as well. There are two other options in the Brewery District, the area directly west of the arena. This is where you will find the former twenty-one-acre Pabst Brewing Company campus. One of the businesses now there is **Central Waters Brewing**. You will read more about them later, but the Amherst-based company took over the space that was built in 1872 as a German Methodist church. It's a beautiful setting, and I have ordered a *Tomorrow River Helles Lager* there a handful of times. Down the street is another unique spot, Chicago-based **Pilot Project Brewing**. They are an "incubator" that provides a launch pad for start-up breweries. If you visit their gorgeous taproom that was previously home to **Milwaukee Brewing Company**, you can try beers from several smaller brewers that all brew their beer there.

Now, we can head just a bit north of downtown, with a stop at **Dead Bird Brewing**. Here, you will find some classic European styles like a Dunkel or an English brown ale; I've even had a barrel-aged Oud Bruin (a Flanders Brown Ale) there, which you rarely see! Interestingly, the building was home to Milwaukee's first grocery delivery service in 1903. About the name: when the co-founders were in college and looking for brewing equipment, they found a pot in one of their parent's attics, and inside was a dead bird! Not far away, our next stop is in the Brewer's Hill neighborhood. **Lakefront Brewery** is one of the originals when it comes to craft beer in Milwaukee. Founded in 1987 by Russ and Jim Klisch, they have seen many "firsts" over the years. The first beer in the country made from 100 percent in-state-grown ingredients, the first certified organic brewery, producing the country's oldest certified organic beer, and the first government-certified gluten-free beer. They also have one of the best tours in the country. The taproom has an open, beer-hall-like feel, and the two-level deck and patio space along the river provides attractive views. They are still one of my favorite breweries to visit, and I enjoy the *Riverwest Stein Amber Lager*, *New Grist Pilsner*, and the *Gosa Rita* (a margarita-style gose). Their food is good too, in particular, the cheese curds and fish fry!

Hop across the Milwaukee River and within shouting distance of **Lakefront** is another of my favorites: **Eagle Park Brewing**. As I mentioned earlier, they started in the Lincoln Warehouse before taking over this Lower East Side location. They now also have a massive complex to the southwest in the suburb of Muskego, where they not only brew beer but also have a distillery. On top of that, they have become well known for their hard seltzers, but of course, I'm more of a fan of their beer. Their IPAs have been popular for many years now, with options such as *Set List*, *Demon Haze*, and *Goon Juice*. But more recently, they have been cranking out some divine lagers like *Vivo Pils* and *Ritmo Mexican Lager*. I'd be remiss not to mention my favorite beer from them: *Booze for Breakfast: French Toast*, one in a series of Imperial stouts that features Vermont maple syrup, Cascara cinnamon, and Madagascar vanilla. Yes, it tastes like it sounds. A little northeast of there is **Good City**'s first location, as well as **Hacienda Brewing**'s taproom. The Door County-based brewery is known mostly for its IPAs but also offers some lagers, stouts, and saisons. It recently was rebranded as Triple Taproom & Kitchen, as they not only serve **Hacienda** beers, but also beers from **Door County Brewing** and Sheboygan-based **3 Sheeps Brewing**.

Just north of this area is the Riverwest neighborhood, and three breweries call this part of the city home. First is the very dog-friendly **Black Husky Brewing**. They started up in Pembine, Wisconsin, before moving their operation here in 2016. The name and theme are inspired by the co-owners' son's sled dog kennel, and they still honor the twenty-three dogs that spent time with them. Continuing north will land you on the block where both **Amorphic Beer** and **Gathering**

Place Brewing are located. **Amorphic** took over a former manufacturing building built in 1915 that features the "Cream City" bricks the area is known for. IPAs have been their most popular style, but I have been more drawn to their sours and lagers on my visits. Specifically, my favorite beer from them was *Bia Hơi*, a Vietnamese jasmine rice lager. Around the corner is **Gathering Place**, which has been a splendid addition to the beer scene since it opened in 2017. They offer a variety of European-style beers that you don't see everywhere else: Kolsch, Dunkel, Weizenbock, Norwegian table beer, Dortmund lager, and Belgian Tripel, to name a few. They also have a second taproom in Wauwatosa.

Finally, I will mention a pair of breweries on the western side of the city, where there are fewer options. First, **Vennture Brewing**. This is a location for beer and coffee nerds to meet, as they are not only a brewery but a coffee roastery as well. They make some of the best beer in the city, too, with a rotating tap list featuring beers like *Doughnut Don* (an Imperial pastry stout collab with a local donut shop), West Coast IPAs, sours, saisons, and much more. They also took over the **Biloba Brewing** location in Brookfield when **Biloba**'s owners decided to retire. One of the coolest places you can visit is right off the freeway inside American Family Field, home of the Milwaukee Brewers. **Leinenkugel**'s, one of Wisconsin's (and the country's) oldest and most noteworthy breweries, took over what was a TGI Fridays in left field. Year-round, you can now stop in to swig a beer brewed on-site with sweeping views of the inside of the stadium. While most of the beers on tap are their regulars, they do have a small pilot system right there in the ballpark where they brew special small-batch releases for the taproom. If you want to watch an actual game from their deck, you need to reserve spots in advance.

My Take: Listen, as much as I love my city, I do try to remain unbiased. I'm not going to sit here and tell you that Milwaukee has the best craft beer scene in the country. But I will say that the "high-end" options here can go up against just about any other city. And there are more than enough breweries to make it a worthy Beercation destination.

Quick Tip: Aside from the beer (and cheese), there are so many activities around the city. The Harley Davidson Museum, Milwaukee County Zoo, Milwaukee Public Market, National Bobblehead Hall of Fame, an array of other museums, and we even have nice beaches when the weather is warm.

SUBURBAN MILWAUKEE, WI

One section wasn't enough, as I wanted to highlight some of the breweries around the Greater Milwaukee Metro area without extending the prior section too long. We've already discussed some of the breweries that have locations in the suburbs: **Eagle Park** (Muskego), **Good City** (Mequon and Wauwatosa), **Explorium** (Greendale), **Vennture** (Brookfield), **Gathering Place** (Wauwatosa), **Third Space** (Menomonee Falls), and **1840** (West Bend). But now it is time to highlight breweries that are only found in the communities surrounding the city.

This time around, we will start in the north, partially because this is the area I call home. I specifically live in Glendale, which is fifteen minutes (or less) from downtown Milwaukee and is home to two similar, yet very different breweries. **Sprecher Brewery** was the first craft brewery in Milwaukee, established in 1984. They moved to a renovated elevator cab factory in Glendale in 1993 and have been there ever since. They make primarily German style beers (I'm fond of the *Black Bavarian Schwarzbier*), but you also may be familiar with their sodas. The fire-brewed root beer, in particular, is tasty.

Not too far away is the brewery closest to my house, **Bavarian Bierhaus**. As the name suggests, this is another place heavily influenced by German heritage. This area was originally leased by the German Clubs of Milwaukee in the 1920s, and they built it up to what it is today. The food, the beer, the "Beer Hall," the "Fest Hall," and the soccer team are all German in nature. Yes, the soccer team! The Bavarian United Soccer Club has teams ranging from young children up to a professional USL League 2 team that plays in a small stadium behind the brewery. The beer is straightforward, and my entire family loves to eat here. This is also where Milwaukee's largest Oktoberfest takes place every year!

A bit further north is a highlight you will want to check out: **Foxtown Brewing** in Mequon. The location they stepped into dates back to 1857 and has a long history of brewing. In fact, right below your feet are two levels of subterranean lager caves. You can sign up for tours and they even offer "Cave Dinners." Yes, those are exactly as they sound, as you can book a dinner party and dine inside one of the caves! The food menu is slightly higher end here, and the interior is gorgeous with high, vaulted ceilings with lots of exposed beams. The beers are exceptional, too, from a wide selection of classic lagers to IPAs, ambers, and stouts. They are planning on opening another large location in downtown Milwaukee, but I did not include it in that section because as I'm writing this there is not a firm opening date set. We will stop there, although if you venture just beyond what I would count as the "metro area," there are breweries like **The Fermentorium** in Cedarburg, **Sahale Ale Works** in Grafton, and **Inventors Brewpub** in picturesque Port Washington.

Working counterclockwise, we head to the west. Our first stop is going to be the city of West Allis, which borders parts of Milwaukee. A trio of breweries have burst onto the scene since 2020, providing locals with an influx of craft options. The eldest is **Layman Brewing**. They took over a corner bar and are going for a traditional "Midwest take" on a public house. It is one of the coziest, most inviting, down-to-earth taprooms you'll find anywhere, and the owners, Kyle and Sarah, are a delight to talk with! Next up is **Ope! Brewing**, which takes a fun approach to the unique linguistics of the region. Many of the beer names play off of this: *'Scuse Me Pale Ale*, *Fer Sure IPA*, and *Dontcha Know Hazy Pale Ale* are just a few examples on tap inside the former Perfect Screw Products building. **Ope!** opened in 2022, and around the same time **Perspective Brewing** set up shop not far away in what was previously a shoe repair shop. The seven-barrel system makes some solid beers, such as the *Travel Fee Hefeweizen*. Our next destination is in Wauwatosa. Although I already mentioned several of the taprooms here, there is one more I need to bring up. Funny enough, it is another transplant. **Lion's Tail Brewing** is based in Neenah, Wisconsin, and although you will read more about them in a later section, it should be noted that they have a standout venue here in the Milwaukee area now, too.

Now, we officially leave Milwaukee County for the neighboring Waukesha County, where the city of Waukesha is home to two quality breweries. They may be the only two available in this city of 70,000 people, but what the city lacks in quantity it makes up for with quality! **Raised Grain Brewing** opened in 2015 before outgrowing their small space and moving to a much larger one in 2019. The taproom features huge windows, and this is another brewery where no matter what style you are looking for, you can probably find something here. But some of the most popular include *Paradocs Imperial Red Ale* (a GABF medal-winner), *Naked Threesome NEIPA*, and *Black Walnut Belgian Stout*. The second brewery in town came around more recently, in 2024. **North Pillar Brewing** is another one that took over an old brewery building—dating back to the 1850s. The towering white pillars inside the space compose half the name (the other half being the location on North Street), and I was impressed with their beers right from the start. This was especially true for the *Early Drumlin Coffee Stout* and *Family Function Red Ale*. Similar to the north, if you stray a little further out west, you'll find even more options: **Delafield Brewhaus** in Delafield, as well as **SteelTank Brewing** and **Brewfinity Brewing** in Oconomowoc.

My Take: As is the case in most metro areas, there is plenty of action to be found in many of the suburbs. This was not fully extensive of every option around the area, but at least gives visitors a good idea of the lay of the land.

Quick Tip: Many of these suburbs are only fifteen to twenty minutes (or less) from Milwaukee. This area as a whole is fairly easy to get around compared to similar cities, so if something strikes your fancy don't be scared to go out to it.

MADISON, WI

The capital of the Badger State is known as a political and education hub, with the capitol building downtown not too far from the University of Wisconsin-Madison campus. It also has a robust beer scene, not only featuring a healthy selection of breweries, but also is home to the Great Taste of the Midwest. One of the premiere beer festivals in the country, it is probably my personal favorite, as there is an insane number of breweries in attendance at Olin Park overlooking Lake Monona. It should not be a huge surprise that I have spent a considerable amount of time here and have grown fond of several of the breweries in the area.

Downtown is located on an isthmus between Lake Monona and Lake Mendota, and two of the breweries I want to highlight are within view of the capitol building about a block apart. **Great Dane Pub & Brewing** opened their original location here in 1994 as Madison's first brewpub, and have since added two more locations in Madison, one in Fitchburg, one in Wausau, and in 2024 they opened one in Japan! I've eaten a meal at the downtown location, and also liked their classic *Old Glory APA*. That first location also has some history to it, as it dates back to 1858 and is the former Fess Hotel building.

Right up the road from this old school spot is some new blood: **Young Blood Beer Company**, to be exact. Since they opened in 2020, they have been a go-to spot for interesting and experimental beers. The downtown taproom is fresh and inviting, with plant life abounding and the brewery situated in a space below for patrons to view. Most of their beers are one-and-done (some do get remade), but expect to find lots of unique fruited sours along with a handful of intriguing IPAs, stouts, farmhouse ales, and lagers. There's also a second location on the northeast side of town. Just a few blocks away is one of the locations for the award-winning **Vintage Brewing Company**. They were named Large Brewpub of the Year in 2019 at GABF thanks to winning gold medals for both their Belgian dubbel and Altbier. Their oatmeal stout and Irish red ale both have multiple medals at GABF and WBC as well. They have another location on the far east side of Madison and a third in Sauk Prairie (about forty minutes to the northwest).

Working our way northeast across the isthmus takes us to our next destination, **Giant Jones Brewing**. This women-owned spot focuses on brewing big, high-ABV beers that are all USDA organic. They opened in 2018 and have a simple, no-frills (and dog-friendly) taproom. My favorite was the *Pale Weizenbock*. A few blocks away is one of the best breweries in Madison, **Working Draft Beer**. They took over a building that was home to RP's Pasta and opened in 2018. Here you will find an assemblage of IPAs alongside European lagers and ales. A little fun fact: the bar and tables are made of old bowling alley lanes from Monona. Continuing northeast, the next stop is the unique **Herbiery Taproom**. They specialize in brewing with no hops, and this distinctive method produces such treats as

Zingibeer (a ginger lager) and *Misty Morning Coffee Kolsch*, which is made with locally roasted coffee. **Starkweather Brewing** is named for nearby Starkweather Creek, and you will find a significant variety here. *Lake Loop Cream Ale* and *Armadillo Madness* (a sour ale with prickly pear and pineapple) are examples.

Karben4 Brewing, located near the airport to the north, is one of the relatively more established breweries, opening in 2012. If you visit the fun, quirky taproom, you will most likely see several people sipping on their flagship *Fantasy Factory IPA*. Right around the corner is Madison's gluten-free brewery, **ALT Brew**. They started up in 2014 and opened up this location in 2016. The story goes that the founder's wife was diagnosed with gluten intolerance, and thus an idea was born. Although gluten may not be allowed in the door, your dog is, so you can bring your four-legged friend while trying a *Copperhead Copper Ale*.

Before moving further out of the city, we swing down to the area south of downtown. One of my other favorites in Madison is located here, **Delta Beer Lab**. It feels like you are stepping into a classroom science lab from high school or college, complete with test tube tap handles, beaker flight glasses, and even sinks on the long tables made to look like workstations! The beer is good too, and features science-like names. Some of the best I had include *BRN.01* (brown ale), *PTR.01* (porter), and *LAG.07* (lager). A bit north of **Delta** is another unique venue, **Black Rose Blending Company**. They took over the space formerly home to Funk Factory Geuzeria, and similarly to their predecessors, you will find beers here that you can't find anywhere else in the area. Their tap list often includes oak-aged wild ales, mixed-culture farmhouse ales, and other lesser-seen styles.

As we leave Madtown, there are a handful of breweries in the surrounding suburbs that deserve to be highlighted. One of the state's longtime stalwarts is located in Middleton, which bumps up to the eastern border of Madison. **Capital Brewery** was founded in 1984 and brewed its first beers in 1986. Since then, they have expanded, won awards, and become well-known for their expansive bier garten. They are another brewery committed to sustainability practices and also founded a bike club that sees over one hundred riders meeting regularly. Flipping over to northeast of the city, **Full Mile Beer Company** is located in a newly built building in downtown Sun Prairie. The modern taproom opened in 2018, and besides having beers like the *Earth & Engine Oatmeal Stout*, they also have an extensive food menu if you are hungry.

Our final stop is a doozy, as Waunakee is home to **Octopi Brewing**. Not only do they make their own beer, but they are the region's leading contract beverage facility. They have expanded multiple times since opening in 2014 and have continued to grow. One of the in-house brands, **Untitled Art**, does collaborations with some of the top breweries all around the country. This is definitely a place to check out if you get the chance. **Lone Girl Brewing** is also in Waunakee, and in 2024 they opened up a taproom in Madison.

My Take: Madison is a vibrant city that is a fun place to be whether or not you want craft beer. But the options here are plentiful, and the fact that so many of them are close to downtown makes it an ideal location to jump around to breweries.

Quick Tip: If you want to attend the Great Taste of the Midwest, you will want to research how to get tickets. Some tickets go on sale in person at a few venues around the area in May, and then there is a week-long online lottery. Often, you can still find tickets floating around other places closer to the event, but this is one festival you will want to plan ahead for.

LAKE WINNEBAGO AREA (WI)

The largest lake entirely within Wisconsin, Lake Winnebago, has several cities around its edge that are home to growing beer scenes. Appleton, Oshkosh, Neenah, and even Manasha are all home to breweries, and while this may seem like it's covering a large area, the furthest apart breweries I'll be mentioning in this section are just over twenty miles apart.

Starting the furthest north in Appleton, the largest of the cities, you'll find a few options. If you are someone who appreciates cask ales, **McFleshman's Brewing** not only had four on tap when I visited, but also feels like a traditional pub inside. Right next to them, you'll find the **Appleton Beer Factory** on the main drag through downtown. Another more traditional experience is across the Fox River at **Stone Arch Brewpub**, which resides in a building that was built in 1858 as a brewery. Moving south along the lake, you'll find the Neenah/Menasha area next, where there is a brewery I recommend checking out. **Lion's Tail Brewing** has become the most popular name in the area (as I mentioned, they have a location in the Milwaukee area now), and they have a neat space inside The Reserve, an old insurance bank. Their *Juice Cloud IPA* won my Best IPA award in 2019, and they make plenty of other tasty options, too. Interestingly this was also the first place I ever tried a "slushie-style" sour ale.

The last stop on this particular journey lands us in Oshkosh. If you are coming from the north, the first spot you'd hit is the dog-themed **Bare Bones Brewery**, complete with a bone-shaped flight board and bone-shaped tap handles that won my award for Best Tap Handles in 2019. Once you're in town, you can stop by **Fox River Brewing**, which is right on the river and one of their two locations (the other is back up in Appleton). My personal favorite in Oshkosh, though, was **Fifth Ward Brewing**. The co-founders both have culinary backgrounds, and it shines through in their beer, such as the *Comb & Crocus Honey Saffron Wheat Ale*.

My Take: Just down the road from Green Bay, this area has emerged as its own destination. Each city has a different vibe, and thankfully, there's at least a brewery or two in each one that can quench your thirst for local beer.

Quick Tip: If you are into airplanes and flight, the EAA Aviation Museum is in Oshkosh and features over 200 aircraft and 20,000 artifacts. The Oshkosh Air Show occurs in July as well.

GREEN BAY, WI

Go Pack Go! As a diehard Green Bay Packers fan (I named my son Lambeau), I have spent my fair share of time here. While the professional football team is far and away the most famous part of the city, this area is also known for its impact on the paper industry and is home to the National Railroad Museum as well. On top of that, as the third largest city in the state, it is not a surprise that a decent craft beer scene has developed. Something else that is not a surprise? Several of the breweries lean into the local passion for the gridiron franchise.

We can start at **Hinterland Brewery**, as they opened up a gorgeous facility right next to historic Lambeau Field. Originally located in a meat-packing warehouse, the newer space was opened in 2017. The best beer to order before attending the game has to be *Packerland Pilsner*. **Badger State Brewing** is not much further from the stadium. They offer around two dozen beers on tap, including plenty of sports-themed options like *Game Day IPA*, *Gold Package Blonde*, *Köld Tundra Kolsch*, and *On Wisconsin Red Ale*. A little north, the aptly named **Titletown Brewing** also features beer names that will appeal to cheeseheads: *Green 19 IPA*, *Dark Helmet Schwarztbier*, and *Johnny Blood Ale*. Established in 1996, they moved the brewery into the former Larsen Canning Co. building in 2015. Bonus: there is a rooftop bar! And across the street is **Copper State Brewing**, which is located in the old meat-packing plant that was formerly home to **Hinterland**! The cozy environment pairs well with beers like their *Chocolate Coffee Peanut Butter Nitro Porter*.

On the western side of Fox River is where you will find the rest of the action. **Stillmank Brewing** got their start in 2011 via contract brewing, but would open up inside the former Builders Supply warehouse in 2014. I had a great time chatting with Brad and Erin Stillmank during my visit. If you want to stick with the football fan theme, order a *Tailgater Blonde*, but I highly recommend the *Perky Porter* or *Wisco Disco ESB*. **Zambaldi Beer** and **Noble Roots Brewing** are also on this side of the city. **Zambaldi** had one of the best children's play areas I've seen at a brewery, and **Noble Roots** has its taproom cozily tucked into a former service station.

My Take: Green Bay is not necessarily a big destination for craft beer, but if you are making the pilgrimage to one of the nation's most historic sporting venues, there are plenty of breweries to keep you busy!

Quick Tip: While going to a game is a must, I also recommend visiting Lambeau Field during the off-season. It is far easier to get around the city, you can meander through the Green Bay Packers Hall of Fame & Museum without the crowds, and walk around the Titletown District (which features a public football field, a tubing hill for the winter months, playgrounds, game courts, and tons of other activities).

RURAL WISCONSIN

I was going to include a short blurb in the "Other Cities and Areas" section, but then decided I wanted to write a bit more than that. While I understand that it may seem I'm diving too deep into the Wisconsin beer scene, I can't help but highlight what my home state offers.

And one of those that is located out of the way is one

of my favorites, **New Glarus Brewing**. This stalwart is well-known for being one of the largest craft breweries in the country but only distributes in the Badger State. As soon as you cross the border, you can stop at any gas station or grocery store, and you'll find multiple options of theirs. Visiting their beautiful location just outside New Glarus is a worthy pilgrimage for any beer lover. While the *Spotted Cow Cream Ale* is the flagship they are best known for, my two favorites are probably the *Kid Kolsch* and *Raspberry Tart*. The entire experience there is phenomenal, as the outdoor beer garden area is gorgeous, and you can also give yourself a self-guided tour through part of the brewing facility.

The next brewery I want to highlight is **Potosi Brewing** located in the far southwest corner of the state. I find this to be one of the most interesting breweries. Originally founded in 1852, it closed in 1972 before being re-founded at the original site in 2008. Not only is this classic location back open and serving up beer, but it is now home to the American Breweriana Association (ABA) National Brewery Museum. The huge collective of beer memorabilia is spread out across several rooms and multiple floors. Bottles, trays, coasters, advertising materials, historical write-ups, and much more are all there for guests to take in.

The southwest corner of Wisconsin has some other unique breweries, including my "Most Interesting Brewery" for the 2024 awards, **Commerce Street Brewery Hotel**. Formerly called Brewery Creek Inn, they changed the name and made it even more literal. The joint business description is preceded by the name of the street it is located on in the town of Mineral Point! The historic building downtown was built in 1854 to help serve the local mining industry boom. So, if you are passing through, you can indulge in some beers brewed on-site before going upstairs to catch some z's!

A bit further north is the town of Cashton, which was my home from the age of one until around eleven, and there are now two interesting breweries located a little outside of this small town. **Footjoy Farm and Brewing** in unincorporated Melvina is another brewery that has a descriptive name, as they grow 100 percent of the grains used in their beers on the owner's family farm! The building they call home was originally built as a grocery store and dance hall, but had been a bar for over 100 years. I enjoyed the pizza and chatting with owner Chad Forsberg. Just a little further up the road from them in unincorporated Leon is **Alchemy Brewpub**. Opened in 2020, they renovated a large garage to serve the needs of brewing and serving beer. Their food menu includes something you don't see often: beer-battered green beans.

We will stay in the southern section of the state but veer to the east. Burlington is about forty-five minutes southwest of downtown Milwaukee, and I had a wonderful day popping between the two breweries there that both opened in 2020. **Low Daily Beer** is located downtown in a building previously home to the Burlington Standard-Press. Now, instead of finding newspapers, you'll discover a nice selection of beers. Personally, I would go for their Kolsch called *Banjo* if it's on tap, but otherwise, one of the IPAs or sours will do the trick. A quick walk will take you to **The Runaway Micropub & Nanobrewery**. The name comes from the fact that when Burlington was first established, horse carriages were popular, and when a horse broke free, it was called a "runaway." The Schwarzbier was a proper choice. If you want some fresh air, head to **Duesterbeck's Brewing** just outside of nearby Elkhorn. A farm that had been around for 150 years and five generations was turned into a brewery. The main facility looks and has the feel of a barn, and there are plenty of rustic touches all over. Walking to the outdoor space, you'll be looking out at cornfields.

Beginning to move toward Madison, **Second Salem Brewing** is in Whitewater. An interesting fact about Whitewater is that it is known as "Second Salem" thanks to its colorful history that includes a spiritualism institute along with rumors revolving around witches and strange happenings. I had a fun brown ale there that was modeled after the Cinnamon Toast Crunch cereal. Let us now bypass the Madison area since we already discussed it, and instead head due north from Whitewater to the rural **Hubbleton Brewing**. I had the chance to talk with the owner, Dan, who founded the brewery in 2017 and turned some pole buildings into "Beer From the Middle of Nowhere." They have a space along the long driveway to grow hops and, more recently, opened a nearby "Taproom and Grill" location. Further north in Beaver Dam, **Ooga Brewing** is named for the sound an old car horn makes. Yes, really! They even have one in the taproom for the last call. It makes sense since they opened up inside a former car dealership and gas station back in 2019.

Continuing north, our next destination is Waupaca. **H.H. Hinder Brewing** opened in the fall of 2018 and took over the space formerly home to the Waupaca Family Center. The curved wooden ceiling and beams are beautiful, and they had sixteen taps with a wide variety (such as a smoked wheat lager called *Smoakey the Beer*). We bypass Plover County (more on that later) and head up Highway 39 to Mosinee. Inside a former general store and IGA store is **Mosinee Brewing**. The woodsy interior and terrific beers, such as a peanut brown ale, made this a surprisingly splendid stop. And not much further, **Red Eye Brewing** was my 1,200th brewery visit in 2023! They breathed fresh life into a vacant warehouse near downtown Wausau, and the *Xanadu Hefeweizen* was the highlight of the stop. **Mosinee** isn't the only woodsy location in this area by the way. **Sawmill Brewing** in Merrill took over a rustic building from the 1940s that served as the town's DNR headquarters. As you can probably picture, it is situated on a wooded lot, and a fun fact is that the flooring consists of thirteen species of wood.

We may as well complete our journey to the north, where

we truly get to some small-town stops. **Rocky Reef Brewing** in the touristy area of Woodruff has cool flight boards based on the white arrow road signs you see all around this part of the state. They also have a large northwoods mural on the outside of the building. Up even further north is **Some Nerve Brewing** in Manitowish Waters. Formerly Gallery 51 and a video arcade, a cool feature here is that the owners, Bill and Jessica, have been to almost every brewery in the state (and display glassware and stickers from their visits to prove it). Earlier in the book I talked about interesting ways breweries get names. Well, **Tribute Brewing** is one of them. The owner helped start the Great Northern Beerfest prior to opening the brewery in 2012 and drove a Mazda Tribute. Now, all the beer names are "tributes" to local things.

And finally, we will cap off Wisconsin with one last trio. Eau Claire isn't really rural (the population is almost 70,000), but I'm tossing in my one stop there in this section. **The Brewing Projekt** has a large facility along the Chippewa River that used to be a meat canning factory, and their bold and flavorful IPAs and sours have become their calling card. Heading west on I-94, Menomonie has some quality breweries, including **Brewery Nønic** and **Zymurgy Brewing**. The former is inside an old train station built in 1906, and along with many original elements inside, they make quality beers across the board, from a red IPA to a Schwarzbier. **Zymurgy**, meanwhile, is right across the street from Lake Menomin, and the name refers to the process of fermentation in brewing. *Ramblin' Rose*, a cranberry honey hefeweizen, was my top selection.

My Take: I realize that was a deep dive into Wisconsin, but I can't help but promote the remarkable breweries in the state I call home. As I mentioned, **New Glarus** should be on every beer lover's bucket list, but there are quality choices no matter where in the Badger State you are.

Quick Tip: Northern Wisconsin is a wonderful travel destination in the summer months, but just be prepared to deal with crowds and traffic that you wouldn't normally see in towns of just a few thousand people. Don't forget to try cheese curds.

MINNEAPOLIS, MN

I decided to split up the Twin Cities, as although they are very close together, they offer distinct experiences when you visit them. Minneapolis is the larger of the two (both in terms of population and simply the number of high-rise buildings), and many people feel it is the livelier of the two. However, as you are about to read, both of them offer residents and visitors alike a significant craft beer scene to explore.

We can start in the beer-drenched North Loop, where five breweries are all within a short walk of Target Field, home of the Minnesota Twins. My favorite of the group is probably **Inbound BrewCo**. The modern industrial taproom offers up to thirty craft beer tap lines, so you are certain to find something that catches your eye (I loved the sours). A block away is **Fulton Beer**, which interestingly sponsors people participating in competitive running, cycling, and skiing. Their *Cold Press Proper Porter* was what I sipped on during a Pintwood Derby they were hosting. **Modist Brewing**, as in a person that modifies, had a cool vibe with some colorful murals, and nearby is a newer location for Burnsville-based **Bricksworth Beer**. I'm a big fan of **Bricksworth**, especially in terms of their Kolsch and IPAs. The other option is one I have not visited yet, **StormKing Brewpub & Barbeque**.

A short trip just north of this neighborhood takes us to **Pryes Brewing**. Located along the Mississippi River, their taproom features the unique game of feather bowling. It's a mix of curling, bowling, and bocce ball, and I had a blast playing. After you're done trying that out, hop across the river to Northeast Minneapolis to check out **Fair State Brewing Cooperative**, which was the country's third cooperative brewery when it was founded. One wall features photos of the members, and they make standout beers like their *Vienna Lager*. If you head south a little way from there, you can find **Bauhaus Brew Labs**. My visit here was unique, as I was there for their massive Schwandtoberfest event in October: live music, food trucks, games, and a fun atmosphere in and out. They turned the former Crown Iron Works Building into a very cool space. Just west of there is **Falling Knife Brewing**, one of my favorites in the city. Their *Chocolate Velvet Milk Stout* was one of my nominees for Best Dark Beer in 2021, and I loved their tap handles shaped like knives (they won Best Tap Handle that year).

Continuing to work our way clockwise around the city, our next stop is **Insight Brewing**. Founded in 2014, one of their flagships is *Banshee Cutter*, a golden ale brewed with organic Ethiopian Coffee. This is another spot with neat murals, too. The most nationally famous brewery in the Twin Cities is still probably **Surly Brewing**, located in Prospect Park. Originally founded in 2006, they opened their large destination brewery in 2014. The beer hall is impressive, as is the outdoor space that hosts a variety of events. *Furious IPA* and *Axe Man IPA* are a couple of the hoppy flagships that helped them grow, but my favorite was their gose.

Circling south of the city, **Arbeiter Brewing** is brewing a plethora of delicious beers. Named for the German word for "worker," I highly recommend *Arby Lime*, a blonde ale with lime. A little further south, **Venn Brewing** is named for the word "friend" in Norwegian. They are also a coffee shop if you need a kick of caffeine, but I stuck with enjoying a sour ale called *Cosmosis: Triple Berry*. Finally, we complete our journey at **Wild Mind Artisan Ales**, where the focus is on barrel-aging and blending. You can even get a look at where they make their foeder-aged beers like *Kuanos*, a fruited foeder sour IPA.

My Take: Minneapolis is a fun city to visit. While the North Loop is a convenient neighborhood for some brewery hopping that only involves your feet, many of my favorites are scattered around different parts of the city.

Quick Tip: Minneapolis is fairly well-known for its art scene. The Walker Art Center and Minneapolis Sculpture Garden are both worth a stop, and you'll get a peek at the famous Spoonbridge and Cherry.

ST. PAUL, MN

The smaller and quieter of the Twin Cities, St. Paul, still has a lot going for it. Besides being the state capital, they have wonderful parks and restaurants, and it's also home to the popular state fair each summer. In my eyes, its craft beer scene is just as good, if not better, than its larger counterpart to its west. The breweries mainly congregate around downtown, along the river, or over on the city's western edge close to where the Twin Cities meet.

One brewery that is not around anymore (but had a huge impact on the city) was Hamm's Brewery. Founded in 1865, it would become the fifth-largest brewery in the country. While it may have shut its doors in 1997, there is a new brewery inside one of the historic buildings it called home. **Saint Paul Brewing** utilizes multiple rooms and spaces inside and outside the building. The large beer garden resides in the ruins of the old stables! And the beer was very good, in particular the *Croom Haven Rye Porter*. Another history lesson can be found nearby at **Yoerg Brewing**. It originally dates back to 1848, when it became the state's first commercial brewery. While it closed in 1952, it was brought back to life in 2016. The intimate space is also a dependable spot to find imported beers.

Making our way downtown, there's a trio of breweries within a few blocks of each other. Sports fans and music fans alike will be drawn to **MetroNOME Brewery**. Located in the Tighe Building that was built in 1902, they are directly across the street from CHS Field, home of the Saint Paul Saints (AAA affiliate of the Minnesota Twins). But inside, you'll find a music-themed spot where some of the proceeds go toward musical instruments, lessons, and education for area youth. Besides the upstairs taproom, they also have a basement where they host live music on the weekends. Probably my favorite brewery in the Twin Cities in terms of the beer is right close by, **Barrel Theory Beer Company**. A majority of the beers you'll experience there are IPAs, sours, or stouts, and everything they do is exceptional. One of my favorite dark beers I've ever had was *Island Fudge*, an Imperial stout with cacao, coffee, hazelnut, and vanilla. To complete this trifecta, **Gambit Brewing** is located on the lower level of the Pioneer Endicott Building. It previously was **12welve Eyes Brewing**, and both featured a very relaxed taproom. Also want to give a quick shout to **Wabasha Brewing**, just across the river from here in the West Side neighborhood. Funny enough, the building they call home was built in the 1860s and was home to the original **Yoerg Brewing**! They now also have an Airbnb upstairs above the taproom.

If you thought your history lesson in St. Paul was done, think again. **Waldmann Brewery** is located in the city's oldest surviving commercial building, built in 1857. It was an old lager beer saloon back then, and now you can try some house-brewed beers. **Waldmann** resurrected this space in 2017, and it still has a historic feel with small rooms, wood stoves, period maps, and whale oil lamps. Across the street is another of the city's popular breweries, **Bad Weather Brewing**. They opened this space in 2015, and the industrial taproom is dog-friendly, family-friendly, and even hosts "Retro Video Game Day" twice a month. This is also a spot that has a wide variety of choices when it comes to styles, whether it's a Kolsch, a sour, an IPA, a stout, or something in between.

A little southwest and further upstream on the Mississippi is one of the original Minnesota craft breweries, **Summit Brewing**. Founded in 1986, they have been cranking out their flagship *Summit Extra Pale Ale* for nearly forty years. They've won a variety of awards throughout the years and also partnered with several local organizations across the area. The furthest south we will go is to **Wandering Leaf Brewing** in the Highland Park neighborhood. And they are not lacking in the "leaf" category. This place is stuffed with plants. The floor, walls, and ceilings are all home to plants (real ones, mind you!), giving this taproom a unique vibe. They even sometimes have a terrarium building class. Opened in 2023, one of the co-owners is a trained horticulturist, hence the strong theme. I enjoyed *If In Doubt*, a sweet stout with black cherry and cocoa nibs.

Now, we head to the Hamline-Midway neighborhood located between St. Paul and Minneapolis. **Burning Brothers Brewing** was the first gluten-free brewery I visited when I stopped by in 2017. The co-owners, Dane and Thom, were planning to open a microbrewery when Dane was diagnosed with celiac disease. That caused a pivot that led to this fully gluten-free facility. Moving west closer to Minneapolis is **BlackStack Brewing**, which you may have heard of if you are into IPAs. While they do offer a variety of styles on tap, they are best known for their IPAs, and that is what a majority of the tap list generally sports. They are one of the best in the Cities, and the flagship *Local 755 NEIPA* is a must-try. Oh, and the name? Yes, the giant smokestack towering above the building may have something to do with that. Interestingly enough, the building once produced cans for Schmidt's and Hormel.

Funny enough, these breweries we are discussing are closer to downtown Minneapolis than St. Paul. But if you know how strange city boundaries can be, it is common for the lines to be confusing. Either way, the next two breweries are so close together you could throw a rock from one to the other. The larger of the two spaces was a former stable for St. Paul Police horses but is now home to the state's first women-owned brewery, **Urban Growler Brewing**. Opened in 2014, they also sport a food menu that features vegan and gluten-free options. Out behind their space is a second brewery that is incredibly memorable, **Bang Brewing**. Housed entirely in a grain bin, this compact space makes organic beers. Don't worry, they also have outdoor space for visitors! I fancied sipping on the *Nice STP Dark Ale* during my visit. The brewery that leans into this area between the two downtowns is **Dual Citizen Brewing**, which is located on the ground floor of the C&E Flats Building. Their hoppy pale lager named *Wouldn't You Like To Know?* was recommended by the bartender and I was happy he let me know about it.

My Take: If I had to pick one, I honestly would give a slight edge to St. Paul over Minneapolis when it comes to the breweries. While both have plenty of quality choices, **Barrel Theory** and **BlackStack** are probably my two favorites between the cities.

Quick Tip: My family has enjoyed multiple trips to the Science Museum of Minnesota. The multi-level facility has exhibits for all ages and interests. Plus, you get some views of the Mississippi River.

DULUTH, MN

The shore of Lake Superior is home to one of my favorite small craft beer cities, and there's even a bit of local beer history here as well. Minnesota's oldest brewpub (**Fitger's Brewhouse**) opened here in 1995. It's also home to one of the largest freshwater aquariums in the world. My family spent a weekend here during the Summer of 2019, and we all had an extraordinary trip.

We will start south of downtown, as my two favorites in the city are there. First is **Bent Paddle Brewing**. They are one of the most popular breweries in the state and have transformed a former furniture warehouse into a nice taproom space. Their *Cold Press Black Ale* with local coffee was my favorite, but if you ask my father, he would tell you to get the *14° ESB*. Not too far from there is **Ursa Minor Brewing**. Like **Bent Paddle**, they have a huge variety on tap, and pretty much anything you pick inside this rustic venue will be a winner. I'll note that my favorite was a cherry sour, which was one of my nominees for Best Sour in my Third Annual Review.

Venturing up north to the Canal Park area, you will find the best view at aptly named **Canal Park Brewing**. Located right along the lake with a nice outdoor area, you're bound to have a blast there, and then a quick walk can put you at **Hoops Brewing**. With huge Douglas Fir beams from 1889, you get a North Woods vibe at this place. I'd also recommend taking the short journey downtown to visit **Blacklist Brewing**. While they do offer a variety, their Belgian styles are a focus. In particular, I would highly recommend getting the *Aquavit Crabby Abbey* (a Belgian Tripel aged in Aquavit barrels) if they have it. They also have axe-throwing.

I want to give a shoutout to a personal favorite brewery of mine, which is located about half an hour north along the lake in Two Harbors. **Castle Danger Brewing** does exceptional work, especially with nailing to-style beers. Their *Cream Ale* and *Pale Ale* were both just immaculate. Another nearby quality option is across the state border in Superior, Wisconsin. **Earth Rider Brewery** has found some GABF success, and I loved sipping on their *Tap Shack Caribbean Lager* inside their taproom, which feels like an old dive bar!

My Take: I featured Duluth when I wrote an article about some of the most underrated beer cities in the country. I feel that holds true, as its size and location (it takes over two hours to get to the Twin Cities from there) make it a bit of an outlier. But it deserves your attention!

Quick Tip: Canal Park is an eventful place to walk around, aside from the breweries. There are shops, restaurants, a distillery, a small museum, and a waterfront pathway that leads up to the iconic Aerial Lift Bridge. So, if you can, take some time to explore the neighborhood.

CEDAR RAPIDS, IA

Cedar Rapids is one of a few mid-sized Iowa cities with some quality breweries. While there are just five breweries that call it home, they do benefit from the fact that four of them are all located in and around downtown. That makes for some easy brewery hopping!

My personal favorite is **Lion Bridge Brewing** in the Czech Village neighborhood. They have several beers that have medaled at GABF, including their dark mild, *Compensation*, which has won multiple golds at the festival. It is a delicious beer that highlights an underrepresented style. If GABF medal-winners are your thing, you can pop across the river to **Iowa Brewing** and order *Tragedy of the Common*, their California common that won a silver in 2018.

A couple blocks from there is **Clock House Brewing**. Unsurprisingly, they are located inside the historic Clock House Building, which has served many lives for over 100 years. The brick and wood inside the taproom showcase the space's age, and the flight board is a clock face! The beer was well-made, with the best of the bunch being *Witch Slap*, a New England IPA. Then, complete the downtown crawl by stopping in at **Quarter Barrel**, where you can have a house-brewed beer and pizza and play one of their thirty-nine arcade games.

The one outlier located on the far north side of the city is **Third Base Brewery**. With the feeling of a sports bar, they exceeded my expectations with some quality beer and delectable food. If you are willing to travel that far away from downtown, you may be interested in heading south to **House Divided Brewery** in Ely or the popular **Big Grove Brewpub** in Solon. **House Divided** has a very small taproom but a nice beer garden in front, while **Big Grove** is one of the more well-known names in the state and makes quality beers across most styles.

My Take: Cedar Rapids has enough for a nice little weekend beer trip. The downtown breweries offer enough to keep you busy, and there are some options further out if you want to venture outside of that area.

Quick Tip: If you are in Cedar Rapids, you are not far from Iowa City/Coralville. There, you would discover **ReUnion Brewery**, **Backpocket Brewing**, and another **Big Grove Brewing** location.

QUAD CITIES (IA/IL)

The metro area closest to where I grew up (at least for middle and high school) straddles the Mississippi River in Eastern Iowa and Northwestern Illinois. The main four cities that compose the "Quad" are Davenport and Bettendorf on the Iowa side and Rock Island and Moline on the Illinois side. Like many areas, they have seen a significant bump in recent years in terms of the number of options for local craft beer, but they do also have some history as well.

And for that, we will start in the largest of the cities,

Davenport. **Front Street Brewery** is Iowa's oldest brewpub and second oldest brewery. Opened in 1992, they were the 300th craft brewery to be established in the entire country. They now have a larger location nearby, but you can still visit the Pub & Eatery, where they originally started with a seven-barrel brewhouse in the basement. You can catch a glimpse of the Mississippi River out the front window as well. Right near there is a newer brewery, **Stompbox Brewing**, which opened in 2020. It's another spot where you can catch a view of the bridge that crosses the river, and they offer a great variety of styles. My favorite on my visit was a porter, but I also would get the hazy IPA again.

The most growth in the area, though, has occurred to the east in Bettendorf, both in terms of population and breweries. Now, they are spread out, but there are four breweries here that are worth a visit. The closest one to the Davenport spots is **Adventurous Brewing**, which was established in 2017, but the taproom opened in 2021. I was very impressed by the beer here, and *PB & C*, an Imperial stout with milk sugar, cocoa nibs, peanut butter, and coconut, was one of my finalists for Best Dark Beer in 2022. Closest to them would be **Crawford Brew Works**, which features an expansive two-level taproom attached to a bicycle store. I had a nice *Cranberry Saison* there. One of the fastest-growing local breweries, **5ive Cities Brewing**, recently upped its production from around 1,200 barrels a year to 16,000 barrels thanks to a new production facility in Le Claire. But you can still visit their taproom on the north side of Bettendorf. **Twin Span Brewing** was part of a newer development just off the interstate, and I dug the lagers here like *Ten-Forty German Pils*.

Hopping across one of the bridges to Illinois, we first stop in Rock Island. **Wake Brewing** is probably my favorite of the bunch, and their music theme comes from the fact that the brothers who opened it formerly traveled the country playing in a rock band. The *Fisted Frost Hammer IPA* was a fitting choice on my visit. Located near Augustana College, **Radicle Effect Brewerks** calls itself the Quad Cities' first nano brewery. Along with their house beers, they also offer a large number of guest taps. Down the road in Moline is the brewpub location of **Bent River Brewing**. My preferred choice here was *Jingle Java Stout*, and they also have a facility back in Rock Island. Also in downtown Moline is **Rebellion Brew Haus**, another small brewery with a cozy interior where they are consistently cranking out something different.

I also want to shout out some nearby options, including **Midwest Ale Works** in East Moline. It is part of the Rust Belt Complex that includes a concert hall, boutique store, restaurant, and fitness center. It was an automobile manufacturing plant in the early 1900s, but now you can go and try beers like a chocolate raspberry stout. Up the river in Le Claire is **Green Tree Brewery**. Sweeping views of the Mississippi gave it the win for my Best Taproom View in my second annual review, and it takes its name from a famous local elm tree that lived to be 225 years old. They are also next door to Mississippi River Distilling Company if you need to get your liquor fix.

My Take: It is not necessarily a place that many people would consider for a "Beercation," but it's one I have pointed out to people since it is fairly inexpensive and easy to get around compared to some larger metro areas. With more breweries continuing to open, I imagine the popularity of local beer there will only grow.

Quick Tip: Baseball fans will want to take in a game at Modern Woodmen Park in Davenport, home of the Quad Cities River Bandits. It's one of the best views in the minor leagues, located right along the river next to the Centennial Bridge. The historic ballpark dates back to 1931 but has seen many renovations and updates. That includes an amusement park behind the left field wall which features a Ferris wheel, kids roller coaster, and a carousel.

RURAL EASTERN IOWA

Rural Iowa may seem like an odd place to highlight, but this is the area where I went to high school, attended college, met and married my wife, and still return frequently to visit my in-laws. It may come as an even larger surprise to learn there are a number of quality breweries that have popped up in different communities here in the last five to ten years.

Jackson County is specifically where I spent the second half of my childhood and also the place where I return multiple times a year. As recently as 2016, there were no breweries, but there are now three in this county that features a population of less than 20,000. The oldest was established in 2016 in Bellevue, **River Ridge Brewing**. In 2021, they moved from their first location to a much larger one, directly on the Mississippi River. The views from the former International Harvester showroom are immaculate, and I thoroughly enjoyed the *Lock 12 Lager*.

The largest town and county seat is Maquoketa, and **Maquoketa Brewing** has been doing its part to revive downtown. They saved a dilapidated 1919 building that originally opened as a department store. The floor and ceiling are original, and I've visited a handful of times to drink beers like *Biergarten Lager* and *Raspberry Blonde Ale*. We have one more stop in Jackson County, just a bit north of Bellevue in St. Donatus. **Beer in a Barn Brewery** is exactly that: a brewery in a barn. But it isn't just any barn. It is inside the Gehlen Barn, which is the oldest standing barn in all of Iowa, dating back to 1839. All original limestone, it is a fabulous space both inside and out. There are multiple levels and rooms, some large enough for events and others intimate with only a couple of small tables.

If repurposed buildings are your thing, I have several more for you in other counties. **TLC Brewing** took over a bank in the tiny town of Holy Cross, and I loved *Jan's 401K*, a maple pecan brown ale. Not far from there in Dyersville is the impressive **Textile Brewing**. They are located in a sewing factory built in 1906, and the rustic interior and decor flow seamlessly together. Order the *Flapjacks Brown Ale* if it is on tap. Following Highway 20 to the west takes you to Manchester, where the old Masonic Lodge is now **Franklin Street Brewing**, complete with views of the Maquoketa River from the patio. **BIT Brewing** took over two adjacent storefronts dating back to the 1890s in Central City, and finally, **Great Revivalist Brewery** breathed new life into an old Episcopal Church built in 1898 in Clinton. **Great Revivalist**, in particular, was one of the best repurpose jobs in a church I've seen. The huge mosaic above the altar is intact, the stained glass windows are gorgeous, and brick walls and peaked wooden arches make for a stunning setting. Oh, and the beer at **Great Revivalist** is phenomenal, too, such as *Peach Wrangler Sour Ale*, *Dirt Road Peanut Butter Brown Ale*, and *Cloud Trippin' NEIPA*.

My Take: Listen, I know this is not a "destination" people visit. But part of writing this book is showcasing the amazing breweries that can be found in unsuspecting places. While I have not lived in this area for over a decade, it still holds a special place in my heart.

Quick Tip: If you want some pizza, go to Geno's Pizza in Preston, IA. As someone who grew up in Preston, my first job was making pizza and waiting on tables at Geno's. People travel from all over the area (and beyond) to get pizza here, and I still love going back!

ST. LOUIS, MO

My good friend Brian Marigotta is the creative director for the St. Louis Brewers Heritage Foundation and operates the STLbeer accounts across social media. He is a better source of information than I am when it comes to beer in the 314 area code. After all, he took me on a brewery tour during my second visit. But I have made a couple of trips to this city with a long brewing history and can vouch for the quality of options it boasts. Two breweries, in particular, have cracked prestigious lists at different times in the past, and there are plenty of other options throughout the city as well. While the Gateway Arch might be the most iconic and famous part of the city, they sure are making some good beer there besides Budweiser.

My personal favorite is also located the furthest south of those I visited. **Perennial Artisan Ales** is one of the breweries that has received many accolades. Housed inside an old Coca-Cola syrup plant, all the beers here were delectable. I'd like to highlight *Owen*, a dry-hopped saison conditioned with brettanomyces (a type of yeast that can give a beer a funky or tart taste), as well as *Intentionally Indulgent*, a tiramisu-inspired Imperial stout with vanilla, coffee, and chocolate sauce that won my Best Dark Beer during my Third Annual Review. We will swoop northwest next to the nearby suburb of Maplewood to hit the other highly touted option, **Side Project Brewing**. **Side Project** has been ranked as the second-best brewery in the world by RateBeer, and these barrel-aging masters have become incredibly sought after. For my taste, the *Blache #2* (a tart Witbier aged in Chardonnay barrels) was the best. The Bottleworks location of the historic **Schlafly Brewery** is not far from there. The abandoned supermarket became their second home in 2003 to help meet the growing demands since its founding in 1991.

We can head back into the city now and pop into the Tower Grove South neighborhood to find another place I recommend, **Civil Life Brewing. Civil Life** is your destination for traditional beers that are expertly made, like a Czech pilsner or American brown ale. They also have a beautiful outdoor area to complement the more customary taproom space.

In that same neighborhood is **Alpha Brewing**, which moved there in 2017 after starting off downtown in 2013. This is the place I would send you if sours are up your alley. For a history lesson, be sure to visit **Earthbound Beer** in the neighboring Gravois Park. Located inside what was once part of the old Cherokee Street Brewing Company that was established in the 1860s, it's a beautiful taproom with beams, pillars, and a curved ceiling. A catwalk provides some bonus seating above the main space, and the owner hand-excavated one of the old lager caves below the building.

Closer to downtown, **4 Hands Brewing** turned a former machine shop into a sneaky cool two-level taproom. The lower level features a bar area that somehow mixes a traditional and quirky feel, while upstairs is a larger, more open space with different activities and games. *City Wide Pils* and *Divided Sky Rye IPA* are two of the popular choices there. Head northwest from there and make sure to stop in at **Wellspent Brewing**, which is inside a former theater. Their Czech dark lager (named simply "*Dark*") was delicious and probably my favorite beer during my second trip to the city. One of **Urban Chestnut Brewing**'s locations is also near there, where you can get your fix of more traditional European styles inside an old 1920s garage.

Finally, I need to shout out **2nd Shift Brewing**, as the Criders are not only making quality beers like *Technical Ecstasy Czech Pilsner* and *Sunny Cat New England IPA*, but they are also amazing people doing whatever they can to help the community. Founded in 2009, 2nd Shift got their start in rural New Haven before moving to St. Louis in 2016 to open their family-friendly and dog-friendly location. They are consistently hosting a wide range of events, and I definitely recommend including them in your St. Louis itinerary.

My Take: St. Louis is another Midwest city that flies under the radar when it comes to craft beer, although trendy names like

Side Project and **Perennial** are helping to combat that. But even outside those two, there are numerous worthy breweries that make planning a Beercation here worth your time. After all, they did win my award for Best Beer City (Large) in my Third Annual Review!

Quick Tip: Whether or not you have kids, visit the City Museum if you have the time. One of the more unique places I've been, it's a multi-level exhibit that utilizes repurposed architectural and industrial objects to create essentially a children's museum for adults.

KANSAS CITY METRO (MO/KS)

The City of Fountains may be better known for barbeque and the recent success of their football team, but they have a top-notch brewery neighborhood and a nice beer scene overall, too. They also have a nationally-known brand in **Boulevard Brewing**, with its multi-level location south of downtown providing visitors with skyline views to treasure while sipping on a *Tank 7 Farmhouse Ale*.

But just to the northeast of Boulevard and bumping up to downtown is the Crossroads neighborhood. Eight breweries are within a few blocks of each other, along with a couple of distilleries and a cidery. The furthest to the east is **Torn Label Brewing**, which was founded in 2014. The chill taproom was a great place to enjoy *The Witch*, a black ale with black currant, rosemary, and sage. Down the street is **City Barrel Brewing**, where the open-concept taproom features reclaimed wood from the Nelson Atkins Museum of Art that dates back to 1930. Had a tasty *Golden Sour* there. I also stopped by **Double Shift Brewing**, where the relaxed atmosphere and *Tessellation IPA* went together well. I need to go back and visit places like **Casual Animal**, **Nimble**, and **Brewery Empirical**.

I did, however, manage to also stop in a pair of breweries across the state line in the suburb of Shawnee, Kansas. Both are along the same street downtown and opened around the same time in early 2019. **Servaes Brewing** (which is the owner/brewer's last name and pronounced "service") makes very interesting beers, especially in regard to fruited sours. They rotate through beers consistently, so there are always new flavors to try. Meanwhile, **Transport Brewery** converted a former law office into their taproom and has a more traditional take, with beers such as the *Broken Rail Brown Ale*. Fun fact: the name Transport comes from Johnson Drive, where they are located. It was a major transportation hub when it was part of the Sante Fe and Oregon Trails.

My Take: Kansas City's beer scene is a nice combination of having a recognizable name and a growing number of hyperlocal options. Anytime you have a neighborhood like the Crossroads, I will be interested in visiting! Some other names I've heard good things about are **KC Bier Co**, **BKS Artisan Ales**, and **Alma Mater Brewing**.

Quick Tip: Sports fans should check out the Negro Leagues Baseball Museum. I went with my family and wished I could have spent even more time, but sometimes, when you have a toddler and infant with you, that choice isn't up to you.

CHICAGO, IL

The Windy City has long been the major hub of the Midwest. Whether it's entertainment, culture, food, or really any type of activity, you are going to find some of the nation's best here. And that holds true when it comes to beer as well. My proximity to Chicago while living in Milwaukee has given me the opportunity to not only visit many of the breweries there but also get to drink more of their beers in distribution!

Let's begin in Lincoln Square with one of Chicago's most well-known options, **Half Acre Beer Company**. Founded in 2007, they interestingly started brewing in Black River Falls, Wisconsin before officially calling Chicago home the following year. Best known for hoppy beers like *Daisy Cutter Pale Ale* and *Bodem IPA*, I personally enjoyed getting to try some taproom exclusives like a mixed culture Witbier called *Big Basin*. Right next door is **Spiteful Brewing**. Opened inside a former dojo in 2016, I was very pleased and surprised by the quality of the beer there, particularly the *Gridiron Golden Lager*.

Speaking of quality, you won't find more of it than at **Dovetail Brewery**. They call an old industrial building in the North Center neighborhood home and make incredible lagers. The *Helles* was my favorite, but their *Kolsch* and *Hefeweizen* are incredible, too. Just west of there is **Hop Butcher For The World**. This is another brewery for IPA fanatics. They do an incredible job of creating delicious varieties within the style. Continuing west is **Old Irving Brewing** in the neighborhood that bears the same name. **Old Irving** was my 400th brewery visit and my wife and I delighted in a brunch, some excellent service, and I had a nice Double IPA.

Next, we go to the Logan Square neighborhood for another array of breweries. **Maplewood Brewery** was opened as the first brewery/distillery in the state, and you can still get your fix of either craft beer or craft cocktails under one roof. And for my money, one of the best sours out there is their *Softcore Mutation* (a series of foeder sours). I do want to give a brief shoutout to the now-closed **Metro Brewing** that was not far from here, as they made awesome lagers right on the river. But a brewery that is still around (and has been for a while) is **Revolution Brewing**. Opened in 2010, I visited their original brewpub, which has beautiful tin ceilings and a gorgeous bar. The colorful fist-shaped tap handles were fun, too. Down the road is the funky and unique **Bungalow by Middle Brow**, as well as **Pilot Project Brewing**'s original brewing facility. As I discussed in the Milwaukee section, their model of allowing multiple small breweries to brew and serve beer in-house (along with helping with distribution, marketing, etc) makes it one of the more unique venues you will visit.

One of my favorite spots in the city is **Off Color Brewing**'s home, affectionately called The Mousetrap. This former train station along the North Branch Canal of the Chicago River features a brewery with amazing beer, branding, and people. Their "*Beer For*" series is probably my favorite beer branding in the country. I enjoyed the *Beer for Tacos*, a gose with lime and sea salt, during my visit, but some of my favorites for artwork include *Beer for Hoops*, *Beer for Huddles*, and *Beer for Ball Games*. Did I mention I am a sports fan? Shifting from northwest of downtown to due west, there are a pair of breweries within walking distance that I can suggest. The first, **Midwest Coast Brewing**, is in a former paint shop and features a beautiful taproom with exposed beams. They make a variety of well-made beers like *West Town Brown Ale* and *Secret Farm Hefeweizen*. Down the street is **Great Central Brewing**. Named after Great Central Train Station, they have a focus on German styles and have a beer hall-like taproom.

Rounding out our time in Chicago will be a trio to the south. **Marz Community Brewing** calls a large brick warehouse in McKinley Park home, and there you can find a variety of experimental ales across a wide variety of styles, including a Berliner Weisse with dill called *Diliner Weisse* that I was particularly intrigued by. Just north of there is the world's first two-Michelin-star brewery, **Moody Tongue**. The space has a mid-century modern and slightly upscale feeling, and along with some high-end food choices, you can also try some of their culinary-inspired beers like a *Sliced Nectarine IPA*. Another interesting option is located in the South Loop. **Duneyrr Fermenta Winery and Brewery**, with **Moderne Dune** being a subsidiary. This means you can choose from an array of natural wines and craft beers when you stop in for a drink.

My Take: I am a big fan of Chicago, both in terms of beer and just as a city in general. My wife and I have loved making the short trek south to enjoy all it has to offer, and I would highly recommend its beer scene to anyone who is looking to visit some quality breweries.

Quick Tip: For a free family activity, you can't go wrong with a visit to the Lincoln Park Zoo. And although it is not exactly a secret, I love walking around Millennium Park and along the lake.

NORTHERN CHICAGOLAND SUBURBS:

Milwaukee and Chicago are fairly close together, but there's a large stretch of suburbs and bedroom communities, especially on the Illinois side of the border. With that comes a large number of breweries! Because of the location of our home base, it has been fairly easy for me to check out many of the breweries in this area.

Right across the border is the first stop, **Harbor Brewing**. Their main facility is now in Lake Villa, but they have a lakefront taproom and biergarten in Winthrop Harbor, and the latter is part of the marina within the Spring Bluff Forest Preserve. The next one is south in Waukegan: **Nightshade and Dark's Pandemonium Brewery**. They feature a Ray Bradbury theme (he was born there) and had a staggering twenty-two of their beers on tap. Many were unique, such as *Rosemary's Baby*, a rosemary and blood orange pale ale. About fourteen miles southwest of there in Mundelein is **Tighthead Brewing**. I enjoyed the rugby theme (slogan: "Worth More Than a Try"), and along with the taproom, they also have a large event space with a private bar.

You will arrive in Lake Zurich if you continue in that same direction, where two incredible breweries have made the town home. **Roaring Table Brewing** was named a Breakout Brewer by *Craft Beer & Brewing* in 2022, and they have continued to make phenomenal beer in what seems like an unassuming strip mall. But inside is a taproom with a more modern feel, and beers like *Elizabeth* (a farmhouse ale) and a mouthwatering Altbier give it a unique character you don't find everywhere. But if you want more trendy styles (especially IPAs), I highly recommend **Phase Three Brewing**. Their *Pixel Density NEIPA* won my Best IPA award in 2023. Citra is the star of the show, providing the typical grapefruit, passionfruit, and overall tropical tasting notes, and the body of it was pillowy soft. They are tucked away in a business park, but after going through a small bar area, you will find more spacious seating options throughout the building.

Staying the path south, the intriguing **Buffalo Creek Brewing** is nestled in downtown Long Grove. Their unique building served many purposes, including an art gallery where the brewhouse now sits. *Too Tall IPA* was my favorite beer there. Pivoting east and proceeding to Lincolnshire, **Half Day Brewing** is named for the historic town of Half Day, originally named for Chief Aptakisic. Their space feels like a blend between a taproom, sports bar, and restaurant. I've already mentioned one brewery with a sports theme, so why not another? **Broken Tee Brewing** doesn't bury the lede, as the owner, Paul, had a career as a golf professional. Many of the beers have golf-related names, and the two spaces in the taproom are referred to as the "Front 9" and "Back 9." *Nacht Putten*, a Schwarzbier, was very well done.

We are finally getting close to Chicago! These final three spots are more within striking distance for those visiting the city, and all of them are worthy of attention. But I'll start with my favorite of this section, **Mikerphone Brewing** in Elk Grove Village. I was a huge fan of this music-inspired joint. Guitars, speaker grills, music posters, and microphone tap handles: they go all out. But what makes them special is the beer! One of my favorite dark beers I've ever had was their *Super Imperial Smells Like Bean Spirit* (an Imperial breakfast stout with maple syrup and coffee). Not far from there, right next to the O'Hare Airport is **Short Fuse Brewing**. Besides fun beers like *Bear-ie White* (a pale ale brewed with gummy bears), they have very cool bottle rocket-shaped tap handles and flight paddles. They were also named the 2021 GABF Brewery of the Year. We put a bow on this section with a stop in Evanston at **Sketchbook Brewing**. Living true to their name, they encourage you to draw or sketch on the coasters and then post them on a wall in the taproom. *Catharina*, a Brazilian sour with gaviola, was the winner here.

My Take: This section is a little different since it spans a fairly large area that consists of a large number of towns and cities. But while it may not be the most convenient for brewery hopping, there are some nice spots all around this part of the state. One bonus Chicagoland brewery I want to mention: **Goldfinger Brewing** in Downers Grove to the west. They make incredible lagers!

Quick Tip: For thrill-seekers, Six Flags Great America has a location in Gurnee, which is right by some of the first breweries I discussed. Great Wolf Lodge also has one of their indoor water park resorts in Gurnee as well.

INDIANAPOLIS, IN

The Crossroads of America is well-known for its connection to racing. Although the Indianapolis 500 draws hundreds of thousands of people, it's not the only reason people should trek there. I've made a couple of stops in the city to check out the local beer scene, and there are plenty of quality options. Many of the breweries are grouped fairly close to downtown, particularly to the west, but there are also some noteworthy places spread a little further out as well.

But starting closer to the center of the city, **Sun King Brewery** is one of the largest and well-known breweries in Indiana. In 2009, they became the first production brewery in the city following the start of the craft beer boom. They now have six locations around Indiana and one in Florida. They also have won numerous awards at GABF, World Beer Cup, and other contests. Running the gauntlet on styles they offer everything from a simple cream ale to bold Belgian Tripels and cocktail-inspired beers. Not far from there is the brewery that won my Best Taproom Interior in 2019. **St. Joseph Brewery** transformed a church that dates back to the 1870s into a lovely taproom. It's gorgeous, and as I've already mentioned, I am a sucker for an old church becoming a brewery. Similar to the **Ministry of Brew** in Baltimore, they did an exemplary job of transitioning the building to accommodate a brewery and seating for the taproom while keeping the stunning interior intact.

Just north of there is **Centerpoint Brewing**, which is part of the Circle City Industrial Complex. Originally built in 1929, the structure served many lives, including a USPS mail sorting center and a space that built turbo-charged race car engines. But it now is serving up freshly made suds, including its flagship *Blood Orange IPA*, which I enjoyed. Jetting south will lead you to the Fountain Square neighborhood, where the aptly named **Fountain Square Brewing** can be found. The area is full of local art and music, and they offer a variety of more simple styles with some adventurous options mixed in.

To the west and northwest are some of my favorites in the state, and we will start with **Guggman Haus Brewing** (my top pick in Indianapolis). Their beer hall is located in the old Boyle Racing headquarters, and there's even a room that features an old truck and race car. The food and beer were delicious here. While my favorite was the *Haus Helles Lager*, the *Guggenweizen Hefeweizen* and *Riverside NEIPA* were both amazing too. Further west in Speedway is **Daredevil Brewing**. Just a few blocks from the famous Indianapolis Speedway, they offer many award-winning German-style beers. But they also make a killer American IPA called *Lift Off* that was one of my finalists for Best IPA in 2019.

I want to point out two other breweries in the area located in nearby suburbs. First is **Books & Brews**, with a location in Brownsburg to the northwest as well as one in far northeast Indy. They are a combination brewery and used bookstore. Walking in, you are greeted by shelves of books you can purchase, with the proceeds going to a local nonprofit called Indy Reads (which works on building literacy). My wife is a big reader, so this was one time that she was just as excited as I was for a brewery visit! Further northwest in Whitestown, **Moontown Brewing** took the town's former high school gymnasium and turned it into an award-winning brewery. And by that, I mean they won Brewery of the Year in 2021 at GABF. As a former basketball player myself, I loved walking in the taproom. The larger space back by the brewery itself still has the look and feel of an old gym. Plus, the beer was killer. I enjoyed the *Hefczkowski Hefeweizen* and some of the IPAs.

My Take: Indianapolis has superb options when it comes to beer. I am hoping to hit **Metazoa**, **Bier**, and **Chilly Water** on a future trip. There's enough close to the downtown area to keep you plenty busy, but venturing further out will net you some truly special stops.

Quick Tip: If you have kids, you could spend a full day at the massive Indianapolis Children's Museum (it's nearly 500,000 square feet). I also recommend taking a tour of the Indianapolis Speedway. It's fun to ride around the track and you get to hop out and kiss the bricks.

GRAND RAPIDS, MI

For many years now, Grand Rapids has gone by the nickname Beer City, USA. It has been awarded this distinction multiple times throughout the years, and it's no secret that a ton of breweries call this area home. Beer bus tours, an Ale Trail, an entire downloadable app, and many other events highlight how the city has embraced craft beer culture. This is one place many people think of when considering a "Beercation" destination, and for good reason.

I'll start with my favorite, which was in nearby Comstock Park when I visited in 2019. **Speciation Artisan Ales** is the place to be if you want intense, palate-testing sours. They do phenomenal work in this area, and I was happy to see they have moved into the Baxter neighborhood of Grand Rapids. They now call a 100-year-old auto shop home, and it's much larger than the smaller space they previously had. They also offer up some other styles, such as lagers, stouts, and pale ales, but the primary focus still resides with the tart and wild. *Meiotic Drive*, a foeder-aged sour ale with elderberries, won my award for Best Sour in 2019. Before focusing completely on Grand Rapids, I should also shout out **Perrin Brewing**, which is still up in Comstock Park. They've been around since 2012 and have a huge facility. They became part of CANarchy, which interestingly sold to Monster.

Now back to the city of Grand Rapids itself again! Another favorite of mine was **Brewery Vivant**, located near the current **Speciation** location. Have I mentioned I like churches turned into taprooms? Well, their space was formerly a chapel for a funeral home! Oh, and also a daycare. But in terms of beer, you will see a lot of Belgian and French styles. I particularly enjoyed a golden ale with honey called *Contemplation*. Another fun fact about **Brewery Vivant** is that they are proud of their sustainability and are known as the first LEED microbrewery in the world.

The densest area of breweries lies just west of the Grand River downtown. On one particular stretch of Bridge Street are **New Holland Brewing, Broad Leaf Brewery, Jolly Pumpkin Pizzeria & Brewery, Küsterer Brauhaus**, and a meadery as well. **Jolly Pumpkin Artisan Ales**, in particular, has become well-known for their sour beers and now has seven locations across the state. They were founded in 2004 and are head-quartered in Dexter, but this particular space opened in 2018 replacing a restaurant. My favorite was Apocolocynposis, a sour ale with blackberries and lime.

A quick trot north gets you to **The Mitten Brewing Company**. This baseball-themed spot is located in historic Engine House No. 9. Founded in 2012, they now have two additional locations in Northport and Saugatuck, but I can only speak for the Grand Rapids taproom. Aside from the great interior, the beer is also quality there. I was a big fan of *Peanuts & Crackerjacks*, a peanut butter porter. Although I did not have any, several people have spoken highly of the pizza too. I also want to give some praise to nearby **Greyline Brewing**, as they make some splendid beers like the *Humblebee Honey Oat Ale*.

My Take: To this day, Grand Rapids is still a worthwhile choice for a Beercation. Michigan as a whole is an awesome beer state, and it's safe to say many people consider Grand Rapids to be the epicenter.

Quick Tip: I was hoping to get back to Grand Rapids in 2023, but it sadly did not work out. Some other breweries I planned to see and should be on your radar are **City Built, Arvon**, and **Harmony.**

CINCINNATI, OH

Another Midwest city with a history of brewing that flies under the national radar during conversations about craft beer? What a surprise. Cincinnati is another brewery scene that I have learned more about in part because of friends I have made through beer. David McKinney has appeared on multiple Brewery Travels Podcast episodes and has a pair of beer-themed podcasts himself. During my second visit to the city, he and I hopped around the city to multiple breweries, and I left each one impressed.

The best place to start is the Over-the-Rhine neighborhood near downtown, as not only is it currently a brewery neighborhood, but it was also home to the Brewery District back in the nineteenth and early twentieth centuries. One of the current breweries that call the area home is **Rhinegeist Brewery**, which is far and away the largest locally-owned craft brewer in the area. Founded in 2013, they have shot up the charts and are now one of the twenty-five largest craft breweries in the country. Their huge taproom and rooftop area was formerly the site of Christian Moerlein Brewing's packaging hall. Now the space serves up well-known beers such as *Cheetah Lager* and *Truth IPA*.

Sadly, **Taft's Brewing** closed their gorgeous Ale House location inside a nineteenth-century church nearby, but thankfully they still have their Brewpourium in the Winton Place neighborhood as well as a location in Columbus. The *Vienna Lager* and tri-tip steak sandwich were delectable when I visited. And the amazing space won't be going to waste, as by the time you are reading this, **Mellotone Beer Project** will have moved in. It should be noted **Boston Beer Company** also opened a facility in this neighborhood in the former Hudepohl-Schoenling Brewery, as has Northern Kentucky-based **Braxton Brewing. Braxton** is another brewery where you can find a large variety of options, and their locations generally have 20+ taps flowing.

We will go north next to two amazing but very different breweries. **Brink Brewing** in College Hill is one of the best breweries I've been to in terms of beer quality, so it's no surprise they have won the GABF Small Brewer of the Year award twice since opening in 2017. *Hold the Reins Dark Mild* won one of my Best Beer Awards in 2021, and all five beers I had in my flight (which covered an array of styles) were exceptional. Down the road a bit is **Urban Artifact**, which is world-renowned for its use of fruit. Operating out of St. Patrick's Church in the Northside neighborhood, fruit tart beers like *The Gadget*, *Peaches & Cream*, and *Keypunch* carved a niche in the beer community. If that style isn't normally your type of thing, I would still suggest giving them a try since they truly are experts at what they do.

To the east, you'll find a pair of breweries, **Listermann Brewing** and **MadTree Brewing**. The Listermann's founded a homebrew parts business back in 1991, but would eventually get to brewing themselves in 2008. They have played an integral role in the rise of craft beer in the city, and I was a big fan of their dark beers in particular. *Satisfied?*, a stout with chocolate, caramel, peanuts, and lactose, was a finalist for my Best Dark Beer in 2021. It should be noted Dan Listermann recently retired and sold the brewery, but it still carries his name. Then, further to the west, you'll find **MadTree**'s massive facility, complete with an enormous outdoor area that features fire pits, a stage, a separate bar area, and tons of seating. Inside, you'll find a pizza kitchen, a large gift shop, and a plethora of hanging plants. The *Happy Amber* was my favorite, but *Legendary Lager* was another worthy choice.

My Take: I have enjoyed both of my visits to Cincinnati and would highly recommend it to someone for a Beercation. Besides the Over-the-Rhine neighborhood, the other places I mentioned are a little more spread out, but there are some others in between and with some planning, you won't have any issues hitting them all. Although I haven't yet visited them, I know David would like me to mention **Third Eye**, **Sonder**, and **Fretboard**, which all make excellent beer.

Quick Tip: I mentioned **Braxton Brewing** earlier, and Northern Kentucky has built up its beer scene. With a handful of breweries there, you could make an evening of brewing hopping across the state line if you have the extra time.

OTHER CITIES AND AREAS

Kenosha & Racine, WI: The two mid-sized cities situated between Milwaukee and Chicago have done some work to bridge the beer gap between those two metro areas. Racine has sadly seen two breweries come and go, but now **Littleport Brewing** holds that spot and has a cool space in a former foundry. Then, down in Kenosha, **Rustic Road Brewing** and **PUBLIC Craft Brewing** are within a couple of blocks of one another downtown. *Hazelnut Harvest*, an Amber Ale, and a Belgian Wit were my top picks at those two respectively. Meanwhile, **Kenosha Brewing** is located in a former monastery where monks once brewed beer!

Door County (WI): If you are familiar with a brewery in "The Cape Cod of the Midwest," it's probably **Door County Brewing**. Brewing since 2012, they are located in the quaint town of Baileys Harbor on Lake Michigan and have a wonderfully rustic taproom with lots of weathered wood. Their *Blank Range Hoppy Wheat* was delicious when I visited! On the other side of the peninsula in Egg Harbor is **Shipwrecked Brewpub**, where the nautical theme fits right in with the location across the street from Green Bay (the body of water, not the city).

There are two levels, and we enjoyed lunch there. Also in Egg Harbor, **One Barrel Brewing** has an impressive facility, complete with a nice patio and pizza. The largest city, Sturgeon Bay, is located about halfway down the peninsula and is home to two breweries. **Starboard Brewing** is right downtown and also features a nautical theme, while **Bridge Up Brewing** is directly below Sonny's Italian Kitchen & Pizzeria and has a sweeping view of the bay. Had a great chat at **Bridge Up** with the owner, Trent, when I was there.

Portage County (WI): This county in Central Wisconsin packs a punch when it comes to beer. **Central Waters Brewing** was founded in Amherst in 1998 and was my 500th brewery visit (and 100th in Wisconsin). They are well-known for their expertise in using barrels, and I got a personal tour of their facilities, including the massive barrel-aging building. They make pretty much every other style, too. One of the oldest breweries in the country is nearby in Stevens Point. **Point Brewery** was established in 1857 and now has lines of cider and soda as well as beer. Down the road in Plover is another veteran, as **O'so Brewing** has been around since 2007, and I've purchased their sours many times.

Rochester, MN: **Forager Brewery** is one of my favorites in Minnesota. The kettle sours were my top pick, but I also had a decadent Imperial pastry stout that was inspired by German chocolate cake. Another distinctive brewery is **Little Thistle Brewing**. Named for Scotland's national flower (one of the owners is originally from Scotland), they are making fantastic beer like the *Schwartzenlager* (Schwarzbier) and *Identity Crisis* cream ale. At the time of my visit in 2019, I wasn't as impressed by **Forager**'s neighbor, **Kinney Creek Brewery**, but I have heard from multiple local people that they have drastically improved, so I may need to give them another try someday.

<u>Hastings, MN:</u> Located about half an hour from St. Paul, this small city along the Mississippi River is where my parents have called home for nearly a decade now, and because of all the time I've spent there, I wanted to highlight **Spiral Brewery**. Located right downtown inside a former photography studio and named for the city's original bridge over the river, they have a neat upper deck area that looks out on the river. My dad's favorite beer there is *Hard Left Stout*, and I'd also recommend the *Townie Kolsch*.

<u>Rosemount, MN:</u> If you've enjoyed reading about farm breweries, I have another one for you. **North 20 Brewing** is situated on 20 acres and built a new barn to brew and serve beer. The properly named *Hay Bale Hazy IPA* goes well with sitting on the wrap-around deck that provides views of the land. **OMNI Brewing** is based in Maple Grove but opened up this Winery & Taproom location more recently. Yes, you read that right. They also make wine, just in case you are with someone who prefers that over drinking one of their beers. But you should try *FAD*, their double NEIPA.

<u>Nisswa, MN:</u> This small town of less than 2,000 people is nestled among the lakes of central Minnesota and is a tourist hotspot. Despite its size, there are two breweries for folks to check out. **Big Axe Brewing** is located downtown along bustling Main Street. Founded by a Nisswa native in 2015, they added a kitchen in 2017 (yes, you can order a walleye dinner). South of town is **Roundhouse Brewery**, and the railroad-themed spot has train tracks running under the plexiglass bar. A huge stage outside hosts live music, and they also have axe throwing, an event space, and a kitchen.

<u>Des Moines, IA:</u> The capital city of the Hawkeye State has an emerging beer scene that has changed quite a bit since my last visit in 2019. Three of the four breweries in the city that I visited have since closed (sadly, **Madhouse**, **Peace Tree**, and **1717**

shut their doors), but several others have stepped in (check out **Lua Brewing**, **Confluence Brewing**, and another outpost for **Big Grove Brewing**). **Exile Brewing** is still on the western edge of downtown in an old soap factory and churning out good beer. The *Dankalope IPA* was delectable. Nearby, I also made stops at the agricultural-themed **Barn Town Brewing** in West Des Moines and **Brightside Aleworks** in Altoona, where the *Enlighten-mint Stout* surprisingly won me over (I normally don't care for mint that much).

Dubuque, IA: Considered to be Iowa's oldest city, Dubuque is located along the banks of the Mississippi River and has a nice variety of options. My favorite is **Dimensional Brewing**, housed in a 1916 brick building that was home to several businesses. They have a wide variety, from simple lagers to intriguing fruited sours. Across town are the aviation-themed **Jubeck New World Brewing**, **7 Hill Brewing** (which has opened two other locations in nearby communities), and an outpost taproom of Coralville-based **Backpocket Brewing**, which is one of the breweries I often purchased beer from during my college days.

Decorah, IA: The name everyone knows from here is **Toppling Goliath Brewing**. They have grown immensely and are well known for their barrel-aged stouts and *Pseudo Sue Pale Ale*. Their huge facility outside of town is alone worth the trip. But in town is the Nordic-themed **Pulpit Rock Brewing**. The beer there was just as good as their more famous neighbor in my eyes, in particular, the raspberry Berliner Weisse called *Pillow Talk!*

Rockford, IL: For a fun history lesson, visit **Prairie Street Brewing** along the Rock River. The magnificent brick building built in 1849 was home to Rockford Brewing through the second half of the nineteenth century. **Prairie Street** opened in 2013 and used materials from the refurbishment throughout the process, such as reclaimed wood for the tables. It's a huge building, and some of the rooms are used for different purposes now but carry the name of their original use (such as Grain House and Bottle House). Nearby in Machesney Park is **Pig Minds Brewing** where I was told they claim to be America's first vegan brewpub. The husband wanted to open a brewery, and his wife wanted a vegan restaurant. So, they did both!

Fort Wayne, IN: Are you interested in beers inspired by cereals? Well, **2Toms Brewing** has a series of stouts and sours called *Cereal Killer* that are themed after (and use) real cereals! My favorite was a sour with Boo Berries. Another neat spot is **Fortlandia Brewing**, where three different brewers take turns serving up different styles inside a cozy former pizza joint. You could cap your night inside a brewery that was started as part of Excell Color Graphics (**Dot & Line Brewing**), which is maybe why they have such fun beer label designs on their menu. I'd recommend the *Peanut Butter Cup Stout* at this one.

Cleveland, OH: Housed in the historic Bryant Building downtown that was originally built in 1921 as a car dealership, **Masthead Brewing** is a delight. Besides the beer, they also have a pizza oven! I was a big fan of their *Single Origin Coffee Stout*. Not far from there is **Noble Beast Brewing**, where plants hang from the ceiling and banners of their awards are above the bar. The *Union Pils* was a nice choice there. Across the Cuyahoga River in the brewery-dense Ohio City neighborhood, you'll find **Bookhouse Brewing**. Their building was originally built in 1866 and would be home to Jacob Baehr Brewery until 1901 and then Cleveland & Sandusky Brewing until 1907. They also serve as a library and you can check out books. I only stopped through for one night, but if you have more time there are seven more breweries in the Ohio City neighborhood!

<u>Dayton, OH:</u> My one visit in the Gem City was memorable. **Carillon Brewery** is one of the most unique places I've visited. Part of the Carillon Historical Park, they use brewing techniques and equipment based on the mid-nineteenth century. It's also the nation's only production brewery in a museum. The entire interior has that historical vibe, and there's lots of information about the history of brewing. *Shaker*, an oatmeal stout, was the best choice in my flight.

<u>Toledo, OH:</u> This often-overlooked city in Northwest Ohio has some meritorious breweries. My favorite was **Ernest Brew Works**. Their main location is on the southeast edge of the city, with an additional spot downtown. Their *Pumpkin Spice Ale* was a treat! **Maumee Bay Brewing** is an original of the area. Located in the Oliver House, a former historic hotel opened in 1859 (a place where Abe Lincoln stayed), they've been around since 1995. I had a great time chatting with the staff there and enjoyed the *Oktoberfest*. Just north of downtown is **HEAVY Beer Company**, and their basement location certainly provides a unique vibe.

<u>Youngstown, OH:</u> The three breweries I visited during my visit could not have been more different. We can start with my favorite, **Noble Creature Wild Ales & Lagers**. Located in a nineteenth-century church, the stained-glass windows and pews for seating give the space a sanctuary-like setting, and they make excellent beer on top of having a cool taproom! *Rosalie* was especially notable; I loved the oak-aged wild ale with apple pumice and hibiscus. A quick walk from there is **Penguin City Brewing**. The local college, Youngstown State, has a penguin as a mascot by the way. This brewery with that same name is in a massive warehouse that was once home to a branch of Republic Steel, as well as a drywall factory. Some good, simple beers here, such as *Penguin City Beer*, which is a crushable golden ale. Finally, **Biker Brewhouse**, located out

to the northwest, is the only brewery in the country that is directly attached to a Harley Davidson dealership. In fact, they were originally a smaller part of the showroom but now have a larger space that is adjacent.

<u>Kalamazoo, MI</u>: One of the nation's most well-known breweries that has been around since 1985 is a big draw here. **Bell's Brewery** is a name many of you are probably already familiar with, and some of you may have even visited their Eclectic Cafe downtown. They opened this place in 1993 and it went through an expansion in 2015. Many of their beers, such as *Two Hearted IPA* and *Oberon Ale*, have wide acclaim, but when you visit you can also try more experimental beers, such as a *Brewery Vivant Collab*, which was a dry-hopped sour saison with kiwi and pineapple. Another notable option in town is **Wax Wings Brewery**. Opened in 2018, they quickly became a popular and highly rated spot. I thoroughly enjoyed their *Pulled Into Nazareth IPA*.

<u>Ann Arbor, MI</u>: I've only been to one brewery here, but **HOMES Brewery** was so good that it needed to be included. They were one of my nominees for Best Small Brewery in 2023, and it is because they knock it out of the park with every beer they make. Whether it was one of the numerous IPAs such as Same *Same Different* or a flavorful sour like *Dub Tropical*, I can't recommend them enough. They also have become well-known for their hard seltzer smoothies called Smooj, and another fun fact is that their name is an acronym for the five Great Lakes that surround the state.

A wide-stretching region, we will look at the beer scenes in North Dakota, South Dakota, Nebraska, Kansas, Colorado, Wyoming, Montana, Utah, and Idaho. I'll be the first to tell you there's more to this region than meets the eye.

Denver was the one city in this region that we called home during our travels. Aside from diving into Colorado's beer scene during that stretch, we have made many stops in this region during different road trips.

DENVER, CO

The Mile High City. One of my favorite places for craft beer. If you are someone who travels to breweries you probably are well aware of the wealth of options that Denver boasts. It's no secret that many people make the pilgrimage each fall to attend the Great American Beer Festival (GABF), which is regarded as one of the elite competitions for craft breweries. We were lucky enough to call this city home during the autumn of 2022, which meant I got to attend GABF for the first time and explore many of the breweries around the area.

We have a lot to cover, but we will start in the neighborhood most synonymous with craft beer in the city, the River North Art District (or RiNo for short). Just a bit north of downtown, this neighborhood was not always a hub for tourism and entertainment, but has become a trendy location for breweries, restaurants, shopping, and more. I'll start with a place very special to me, **Bierstadt Lagerhaus**. Established in 2016, they were my 1,000th brewery visit, and I had a fabulous time getting the behind-the-scenes tour. Their indoor Bierhalle is a playground for adults, and they have become well-known for their exceptional lagers. If you follow people in the beer industry on social media, you are barraged with photos of the Slow Pour Pilsner when everyone comes in for GABF week. Another fun fact: their copper brewing system was brought over from Ammendorft, Germany and was built in 1932.

On the eastern edge of RiNo not far from there is **Our Mutual Friend Brewing**. Their colorful building will immediately catch your eye, and both saisons I sampled have won medals at GABF (including one of them winning gold merely two days after I visited). A block north is another stalwart, **Ratio Beerworks**. The taproom features curved ceilings and was formerly home to Mile High Spirits. My favorite here was *Hold Steady*, a dark Scotch ale brewed with coffee from the local Novo Coffee. Across the street is Fort Collins-based **Odell Brewing**, which opened up a cool two-level space with multiple outdoor areas. They actually have two locations here in Denver and two in Fort Collins. Further north, you'll find even more options: **14er Brewing** is themed around all the mountain peaks in the state that are taller than 14,000 feet, **River North Brewing** is named for the neighborhood (and I enjoyed their session West Coast IPA), and **Black Shirt Brewing** is a highlight for those who are also into music (they have lots of shows on their back patio stage).

Although they are technically just east in the Clayton neighborhood, now is a good time to talk about **Cohesion Brewing**. Housed in an old army medical supply depot from WW2, they specialize in Czech lagers. You can even get a flight with the three traditional pour styles: Hladinka, Snyt, and Mliko. For those that may not know, these different pour styles offer widely different experiences. Hladinka is what many would consider a "typical" pour, with about 20 to 25 percent foam. Snyt, or "split," is half foam and half beer, while Mliko, or "milk," is almost entirely foam. The aromas and tasting notes can vary within the same beer depending on the pour style, and the drinking experience is, of course, different, too. Drinkers are supposed to consume a Mliko pour quickly, or even in one gulp! Snyt pours are a happy medium between the Mliko and Hladinka, as they are refreshing and not as filling as a regular pour but provide more body than those that consist mainly of the foam.

Working back south toward downtown, you will find another group of breweries, starting with **Great Divide Brewing**. They have a taproom in RiNo as well, but I visited the location right down the road from Coors Field. With all their GABF medals hanging on the wall, it's not hard to see why they became a popular local staple. A short walk takes you to **Woods Boss Brewing**, and to no one's surprise, it features a woodsy theme complete with logs and saws all over the taproom. Not far from those two spots and more central to downtown, you can discover **Jagged Mountain Brewing** (which is named after a Colorado mountain), a taproom in The Dairy Block for the Idaho Springs-based **Westbound & Down Brewing** (I enjoyed *The Coloradan Lager*), and **Wynkoop Brewing**, which was Colorado's first-ever brewpub when it opened in the LoDo neighborhood near Union Station in 1988.

As we start to look further outside of the immediate downtown area, let's head east along Colfax Avenue. This main vein through the city will lead you to several breweries, with the first stop being one of the locations for **Bruz Beers**. Their primary location is in the Highlands, but this particular space is a split-level taproom built in the 1930s as Denver's first Walgreens. The focus here is Belgian styles, and they do them well. A bit further down is **Cerebral Brewing**, where they take a "scientific approach to beer." One wall is covered with textbook pages, and they use beaker glasses for the flights, and, oh yeah, the beer is excellent. My top selection here was the *Rare Trait Hazy IPA*, a nominee for my Best IPA in 2022. Continuing west, you will find the literacy-themed **Fiction Beer Company** before arriving at **Lady Justice Brewing** in Englewood. **Lady Justice** is a women-owned spot that is known for supporting a variety of nonprofits and community partners that benefit women and girls in the state of Colorado. Their core lineup includes an award-winning ESB.

Back downtown, we will trek south now and hone in on two of my favorite breweries in the entire city. **Baere Brewing** and **Trve Brewing** are less than a block apart in the Speer neighborhood but provide vastly different experiences. One thing they have in common though is making amazing beer! **Baere** is located in an unassuming strip mall and named after an Old English word for barley. They made stunning beers across many styles: Berliner Weisse, saison, and stout, but the big winner was *C3(i)PA*, a West Coast IPA that won my award for Best IPA in 2022 thanks to its perfect execution with a trio of "C" hops (Cascade, Centennial, and Chinook). Trooping down to **Trve**, you are immediately met with a different vibe. The taproom is long, narrow, dark, and has a strong heavy metal theme. In the back is Music City Hot Chicken, but that was not something I partook in. Similar to **Baere**, they do great work across several styles (including mixed-culture sours), but my favorite was *Happy Tuesday*, a light lager with corn grits that was a finalist for my Best Lighter Beer in 2022.

A longer jog to the southwest is another of my favorites that should be on everyone's radar: **Comrade Brewing**. While it's more out of the way than most of the breweries I'll discuss in Denver, they won the GABF Small Brewery of the Year in 2019 and have an array of beers that have medaled in the competition. The best of those, in my opinion, was the Irish red ale called *REDCON*, but I'd also recommend *More Dodge Less Ram*, an IPA that has won gold twice at GABF. The name of that IPA? Oh, just a nod to the fact that a Dodge Ram bull-dozed into their brewery back in 2016.

Heading back north along I-25, our next stop is **Burns Family Artisan Ales**. If you are into high-ABV options, barrel-aging, and interesting sours, this is the place for you. Wayne Burns is well-known for pushing the limits of ABV while still crafting them in a way that makes them irresistibly smooth and balanced. *Zero Over Zero: Talnua* was a barrel-aged Imperial stout I sampled that came in at 13.8%, but two others available were higher than that! Even though that isn't my preferred style, I enjoyed it immensely. But my favorite beer there was *Genie^Logical V11: Blossoms I (Crabapple, peony, begonia)*, a mixed-culture sour with Colorado wildflowers. It won my Best Sour in 2022 and was soft, approachable, and yet intriguingly complex. Two of the breweries with memorable stories on this side of the city have sadly closed, but I wanted to mention them. **Dos Luces Brewery** used Incan and Mayan brewing traditions to produce some unique (and gluten-free) options, while **Wah Gwaan Brewing** was a Jamaican-inspired location with a distinctly tropical feel.

Unlike those to the east and south, most of the breweries I want to discuss to the west are more grouped together. Just across the South Platte River is a triangle of breweries providing three very different profiles. **Denver Beer Company** has five total locations, but this one in the Lower Highland neighborhood is in an old car garage. Considerable variety of beer, but the *Graham Cracker Porter* is what you need to try. On the other side of the freeway is **Prost Brewing Company & Biergarten**. As the name hints, this spacious beer hall focuses on German styles and has a nice outdoor space facing toward downtown. Completing this triangle is **Zuni Street Brewing**, which feels like walking into nature. Hanging plants and vines engulf the taproom space, plus there are tree murals on the front of the building. Here, I would recommend the *Way West Wit*.

Just north of that trio, you'll stumble upon **Diebolt Brewing**, which is inside a former government meat packing facility. Located in the Sunnyside neighborhood, you get a glimpse of the skyline from the patio while sipping on a *Bolt Lager* or one of the other award-winning beers. Then, you could continue your way up to **Crooked Stave Brewing** if you have a hankering for sours. While they do also brew some other styles, those sours are what they are best known for since being founded in 2010. The *Petite Sour Raspberry* was the highlight of my stop. Further west from the places I've mentioned is **Hogshead Brewery**, a unique spot that has a majority of beers on cask inside their cozy taproom. Completing a semi-circle around the western side of the city is **Raices Brewing**. Latino-owned, they want to connect guests through Latino culture, and the bright and colorful taproom in the Sun Valley neighborhood does just that!

I could go on and on. I haven't even mentioned places like **Renegade**, **FlyteCo**, **Banded Oak**, **Spangalang**, and **Novel Strand**—and that's before you head out into the mountains! There's a reason the Denver beer scene is so well covered and a bucket list place for many beer lovers.

My Take: As I said, Denver is one of my favorite beer cities. Not only is there a plethora of options, but there are so many high-quality choices for anyone visiting. It may seem overwhelming at times, but that just means multiple trips are in order!

Quick Tip: I did not get to visit since we were not there during the baseball season, but if you go to a Colorado Rockies game there is a brewery inside the stadium, **The Sandlot Brewery**. It was the first brewery inside a Major League Baseball stadium when it opened in 1995. However, it is only open to ticket holders on game days.

COLORADO SPRINGS, CO

The second largest city in the state, Colorado Springs is a gateway to many amazing outdoor adventures. Taking the train up Pikes Peak is an incredible experience. The Garden of the Gods is awe-inspiring, and not far away is the jaw-dropping Royal Gorge Bridge and Park. But after you are done taking in as much of Mother Nature as you can, you'll certainly be looking for a place (or two) to indulge in some beers. There are options throughout the city, so no matter where you are staying, there are choices nearby.

Starting with the furthest north, there's a pair of breweries close to Garden of the Gods. **Red Leg Brewing** is a veteran-owned spot that fittingly opened on July 4, 2013. The incredible outdoor area is surrounded by different food vendors in repurposed shipping containers. Right down the road is **TRiNiTY Brewing,** which immediately earned a place in my heart as it functions as a Green Bay Packers bar! As I mentioned in my Green Bay section, I am a die-hard fan, so seeing the plethora of flags, jerseys, and signs adorning the taproom was a wonderful surprise. Dug the *Space Force Orbital Warfare IPA*, too.

Working back toward downtown, **Goat Patch Brewing** has a memorable logo. Part of the Lincoln Center complex, it was named for the head brewer's beard. I had a mouthwatering pumpkin beer here. In terms of beer, **Cerberus Brewing** to the west of downtown might have been my favorite. The spacious beer garden is where I fell head over heels for the *No Big Deal Kolsch*. My last two brewery visits of the trip were right up there for best beers though. The *Peanut Butter Stout* at the dog-friendly and mining-themed **Battle Mountain Brewing** hit the mark, and the freshly opened (in October 2022) **Urban Animal Beer Company** was serving great stuff, such as *Surveillance Doe Blonde Ale*, inside the former China Doll restaurant.

My Take: We loved our visit to Colorado Springs. There are so many options for different activities depending on what you fancy, and there's a nice array of breweries available, too. There's a decent contingent of them around downtown that I was not able to get to.

Quick Tip: Sports fans will want to visit the US Olympic & Paralympic Museum. You can even try out some of the skills for different events. I mentioned my wife doesn't like beer, but she loves zoos and we have been to over seventy around the country. The Cheyenne Mountain Zoo is a very good one, but be prepared for some steep pathways!

BOULDER COUNTY (CO)

Separated by just fifteen miles, Boulder and Longmont are two mid-sized cities to the north of Denver located in Boulder County. While the number of breweries may not rival the Mile High City, they each boast their own beer scenes with several breweries, many of which are well-known. I took day trips to both places during our time living in Denver, and although I could not make it to every brewery, I did have enjoyable experiences in those I stopped into.

We'll start first in Boulder, which is slightly closer to Denver. Home to the University of Colorado, this college town has a fun little downtown highlighted by the Pearl Street pedestrian mall. The brewery closest to that area I visited was **Twisted Pine Brewing**, which featured one of my favorite logos in the state. Founded in 1995, they moved to the current location in 2003 and now feature a nice selection of twenty draft lines. I was there in the fall and enjoyed the porter with pumpkin spices, vanilla, and marshmallows named *Pumpkin Porter Peeps*. To the east is **Wild Provisions Beer Project**, which is run by **4 Noses Brewing**. Focusing on lagers and wild beers, everything I had inside the modern taproom was delicious. The *Echo-Rood Blended Mixed Culture* was especially delightful. Two other popular spots are **Upslope Brewing** (they have two locations) and **Avery Brewing**. The latter is now owned by Mahou-San Miguel Group of Spain but has been a Colorado staple since its founding in 1993.

Up in Longmont is where you will find some familiar names. **Left Hand Brewing** was founded in 1993 and became famous as the first brewery to bottle nitrogen beer. Their milk stout is one that many people have had, and I tried a French Toast version at the taproom. Another big name in Longmont is **Oskar Blues Brewing**. Established as a brewpub in 1997 and beginning brewing in 1999, their claim to fame is being one of the first breweries to put craft beer like *Dale's Pale Ale* in cans back in 2002. But maybe the most interesting brewery in town is **Primitive Beer**, where they focus on Spontaneous Fermentation Method Traditionale. I had a tremendous time chatting with the brewer and owner, Brandon, and learning about his process. Their unique approach is highlighted by all the barrels inside the taproom, along with a koelschip (an open-top and flat brewing vessel that allows the wort to cool rapidly). Unfortunately, that taproom is no longer open, but there is still beer being made! Now you have to keep your eyes peeled for special releases.

My Take: This area has a marvelous mix of nationally recognizable names with familiar flagships and smaller, more intimate spots brewing unique beers. I honestly recommend going to both types, as you'll be able to try classic at both **Left Hand** and **Oskar Blues**, while places like **Wild Provisions** and **Primitive** will test your palate.

Quick Tip: You are closer to the mountains here than in Denver, particularly in Boulder. So, make sure you take advantage of that by checking out some of the nearby state parks and hiking trails while in the area.

MISSOULA, MT

Missoula is an outdoor lover's paradise. Mountain trails and rivers for fly fishing, plus it's a reasonable drive to get up to Glacier National Park. The natural beauty alone is enough to entice travelers to visit, but add onto that a flourishing local beer scene and you have a winner! Montana has long had tough laws surrounding beer (it wasn't that long ago breweries couldn't sell beer in a taproom), and even today, there are hurdles to overcome (brewery taprooms can't stay open past 8 pm). But that hasn't deterred those who wanted to bring craft beer to Big Sky Country.

And speaking of **Big Sky**, that is the largest brewery in the state and is conveniently located out by the airport. They've been making their popular beers since 1995. I'm a fan of their flagship, *Moose Drool Brown Ale*, but the taproom offers plenty of other options. **Kettlehouse Brewing** is another local staple and has an amphitheater outside of town in addition to the main brewery. The *Cold Smoke Scotch Ale* is a staple here and is what I recommend ordering. **Kettlehouse** is another staple of Montana, as they also were founded in 1995.

Continuing the repurposed building theme you've seen throughout this book, **Draught Works** utilizes an old recycling plant. Their *Blood Orange Gose* was delicious! **Imagine Nation Brewing** is not just a brewery but also home to the Center for Community Transformation. Unique beers, a patio just off the river, and an admirable mission makes this a must-stop in my eyes. For classic German-style beers, **Bayern Brewing** is the place to be. Founded in 1987, they are a classic Montana establishment and brew their lagers in accordance to Reinheitsgebot (German Law of Purity that requires beer be made using only barley, yeast, hops, and water). The two-level taproom also serves up food as well, but I was mostly focused on *Dragon's Breath*, a dark Hefeweizen.

My Take: Similar to Duluth, I featured Missoula in my "Underrated Beer Cities in America" article I wrote in 2020, and I stand by the idea that it's a place everyone should visit. Plus, it's a wonderful little city, even aside from the beer.

Quick Tip: If you are outdoorsy, you can work off your beer with a hike up Mt. Jumbo or Mt. Sentinel. Both provide a view of Missoula and the surrounding mountains.

GLACIER NATIONAL PARK (MT)

Remote, difficult to get to, and absolutely worth the journey. We were blown away by the beautiful vistas and untouched wilderness throughout this area in Montana. Hidden Lake at Logan Pass and Wild Goose Island in Saint Mary Lake were two of my favorite views, but truly at every turn it seemed to be a buffet for your eyes. Along the western side of the park are several towns running down from Whitefish Lake toward Flathead Lake, and in some of these towns are breweries serving up appealing beer.

The main city for breweries in the area is Kalispell. Near the airport is **Sacred Water Brewing**, which has a very "Montana feel" to the taproom. Dark woods, taxidermy mountain animals, beautiful pictures of local outdoor scenes, and even an enlarged fishing reel flight board are all present. Back in town is **Bias Brewing**. The *Tea Pale Ale* I had was especially well done. A fun fact about the porcupine logo: the reason they chose it is because they wanted an animal from Montana, but didn't want to be cliche with a bear or moose. **SunRift Beer Company** is not far from there, and the small spot is where I enjoyed a wheat ale and gazed at the map of the Blacktail Mountain Ski Area.

The best view in the area (and one of the best views I've seen at a brewery) is at **Flathead Lake Brewing** in Bigfork. As the name suggests, it sits on a small hill looking out at Flathead Lake with mountains rising on either side. Across the lake in Lakeside is **Tamarack Brewing**, where you'll find Stoner Creek running along the outdoor area and a spacious two-story taproom. The final area brewery that needs a shoutout is **Bonsai Brewing Project** up in Whitefish. The snug taproom in the quaint mountain town has a phenomenal outdoor space and serves up several interesting beers, like a Belgian saison aged in sauvignon blanc barrels.

My Take: This is a stunning part of the country and worth the trip. While the main focus of your stay in the region most likely won't be focused around beer, there are certainly some good options scattered around the area for you to choose from.

Quick Tip: If you want to visit Glacier National Park and stay close to the park, you'll want to plan ahead. There are not many hotels or places to stay in or around the park, and it's twenty to thirty minutes to get to the entrance from the closest town. Kalispell (where the airport is) is about forty minutes away.

SALT LAKE CITY, UT

When it comes to beer, Utah has often been associated with some of its constrictive laws. Until 2019, breweries could not serve beers on draft over 4% ABV. When I passed through in 2021, that number sat at 5% following a law change, giving them more flexibility. But if they made a beer higher than that it needed to be purchased in bottles or cans. Some people may view this as detrimental to a city's beer scene, but I honestly was impressed with the quality of options around Salt Lake City. You could still find just about every style you were looking for, but maybe just a lower ABV than you were accustomed to seeing.

The most central to downtown that I visited also happened to be my favorite in terms of beer. **Templin Family Brewing** is located in the Granary District and has become well-known for its award-winning lagers. Their *Kellerbier* took home silver at GABF in 2022, but my favorite was the *Schwarzbier*. The taproom is also very sleek and modern, with tons of space. Heading south from there is **RoHa Brewing Project**. I had the pleasure of having Rob Phillips (the "Ro" in **RoHa**) on my podcast when I did an episode on Salt Lake City. He teamed up with Chris Haas (the "Ha"), and they opened up in 2017 inside a former office building. I loved the mural in the taproom that was inspired by the terrain of Southern Utah, and my favorite beer was *Americano*, an ale with cold brew coffee.

My other two stops in the city were close together, but a bit further south. In fact, **Level Crossing Brewing** is technically in South Salt Lake. Colorful murals adorned the walls inside and out, plus they are making some solid beers such as a *Belgian Wit* and *Vienna Lager*. As of summer 2023, they have a location in downtown Salt Lake City too! My final stop was an interesting one, as all of the beers at **SaltFire Brewing** were over 5% during my visit. This meant that their taps were not in use and you had to drink the beers from cans. But I did dig both I tried, particularly their flagship, *Fury Kolsch*.

I also want to mention the two breweries I stopped at during my first time in the state back in 2018. These were in Ogden, just a little way to the north, and at that point, it was before the law changed, so all the beers were at 4% (or less). I walked away from **Talisman Brewing** quite impressed with all the flavors and depth they were able to achieve, especially in their *Honey Wheat with blood orange*. The other spot highlighted another odd law in Utah: if you are considered a restaurant, you must order food with any alcoholic beverage. That was the case at **Roosters Brewing**, where I had to get a side order of fries to try a couple of the beers.

My Take: I think people would be impressed with the number of options here. With close to thirty breweries in the city (and many being close to downtown), Salt Lake City has quietly been building a robust beer scene worthy of a visit.

Quick Tip: While they have the odd limit for beers on tap, Utah does not have a limit on what the ABV can be for beers brewed and packaged in cans or bottles. So you can sometimes find beers with even higher ABVs than you are accustomed to seeing.

OTHER CITIES AND AREAS

Fort Collins, CO: With big names like **New Belgium Brewing** and **Odell Brewing**, Fort Collins is another Colorado city that most craft beer fanatics are familiar with. But there are a couple of smaller spots that stole the show for me. **Purpose Brewing**, owned by former New Belgium brewmaster Peter Bouckaert (who pioneered bringing sour beer to America), has an array of new beers released every week. When I visited, *Smoeltrekker #033* (a sour ale) was my favorite. Another nice spot is **Gilded Goat Brewing**, which has two locations in the city, including a taproom downtown. I quite enjoyed *Late to the Partea*, an ESB with Earl Grey tea. Some Denver-based breweries also have spots there, such as **Prost Brewing** and **Crooked Stave.**

Bozeman, MT: Home to my Best Small Brewery of 2022, **Mountains Walking Brewery**. All of their beers were amazing. Their *Porter* won my Best Dark Beer, *Montana Kriek* was a nominee for Best Sour, and the IPA and pilsner I had could have easily made the cut, too. I loved the branding and modern rustic taproom with mountain views. But it was down the road at **MAP Brewing** where I found my Best View of 2022. The cabin-like taproom looks out at Glen Lake and the Bridger Range; is absolutely stunning. Both places also have food as well.

<u>Billings, MT</u>: It's not every day you can have a flight of four beers where all of them have medaled at GABF. But that's the case at **Uberbrew**! Housed in what was previously Yellowstone Garage, the *Canu Cream Ale* was my favorite and was a finalist in 2022 for my Best Lighter Style Beer. I also visited **Angry Hank's Microbrewery**, which resides in a 1916 carriage near downtown.

<u>Livingston, MT:</u> A pair of interesting breweries call this small city home. **Neptune's Brewery** is an aquatic and oceanic-themed brewery, which is not something you expect to see in Central Montana. A legit fish tank behind the bar, fake shark and marlin, fish nets everywhere, and plenty of nautical artwork are all inside! Downtown is **Katabatic Brewing**. Located in the Pape Building downtown, it was built in 1883 as a liquor wholesale and public hall. Later on, it would be rebuilt after a fire in 1904 and would house a saloon and National Park Steam Laundry

<u>Cheyenne, WY</u>: Sadly, my favorite brewery here closed its doors. **Danielmark's Brewing** brewed some exceptionally well-made beers inside a house built in the 1880s. They have been replaced, though, **Blue Raven Brewery**. There are some other worthwhile stops, such as **Black Tooth Brewing**, housed in the former Pioneer Printing Building (they also have a location in Sheridan, WY) and **Accomplice Beer Company**. The latter is part of the old train depot, and there's a patio in the back by the railroad tracks.

<u>Coeur d'Alene, ID</u>: You can pair these breweries up with a visit to Spokane, which you'll read about later. This small city up in Gem State's panhandle has a nice handful of breweries, with my favorite being **Trails End Brewery**. Suitable beer across the board, in particular the *Right as Rain Golden Ale*. To no one's

surprise, there's a bit of a woodsy theme here. **Daft Badger Brewing** had been named "Best Local Brewery" five years in a row by the Business Journal of North Idaho when I visited in 2022, and I certainly enjoyed the *Blood Orange IPA* and food menu. **Paragon Brewing** was my other stop. It's located inside a former pub and also has an outdoor beer garden for cornhole and live music.

Omaha, NE: Nebraska as a whole has a sneaky good beer scene. In my opinion, it's spearheaded by Lumen Beer Company, located in the Little Bohemia neighborhood of Omaha. The rustic, airy taproom was serving up delicious beer, and *Bounce Hazy IPA* was a finalist for my Best IPA in 2022. Just to the Southeast in La Vista, you'll find some other spots like **Kros Strain Brewing** and **Pint Nine Brewing**. **Kros Strain** has a colorful taproom with several award-winning beers, and **Pint Nine** was a finalist for my Most Surprising Brewery in 2022.

Lincoln, NE: The state capital may be more well-known for Cornhusker football, but there's a nice string of breweries through downtown, with some others scattered around the outskirts. Named for Morse code because they are located in the old telegraph district, **Code Beer Company** has transformed a former machine shop into a nice taproom and makes a slew of different styles. Located in the old boiler room of what was previously the US Courthouse and Post Office downtown, **Boiler Brewing**'s *Hot Sauce Barrel Aged Chili & Cinnamon Roll Pastry Sour* might be the most unique and interesting beer I've ever had. Ya, you probably want to read that again. While their downtown taproom is now closed, **White Elm Brewing** still has its main location to the south, and I thoroughly enjoyed the *Positive Mental Attitude Pale Ale*.

Grand Island, NE: Continuing west along I-80 from Lincoln, you will eventually stumble onto Grand Island. Their two breweries are both downtown, right across the street from each other. **Kinkaider Brewing** is based in Broken Bow, but it's hard to imagine it's in a cooler building than this one. They took over a former theater and turned it into a gorgeous space to try their beer and food. A balcony wraps around the top and I fell in love with the *Caramel Peanut Butter Amber Ale*. Not to be outdone, **Prairie Pride Brewing** serves Nebraska-shaped flight boards of beer inside a 1930s building that served as a jail, plumbing facility, and furniture store.

North Platte, NE: I have only one brewery to highlight here, but I wanted to include **Pals Brewing** because they were excellent hosts for my milestone 600th brewery visit! Located just south of town, they took advantage of their location and have a two-acre outdoor area adjacent to the large shed-like taproom. My family enjoyed eating lunch here, and my top pick for beer was *Football Sunday*, a cream ale. They also opened a second location in Wisconsin Dells, WI in 2024.

Sioux Falls, SD: I last visited the largest city in the Mount Rushmore State in 2018, and like many places, I know they have added several new breweries since then. I did visit a handful, though, including **WoodGrain Brewing** right downtown, **Remedy Brewing**, where the *Queen Bee Imperial Cream Ale* was a delight, and **Fernson Brewing**, with two locations to check out beers like *Lion's Paw Lager* and *Shy Giant IPA*.

Fargo, ND: The Viking-themed **Drekker Brewing** is a destination on its own, as they have become uber-popular thanks in part to their smoothie sours and Imperial IPAs. Formerly located downtown, they are now in an 1880 building originally built as a locomotive repair building. Called "Brewhalla," it's part of a massive complex that includes a food market, specialty shops, and even a hotel where the rooms are each themed around one specific **Drekker** beer. But don't ignore the options across the Red River in Moorhead, MN. **Junkyard Brewing** makes amazing sours as well, and the larger section of the taproom was previously an alley next to the original space. Close by is **Swing Barrel Brewing** inside an old car dealership (the floors are even original). Here, I had a soft spot for *Sweet Melissa*, a honey peach wheat ale.

Bismarck, ND: Maybe one of the most surprising "beer cities" I've been to; I went in with little expectations and left very impressed. The biggest winner was **Gideon's Brewing** downtown, where they were knocking every beer out of the park. The *Soul Glo Hefeweizen* is one of the best of that style I've had. The original craft brewery in town, **Laughing Sun Brewing**, was founded in 2012, and I enjoyed sipping my *Red Dwarf Raspberry Sour Ale* from my North Dakota-shaped flight board. Oh, and they have axe throwing and live music, too. **Stonehome Brewing** was another big surprise as this brewpub/sports bar hybrid attached to a large bank (you walk through the bank's lobby to get inside) had prime beers like the *River Otter Red IPA*. Don't sleep on Bismarck!

Oklahoma, Texas, New Mexico, Arizona, and Nevada make up the quintet of states for this section. Some more "under the radar" cities are featured.

This is the one region in the book where we have not lived during our travels. But aside from passing through many times on road trips, Austin is the place where I planned my most extensive "Beercation."

AUSTIN, TX

This is another city where I have quite a bit to discuss. In 2022, I awarded Austin with my Best Beer City (Large) during my annual review, and for good reason. There are many quality breweries, and in my opinion, it has the strongest beer scene in the Lone Star State. It's a quickly growing metro area, so I don't expect locals to run out of options for beer anytime soon. What made my time in Austin extra special is that my father joined me for an extended Beercation.

We will start outside the main city in Hill Country, as **Jester King Brewery** is most likely the place that people outside of the area are familiar with. The farm, the beer, and the goats make this an absolute must-stop. The grounds are expansive, complete with multiple buildings and a hop yard.

Less Dots, a farmhouse ale with spent black currants, was my favorite of the visit. Also out in Hill Country is **Oasis Texas Brewery**, home to one of the best views you'll find at a brewery. Up on the third level of a complex perched high above Lake Travis, there's a great flow from inside to the outer deck so you can soak in the panorama.

Back to the city, I'll start in North Austin and work my way down. **Austin Beerworks**, one of the other big names locally, has a cornucopia of options (twenty-nine beers on tap when I visited). The Russian Imperial coffee oat stout called *Sputnik* was phenomenal. **Hopsquad Brewing** is a nearby colorful spot close to Q2 Stadium. They had one of the most unique beers I had that year, *Pepito's Pepino*. A cucumber basil wheat ale, it somehow managed to taste similar to a pasta sauce while remaining incredibly refreshing. In that same area, you can check out the worker-owned **4th Tap Brewing Cooperative** and long-standing **Celis Brewery**, which originally opened in 1992 before getting more recently revived by the family of the original founder.

Working toward downtown, you'll find one of the **Pinthouse Pizza & Brewing** locations in the Brentwood neighborhood. With the classic *Electric Jellyfish Hazy IPA* on tap, you'll want to plop down and enjoy a pizza or order of queso. In that same vicinity, **The Brewtorium** and **Draught House Pub & Brewery** both offer an ample variety of beer with nice outdoor areas. Just to the east is a pair of neighboring breweries I would recommend, **Batch Craft Beer & Kolaches and Oddwood Brewing. Batch** explains its business in its name, as you can munch on a delicious pastry stuffed with meats and cheese or sweets while quaffing a beer in their outdoor space. **Oddwood** transformed a restaurant and nightclub into its venue that supplies beers like the *Perfect Strangers Golden Sour* to coincide with Italian-inspired food.

Around downtown and East Austin you'll stumble onto another helping of breweries. **Central District Brewing** is the most centrally located and has a modern space with plants and a drop-down projection screen. Just to the east are two of my favorites from the trip, **Lazarus** and **Blue Owl. Lazarus Brewing** was founded by a former pastor and had a great selection of beer, seating options, and scrumptious tacos! The *Prodigal Pils* and *Farm Girl*, a farmhouse-style wild ale with lemon, lavender, and wild honey, were both amazing. If you are into sours, a stop at **Blue Owl Brewing** is necessary. That's the focus there, and I also loved that they had a Little Free Library in their taproom. And back by **Lazarus** is **Zilker Brewing**. The folks there converted a former auto shop and used the floor of a 1930s boxcar to create some of the tables.

Across the Colorado River, we continue south, and if you've got a hankering for award-winning lagers, I would tell you to run, not walk, to **The Austin Beer Garden Brewing**. They won the GABF Best Big Brewpub of the Year for three straight years from 2016 to 2018. I had four lagers during my visit that had won a gold medal at GABF, including *Hell Yes*, the aptly named Helles lager. **St. Elmo Brewing** is in the neighborhood that bears the same name. This was one of the biggest surprises for me, as the coffee cream ale was a major success. If outdoor spaces are your thing, **Meanwhile Brewing** will dazzle you. Artificial turf, a large stage, and a huge wooded area with a playground provide a complete experience.

If you are craving more outdoor areas, stopping at **Live Oak Brewing** is the move. It should be the move no matter what, as they make some of the best beer in the area. Established in 1997 and located near the airport, they had a tremendous space with multiple levels of shaded picnic tables and disc golf. The *Grodziske Smoked Polish Beer* was an absolute treat, but any of their beers will satisfy you.

My Take: I highly recommend Austin for a Beercation. You'll need a full vacation to visit all the worthwhile breweries in the area, especially since it can take a while to travel around the metro area.

Quick Tip: I mentioned the food at a couple of breweries, but many others had tasty options to eat as well. Whether it's BBQ, tacos, pizza, or something else entirely, you'll be able to find something to fill up your stomach.

ALBUQUERQUE, NM

My uncle lives in Albuquerque, so I visited the largest city in New Mexico a few times growing up. I always had a blast going up to Sandia Peak in the Sandia Mountains, and I remember my family enjoying the zoo there as well. I've been able to pass through twice since starting my beer travels and have had gratifying times at the breweries during each visit.

I could write an entire section on **Bow and Arrow Brewing**, as my experience at this Native American women-owned brewery was phenomenal. This was actually the *first* brewery opened by Native American women in the country! It won my Best Small Brewery in 2021, thanks in large part to their *Denim Tux Blue Corn American Pilsner* taking home Best Lighter-style Beer and *Cactus Flats Sabro Hazy IPA* being nominated for Best IPA. It should not be a surprise that they use a lot of local ingredients and Native traditions play a large role. The branding, the taproom, the backstory, it all makes for a must-stop brewery. They also have a taproom in Farmington if you are in that region of the state.

But there is so much more to the beer scene here. I think people would be surprised just how many breweries are in the city. This is especially true for downtown and the Wells Park neighborhood just to the north (which is where **Bow and Arrow** is). **Rio Bravo Brewing** is also in that neighborhood and has a nice covered patio. I enjoyed the *Peanut Butter Hazelnut Brown Ale* there. Although I visited their location to the east (they have four in total), **Tractor Brewing** also has a taproom next to the first two I mentioned. **Tractor** makes cider that they serve alongside their beers, but I'd recommend one of the sours.

Across the freeway are a pair of classic breweries that have been New Mexico stalwarts. **La Cumbre Brewing** displays all their Great American Beer Festival and World Beer Cup medals in their taproom, and I can vouch for the *Slice of Hefen* (a Hefeweizen) and *ESB*. Meanwhile, **Sante Fe Brewing** (the original New Mexico craft brewery opened in 1988) has a location at Green Jeans Farmery. With two levels that offer indoor and outdoor seating, you can get whatever vibe you want while consuming a *Happy Camper IPA*. Throughout the city you can also find three locations of **Marble Brewery**, which won Small Brewery and Small Brewery Brewer of the Year at GABF in 2014. Their *Wildflower Wheat* and *Smoked Helles* were both delicious.

My Take: People may not think of Albuquerque as a potential destination for a Beercation, but I will stand on the table and tell everyone it is worth the visit. The number of breweries (and their quality) deserves more attention. I need to get back to try more spots. Plus, it is a very beautiful area!

Quick Tip: Be prepared to answer "Red or green?" as New Mexico became the first state to adopt an official state question. They are asking you which type of chile pepper you prefer.

OKLAHOMA CITY, OK

The largest city in the Sooner State was not one of the early adopters of the craft beer movement, but in the last ten years they have seen a boom thanks to some new legislation. And it now has a thriving beer scene! The growth has occurred mainly in the city itself, which makes it easier to do some brewery hopping.

While it is a newer craft beer scene, the oldest craft brewery in the state is downtown in the Bricktown neighborhood. **Bricktown Brewery** dates back to 1992 and is a traditional brewpub that has 22 locations scattered across six states, although most of them are in Oklahoma. We ate there as a family, and I had a tasty burger and nachos. On the other side of downtown, **Stonecloud Brewing** is located in an old laundromat and makes solid beers such as *Astrodog IPA* and *Havana Affair Pilsner*.

On the northern edge of downtown, there's an alluring group of breweries. Maybe the most well-known Oklahoma brewery has its taproom here, **Prairie Artisan Ales**. While they make many styles well, their unique sours are what stuck with me. From *Rainbow Sherbet*, a sour ale with, you guessed it, rainbow sherbet, to *Red Hot Spectrum*, a sour ale with hibiscus, cinnamon, chiles, and Red Hots candy, there are so many different flavors to explore. You should also swing by **Vanessa House Brewing** in this neighborhood, as the former auto shop is now a bright, colorful taproom with arcade games, action figure tap handles, movie merchandise displayed, and good beer. Although I did not get to them during my trip, I have heard good things about **The Big Friendly** and **Skydance Brewing**.

My Take: Like some other cities in this section, they are often overlooked on a national scale when discussing craft beer. But there are a lot of options, and you can check out the Oklahoma Ale Trail for more information, too.

Quick Tip: If you have time, stop at the Oklahoma City National Memorial & Museum. Commemorating the victims of the 1995 Murrah Building bombing, it is a powerful and worthwhile experience.

TUCSON, AZ

The soul of the Sonoran Desert, Tucson is a fun little city situated next to Saguaro National Park. With how hot it can get here (especially in the summer), it's no wonder that the craft beer scene has been taking off. I can always appreciate when a city's brewery scene has a focus on the downtown area, which is the case here in Tucson!

Crooked Tooth Brewing is part of this area, and turned over a former automotive shop. They featured maybe my favorite flight board: a skateboard! The wheels didn't move (thank goodness), but it was such a cool and unique look. Plus, I enjoyed their *Mexican Lager*. Heading to the southern side of downtown next you'll find **Barrio Brewing**, which opened in 1991 and is Arizona's oldest craft brewery. They transformed a space that was a meat market and storage unit, and my entire family had a scrumptious dinner on a Taco Tuesday here.

Not far from there is **Moto Sonora Brewing**, which features two vintage motorcycles inside the taproom and a striking mural outside of a lizard driving away in the desert and waving at a scorpion. This space was formerly a tile warehouse, and dog owners will be happy to find out that there is an off-leash area in the beer garden. *Pink Pilots*, a hoppy saison, was excellent. Although they were not open the night I was there, I have heard great things about **Pueblo Vida Brewing**, also downtown.

My one stop outside of the downtown area was to the northwest at **1912 Brewing**. This was one of the most unique stops I made that year (they were a nominee for Most Unique Brewery in 2021), and if you are a fan of goses, you will enjoy this one. When I visited, NINE of the eighteen beers on tap were goses, and each one was a different recipe, ranging in ABV from 4% to 9% with a variety of different flavors. My personal favorite was *Rebanditas*, a strawberry watermelon Mexican candy gose. Another example was one featuring dragon fruit, pineapple, and soursop.

My Take: Tucson is a fun city to visit, beer and otherwise. It's big enough that plenty is going on, and in terms of breweries, there are many options. But it's small enough that it's easy to get around and bounce between those breweries.

Quick Tip: As I said, it can get HOT here. Although everyone probably already knows this, make sure to take plenty of water if you are going hiking in the national park. But don't fret, you aren't too far from the city in case you need to run back.

OTHER CITIES AND AREAS

Dallas, TX: The massive metro area is home to some quality breweries. My personal favorite was **Peticolas Brewing**, with its three-tiered taproom and the decadent *Velvet Hammer*, their flagship Imperial red ale. Michael Peticolas, the owner, also happens to be a lawyer and fought for the rights of craft brewers across Texas. A couple of other names to keep in mind: **Celestial Beerworks** and **Vector Brewing**.

San Antonio, TX: My lone brewery visit was **Künstler Brewing**, but it was a laudable one! Housed in a former mattress recycling facility just a bit south of downtown, there's a strong German influence here. While you'll find pilsners, Kolsch, and other lagers here, I was a big fan of the West Coast IPA I tried called *Texas Tube Float*. **Weathered Souls Brewing** is another place worth a visit.

Amarillo, TX: Located up in the Texas Panhandle, I enjoyed stopping through here and visiting some of the tourist spots like Cadillac Ranch and the Big Texan Steak Ranch. The latter is also home to **Big Texan Brewing**, so you can grab a pint brewed in-house to go with your massive steak. My favorite local stop was **Pondaseta Brewing**, which turned an old tire shop into a taproom space with a nice outdoor area. I recommend the Irish stout there. Downtown is home to **Six Car Pub & Brewery**. It features two floors and an upstairs deck that looks out on the city.

Phoenix, AZ: Dipping back into the Grand Canyon State, Phoenix is, of course, the largest metro area and has a lot to offer. Unfortunately, I have only spent one night there (back in 2018), but I did thoroughly enjoy **Wren House Brewing**. The cozy taproom was formerly a house (the fireplace is still near the bar), and I dug *Jomax*, the coffee oatmeal stout. The other two breweries in Phoenix I visited have since closed, but some other breweries in the area to keep in mind: **Kitsune Brewing**, **Arizona Wilderness Brewing**, and **Simple Machine Brewing**.

Flagstaff, AZ: En route to the Grand Canyon we spent a night here, where instead of skyscrapers, the San Francisco Peaks provide a different type of skyline. **Dark Sky Brewing**, founded in 2014, was my favorite stop. Dog-friendly, they are constantly cranking out new beers such as the decadent *Astro Cookie*, an Imperial Oreo stout. My other stops were **Mother Road Brewing**, where I enjoyed their *Kolsch* and looking at the old maps of the area, as well as **Lumberyard Brewing** which is—no surprise—housed in a former lumberyard building.

Las Vegas, NV: While many people are visiting Sin City for reasons other than beer, there are some nice options for those who do want to partake in visiting local breweries. I enjoyed **Tenaya Creek Brewing**, which is not far from downtown and has some award-winning beers. The brown ale was particularly good. I was there in 2018, and the scene has grown a lot since then with newer spots like **Neon Desert, Able Baker**, and **Astronomy Aleworks**.

<u>Reno, NV</u>: The Biggest Little City in the World has seen a boom in brewing! There were several spots I visited that are worth a mention, but my top pick would be **IMBIB**. The sours were the stars here, and I loved the *Blue Apricot Nevada Weisse*. **Brasserie St. James** has a very classic, traditional feel, and their *Sierra Candy West Coast IPA* was a finalist for my Best IPA in 2021. If you want to dip your toe into other beverages, **10 Torr Distilling and Brewing** will allow you to do that inside an old grocery store.

We wrap up out west with California, Oregon, and Washington, all of which have been integral in the growth of craft beer. I will also be including Alaska and Hawaii in this section, which were the final two states I visited breweries.

Aside from the Midwest, this is the region where I probably have the most experience. We have lived in Eugene, Oregon; Seattle, Washington; and Bonita, California, just outside San Diego. I also have family living in the San Diego area and Napa, and with many trips out there, The Golden State is where I have the second most brewery visits.

SAN DIEGO, CA

Kicking off the West Coast with a bang! As you can imagine, this is going to be another longer write-up. San Diego has long been a major player in the craft beer game. It have numerous old-school breweries that have led the charge, now complemented by a staggering number of more recent additions. My grandparents live in Bonita, a suburb to the southwest, and we lived with them for three months during my wife's first stint as a travel nurse. While that part of the metro area is not as brewery-rich as others, I was close enough to the action to experience what the city has to offer.

I figure the easiest way to get started is to begin around the downtown area and then work outwards (and, as you'll soon learn, up). Just south of downtown in the historic Wonder Bread factory is **Mission Brewery**. Originally established in 1913, they would go out of business during prohibition before the brand was brought back in 2007. The taproom is awesome, and I loved the *Margarita Sour*. In the East Village just blocks from Petco Park (home of the San Diego Padres), **Half Door Brewing** has possibly the quirkiest taproom in the area. Inside an old Victorian house, it certainly sticks out, and I got to try a coffee IPA there. A block and a half north is Knotty Brewing, which interestingly has two locations right next door. Besides the brewery taproom, they also have the **Knotty Barrel**, a gastropub where you can grab a bite to eat. A little way north is the delightful **Resident Brewing**. They share a space with The Local Eatery, and the surfboards on the wall remind you that you are, in fact, in Southern California.

Sticking around downtown, we now turn our attention to two of the aforementioned stalwarts of the local brewing community. First up is **Karl Strauss Brewing**, which was founded in 1989. I visited their location downtown, but they have nine locations scattered from San Diego up into the Los Angeles area. The namesake is Master Brewer Karl. M. Strauss, who was a cousin of one of the founders. They've won more medals than you can count, and in 2016, they were named the GABF Mid-Sized Brewing Company of the Year. The other long-standing brewery in nearby Little Italy has had a more colorful and turbulent past. **Ballast Point Brewing** was founded in 1996 after starting as a homebrew supply store four years earlier. By 2015, it was the seventeenth-largest brewery in the company and had numerous locations. That same year, they were bought by Constellation Brands for $1 billion, much to the chagrin of locals. But then, in 2019, it was shockingly purchased by a small Chicago-based brewery, **Kings and Convicts**, and once again became independent. Either way, their *Sculpin*

IPA and *Victory at Seas Imperial Porter* are classic choices.

Next, we head to one of the most well-known brewery neighborhoods in the area, North Park. You could spend a week in this one neighborhood, walking to all the breweries, restaurants, and bars that have turned this area directly northeast of Balboa Park into a destination. We begin on the southern end with **Mike Hess Brewing**. They have seven locations, but this one in North Park has the cool feature of walking in on a catwalk directly above all the brewing equipment. Founded by former US Navy Officer Mike Hess in 2010, I was a big fan of the beer, in particular the blood orange IPA *Into the Sunset* that won my Best IPA during my 2nd Annual Review. And right around the corner is one of the hotter names locally, **North Park Beer Company**. A tap list full of lagers and IPAs await visitors, and they have won the awards to back up the hype. They have been around since 2016, although the homebrewing behind the scenes goes back to 2004. On the same street (University Avenue), **Original 40 Brewing** has a vintage yet modern space serving up desirable food and beer. They also have cocktails, wines, seltzers, ciders, and NA beers if you have a diverse drinking group.

We need another paragraph for North Park, so we continue our trek north and stop at one of the four **Belching Beaver Brewery** locations. Their *Peanut Butter Milk Stout* is a personal favorite of mine, and they also now make hard seltzers. Heading up on 30th Street, you can discover the next two destinations, **Poor House Brewing** and **Fall Brewing. Poor House Brewing** has a dive bar feel to it, which makes it stick out locally. It's a fairly basic bar area with plenty of games to play, such as pool, darts, shuffleboard, and foosball. I actually played a couple games of darts with my Bill, who at that time had visited every taproom in San Diego County! **Fall Brewing** was a dog-friendly spot that featured local art and photographs. I would order their *Goo Goo Muck IPA* again.

Next, we veer just a bit west to the University Heights

neighborhood. If you are from New Zealand or simply like New Zealand, you will feel at home visiting **Kairoa Brewing**. The folks there have roots in the country, and the name is a combination of Kaikoura and Akaroa (two coastal towns in the country). The food and beer are inspired by New Zealand, and I had a delicious New Zealand pilsner called *Paddock* during my visit. Oh, and they have a rooftop deck! In the same area is the awesome **Taproom Beer Company**. When I visited, they had eighteen of their beers on tap and twelve guest taps as well. The indoor and outdoor spaces flow seamlessly together, and the overall vibes are engaging. Also in the neighborhood is **Hillcrest Brewing**, an LGBTQ-owned spot that serves up pizza.

Next, we zip west toward Ocean Beach, but first a pit stop in the Midway District at **Modern Times Beer**. They quickly became one of the trendiest breweries on the West Coast, and although they went through a contraction and eventual sale, you can still visit one of the three San Diego locations. The location here in Point Loma is the production facility and original taproom, and like all three spots, has a bunch of fun decor and features. Besides their popular IPAs, I enjoyed *New Atlantis*, a wine barrel-aged pale sour. Now, getting to Ocean Beach, we arrive at **Ocean Beach Brewery** (no mystery where they got this name). With multiple levels and a rooftop that allows for views of the ocean, the strong coastal theme here fits perfectly. Not far away is one of the **Pizza Port Brewing** locations, which was originally established in 1987 and began serving its own beer in 1992. They have been a staple in the local beer scene since then and have won numerous awards, including the GABF Brewpub of the Year several times.

Now is the time when we truly start making our way further north, as I hinted at in the second paragraph. Kearny Mesa is a sprawling area between two of the main freeways, 805 and 15. Here is where we find the next grouping of breweries. The most southern of the group is **Ataraxia Aleworks**.

Like many of the breweries in northern San Diego, it is part of a business park. The long, narrow taproom has a fun mural and a fake plant wall. The Helles lager and Belgian pale ale were delicious. My favorite in this neighborhood is **Hopnonymous Brewing**, which has been "Saving the City from Thirst" since 2018. Their Irish red ale, *Leaving Without Saying Goodbye*, was impressive. You could throw a rock to hit the next stop, **Kilowatt Brewing**. They have two other locations in the metro area, and the *Chocolate Macadamia Nut Stout* won a bronze at GABF in 2018. **Societe Brewing** also has a tasting room in Old Town, but the main brewery and tasting room is right down the street from the previous two breweries. Aside from offering plenty of IPAs, you will also be treated to a variety of Belgian styles, such as the Belgian amber named *The Debutante*.

Further north, we go to our next area, Miramar. It has been a brewery hub for many years, earning it the nickname "Beeramar." One of the old-school options holding it down is **AleSmith Brewing**. Established in 1995, they are one of the few breweries in the area known for their dark beers, specifically the *Speedway Stout*. Their spacious brewery and taproom are a must-visit in the neighborhood. Although **Pure Project** now has taprooms in North Park, Balboa Park, Vista, and Carlsbad, this smaller, original location is where they got started. They are probably my favorite brewery, not just in San Diego but possibly in all of California. Many people know them for their IPAs, but I want to highlight two different styles. *Madeline* was a barrel-aged mixed-fermentation farmhouse saison, while *Log Cabin* was a maple bourbon barrel-aged Imperial stout with cocoa and coffee. Both were delectable.

Sticking around Miramar, we have one of the most unique places we will discuss in this book, **White Labs**. A yeast manufacturer, they also started brewing and showcasing how beer is affected by different strains of yeast. They do this by brewing a beer with the same base recipe, but using different yeast strains in different batches. So, for instance, when I visited,

I tried a breakfast stout and an IPA. But for each beer, I got two samples, each one using a different yeast strain. The color, aroma, and flavor were all different! So not only can you sip on some beer, but you'll be getting an education too. As I mentioned in the Asheville section, they also have a location there. We'll round out our time in the area with **Rough Draft Brewing** and its wide-ranging menu that has been around since 2012, as well as Duck Foot Brewing, which is named for its snowboarding stance and makes gluten-reduced beers.

This has been a long section, but I want to highlight a few suburban breweries to the south and east. Chula Vista is the population hub to the south, and while there are several breweries there, I want to focus on **Novo Brazil Brewing**. I spent a month in Brazil during my senior year of college and fell in love with it. The owners here are from Brazil, which directly influences your experience. Bright colors abound, and the beer names are inspired by the country (Copacabana, Ipanema, The Carnival, etc). They have grown and now have four locations. Another brewery with a tasting room in Chula Vista is **Groundswell Brewing**. They were in Santee when I was there but now are in Chula Vista and San Diego. I loved the *Guava Tart*. Out east in El Cajon is **Burning Beard Brewing**. Here was one of the surprises of my time in San Diego, as I stumbled upon their *Roggenbier*! Finally, we cap our time in San Diego by hopping across the Coronado Bridge to beautiful Coronado and the aptly named **Coronado Brewing**. You can get views of the San Diego skyline down the street, and they have been making classic beers at their brewpub since 1996,

My Take: The year we lived there for three months, San Diego won my award for Best Beer City (Large), and it still holds true that it is a favorite of mine. The number of breweries is staggering, but while the neighborhoods themselves are densely packed, the scene in its entirety is very spread out, which is something to keep in mind should you visit.

Quick Tip: Besides getting Mexican food and checking out the world-famous zoo, don't forget that San Diego has a major naval base. One of the cooler attractions is the USS Midway Museum, a historical naval aircraft carrier that has been turned into an educational vessel.

NORTH SAN DIEGO COUNTY (CA)

We just talked about San Diego, right? Well, we did, but focused on just the city. San Diego County is an absolute monstrosity, covering around 4,500 square miles (about the size of Connecticut) and is home to nearly 3.3 million people (making it the fifth most populous in the country). That means almost 2 million people live in the county outside the city of San Diego. While Chula Vista to the south has the second highest population, Oceanside, Escondido, Carlsbad, and Vista all have over 100,000 people and are north of the city. Because of this, the northern section of the county has its own beer scene.

I think the easiest place to start is in Escondido, as it is home to arguably the most famous brewery in the area. **Stone Brewing** was founded in 1996 and became instrumental in the surge of the West Coast IPA. While they have multiple locations, I absolutely recommend **Stone Brewing World Bistro and Gardens**, which was my 300th brewery visit. Towering floor-to-ceiling windows allow you to look into the massive brewhouse, and opposite of them, you can look out into the gorgeous gardens. A rock formation is right in the middle by the bar area, and a huge stone wall features their famous gargoyle logo. The *Enjoy By IPA* series is incredibly popular, and I also loved a unique *Pineapple Chili Gose* during my visit. Exquisite food there, too. For a more low-key experience in town, **Jacked Up Brewery** opened in 2017 and has a garage feel to the taproom.

Moving west toward the ocean, I need to highlight **Bear Roots Brewing** in Vista. Not only do they make one of my favorite San Diego Area beers with *Bear Cookie*, a chocolate peanut butter stout, but they are also a homebrew store. They have two locations, both of which are in Vista. Once we reach I-5 and the city of Oceanside, there are a couple of welcome options. You'll find a woodsy-themed brewery that feels like a place you'd find in Maine or Oregon instead of Southern California at **Northern Pine Brewing**. Their *Saison* and *Gose* have won local awards. There is also another **Stone Brewing** location here if you can't make it to Escondido.

If you enjoyed the woodsy taproom at **Northern Pine**, you'll find another one in Carlsbad at **Burgeon Beer Company**. Much of the wood utilized in the taproom that serves some stellar IPAs came from a tree found in Northern California following a fire. Growth has been the name of the game for them, as they now have four locations scattered across the region. Continuing to stray south along the coast, you will find **The Confessional by The Lost Abbey** in Cardiff not far from the water. This well-known spot is a must-stop, especially if you have a hankering for a good sour ale.

My Take: There is still much of the area I have not explored, and as my podcast guests from *I Like Beer the Podcast*, Jeff Spanier and Jeff Riccitelli say, the brewery scene here is worth a visit on its own aside from the city of San Diego. You will have plenty to keep you busy, especially in Vista.

Quick Tip: Just like the rest of Southern California, you're best suited to plan on sticking around one area if you want to be efficient with your time. Vista, Carlsbad, and Oceanside all have plenty of breweries close together, so you don't have to sit in traffic.

LOS ANGELES METRO AREA, CA

The City of Angels. Hollywood. Santa Monica Pier. Griffith Observatory. The Lakers and Dodgers. Los Angeles is the second largest city and metro area in the country and is known for many things nationally and internationally. While I have been here many times, I do not have the personal experience with the beer scene that I would like. For travelers, it's important to realize that it can take a LONG time to get across the city, especially if you choose the wrong time of day. Picking an area (such as the Arts District in Los Angeles, the Old Torrance neighborhood in Torrance, or Northeast Anaheim toward Placentia) will mean less time spent traveling and more time at the breweries.

It makes the most sense for me to start as central in Los Angeles as possible, and it's hard to get much more central than the Arts District. On the eastern edge of downtown, there are a handful of breweries calling this neighborhood home. The most visually striking of the bunch is in the John A. Roebling building, which is where **Angel City Brewery** set up shop. This two-level spot has lots of original features and plenty of space to spread out. The neon sign in front is eye-catching as well. Down the street is a haven for skeeball fanatics. Yes, really. **Arts District Brewing** is home to fifteen skeeball machines, so you can get your roll on while enjoying their diverse beer menu. Another short walk takes you to **Boomtown Brewery**, where they have a fun taproom inside a warehouse with a variety of games. My favorite beer there was *What Gose Around*.

Just north of this area is Chinatown, where **Highland Park Brewery** and **Homage Brewing** are on the same block. **Highland Park** got its start in the back room of a bar in the Highland Park neighborhood before opening up the space here in 2018. Hoppy lagers, West Coast IPAs, and barrel-aged stouts; they do excellent work across many styles. My favorite was *Bortz*, a Schwarzbier Similarly, **Homage** opened up elsewhere first, specifically downtown Pomona. Besides lagers, saisons, and a barrage of other ales, they also serve wines inside their taproom. In the Fashion District on the other side of downtown is **Creature Comforts Brewing**. Yes, the one based in Athens, Georgia. One of the fastest-growing breweries out there, this location opened in October 2023. On top of drinking a delicious cucumber and lime gose called *Tritonia*, I had an excellent time chatting with the bartender, Josh.

Firestone Walker Brewing is another major name when it comes to craft beer in California. While the main location is a few hours north in Paso Robles, they have an R&D Brewhouse in Marina del Rey, just a short drive west of downtown LA. Founded in 1996, they are fast approaching three decades of producing iconic beers such as *805 Blonde Ale*, *Pivo Pils*, and *Union Jack IPA*. My two favorites from my visit were *Parabolita* (a barrel-aged Imperial stout) and the award-winning extra pale ale, *Firestone XPA*. They also host the uber-popular Firestone Walker Invitational Beer Festival each year. Staying on the western side of the metro area, I want to highlight one of the coolest buildings I've been to a brewery in. **Broxton Brewery & Public House** moved into the Janss Investment Company Building (also known as the Janss Dome) in Westwood. Built in 1929, it was home to many things before the brewery, but one constant has been the beautiful features. The gorgeous arches, high ceilings, and towering windows give visitors an incredible setting to enjoy a beer.

One of the more sought-after names in the LA beer scene is **Monkish Brewing** down in Torrance. They also have a location in Anaheim, but Torrance is where they got their start back in 2012. Although they originally did not make them, their IPAs are probably what most people recognize them for now. But they use barrels very well, too. I had an appealing barrel-aged wild ale and decadent bourbon-barrel-aged stout during my visit. Just down the road is **Smog City Brewing**, which began brewing in 2011 and opened its facility in Torrance in 2013. They now have two other locations as well, not too far away.

If you head east from Torrance, you will eventually get to Anaheim, which has enough beer for its own section if I could have spent more time there. **Bottle Logic Brewing** is one of the names people are most likely to have on their radar. Their barrel-aged stouts, smoothie sours, a rainbow of IPAs, and even foam pours of lagers offer a complete experience no matter what you are looking for and are well worth the visit. Also worth the trip is **The Bruery**. The name is a spelling alteration of "Brewery," taking into account the last name of the founder, Rue. They have over forty draft options and over fifty different beers to go, so you will absolutely find something you are craving. My two favorites from my visit showcase their willingness to experiment, as I loved a nitro milkshake blonde ale with passion fruit, orange, guava, lactose, and vanilla, as well as a dark ale with yams, maple, and spices called *Midnight Autumn Maple*. Sours and barrel aging are big here, too.

My Take: While I hit some of the highlights, I still have plenty of unfinished work here. There is a ton to do here besides drink beer, but thankfully there are good options no matter what part of the metro area your trip is focusing on.

Quick Tip: I wasn't kidding about traffic, but if you can travel during the weekend and later in the evening, you may have better luck. Either way, be sure to check the traffic situation before you jet off to somewhere in a different part of the city.

NAPA, CA

Wait, isn't this a book about breweries? Why are we talking about the heart of wine country? Well, believe it or not, there is local beer being made here, even if it is playing second fiddle to the endless vineyards in the area. I was born in nearby Vallejo and lived my first couple of months of life at my grandparents' house in Napa. With consistent return trips throughout my childhood and adult life, I have had many amazing experiences in the area, and since turning twenty-one, that includes visiting the local breweries.

Most of the action is focused around downtown and the surrounding area, and to that point, **Downtown Joe's** is a classic spot right on the Napa River. Established in 1994, it has a traditional bar area in front, but the patio in the back allows you to view the water. A block away is the **Napa Palisades Saloon**, which offers a few of its own house-brewed beers in a gastropub with a rustic feel. Another quick walk takes you to the Oxbow Public Market, which houses a taproom for the Berkeley-based **Fieldwork Brewing**. The *Portrait of Bruin Brown Ale* was my favorite, but they make reliable stuff across the board. Across the street from them is **Trade Brewing**, where a converted house now serves up fresh suds with cool rustic tools up on the walls. *Comfortably Plum*, a wheat ale with plum, showcased a fruit you don't typically see in beer.

A short jaunt north takes you to probably my two favorites in town. **Tannery Bend Beerworks** moved from their old location that was formerly a tannery, but no matter where they are I would want more of their beer. *Capps*, a Belgian Dubbel with candy cap mushrooms, is one of my favorite beers that I've had in Northern California. It won my Best Beer (Other Styles) award in my second annual review. Nearby is **St Clair Brown Winery & Brewery**, which combines craft beer and that other alcoholic drink that uses grapes. The taproom itself is a small glass greenhouse, but a spacious and plant-filled outdoor area is perfect for imbibing any kind of beverage in the famous California sunshine.

My Take: I don't think many people planning a trip to Napa are basing their itinerary around craft beer, but should you find yourself visiting, don't hesitate to visit some of the brewing establishments. With many of them within walking distance of each other, it can make for a fun evening.

Quick Tip: If you like donuts, go to the Butter Cream Bakery, and if that doesn't satisfy your sweet tooth, you can take a tour at the Jelly Belly Factory in nearby Fairfield.

SANTA ROSA, CA

First of all, even with a well-renowned brewery like **Russian River** and the famous *Pliny*, Santa Rosa is still in the heart of wine country, just like Napa. And unless something drastic happens, that particular fermented beverage will always reign king in this area. But there is a solid (and growing) beer scene here!

We should probably address that aforementioned brewery. **Russian River Brewing** is worth the pilgrimage on its own. Founded in 1997 in nearby Guerneville, they have since won Brewery of the Year at both GABF and the World Beer Cup! The brewpub downtown opened in 2004, and you can get a wide array of food, including pizzas, wings, sandwiches, and salads. While *Pliny the Elder Double IPA* is their calling card (not to mention the always anticipated release of *Pliny the Younger Triple IPA*), I had a phenomenal brown sour aged in Pinot Noir barrels called *Supplication* during my visit. In 2018, they opened up a larger brewery and pub just to the north in Windsor, if you can make it up there.

Third Street Aleworks has been around since 1995 and is still cranking out its award-winning beers. They closed down their downtown restaurant in Santa Rosa, but they are still brewing. So you can still find their beers out and about. One of my favorite visits in the area was **Shady Oak Barrel House**, a sour extraordinaire (the *Barrel Fermented Gose* was incredible). Their large warehouse-like space was previously a car dealership and showroom. **Fogbelt Brewing** had some pleasing choices, too (like the *Redwood Lager*). Some of the beers are named for redwood trees around the state such as Stardusk and Del Norte. If it wasn't obvious from my Napa writeup, don't just focus on the wine when you head north from the Bay Area!

My Take: Many people are already making the pilgrimage to the area because of **Russian River**, but as you just read, there are plenty of other breweries here that are worth your time.

Quick Tip: Don't forget about the outdoors! From Santa Rosa, you are within an hour of Point Reyes National Seashore, Muir Woods National Monument, Armstrong Redwoods Natural Reserve, and a host of other state parks and beaches. My personal favorite? Bodega Head, which overlooks Bodega Bay and Bodega Harbor.

EUGENE, OR

Aside from briefly staying with my parents following our wedding, the city my wife and I first called home together was Eugene. The original plan was that I would attend graduate school at the University of Oregon, and while we moved home to Wisconsin instead a year later, we still loved our time living there. Eugene certainly is a college town, and with the campus directly adjacent to downtown and the beautiful Alton Baker Park along the Willamette River, it was a wonderful place to start our life together. Speaking of downtown, many of the breweries are in or near downtown, even more so now than when we lived there.

Starting on the northern edge of that area, you'll find **ColdFire Brewing.** Owned by two brothers, I was impressed by both an Imperial coffee porter and farmhouse ale aged on peaches during my visit. One of my first brewery visits was right on the edge of downtown and campus, where **Elk Horn Brewery** is a family-owned gastropub and cider house. I remember being impressed with the *Raspberry Sour* there, and they have won a handful of medals from contests such as GABF and the World Beer Cup. Not far away is **Falling Sky Brewing**, which has two locations in the city. The *Upside Brown Ale* was the star here, and the brewpub has a nice selection of food.

Looking west, you will find two of the larger names in the area, **Ninkasi Brewing** and **Hop Valley Brewing**. Hop Valley was founded back in 2009 and was purchased by MillerCoors (now Molson Coors) in 2016, literally a month after we moved to Wisconsin. Because of this, it is probably the Eugene brewery that is most widely known on a national scale. They were just acquired by Tilray Brands in August 2024, so it will be interesting to see if that changes anything. **Ninkasi** has also gone through a number of ownership changes, but not of the same recognition as **Hop Valley**. The regional brewery's most recent merger was with Wings & Arrow, a consolidated alcoholic beverage company. They offer a variety of IPAs as part of their core line, including hazy, West Coast, red, and double.

Another local mainstay is **Oakshire Brewing**, which has expanded and now has a location up in Portland. This is one with a large variety of styles on tap at pretty much all times, but my favorite was a Berliner Weisse called *Sun Made Cucumber*. I haven't had the pleasure of visiting **Alesong Brewing** or **The Viking Braggot Company** nearby, but have heard positive things about both. Some other more recent openings include **Manifest Beer Company**, **Gratitude Brewing**, **Freehand Brewing**, and **Drop Bear Brewery**.

My Take: I have a soft spot for Eugene, as it was not just my wife and I's first home, but my first home after college. From attending football games to biking along the numerous trails,

I had a great time living there. The beer scene has seen more growth in the last five years or so and now bolsters a strong number of options.

Quick Tip: Voodoo Doughnuts is a Portland staple, but they also have a location right in downtown Eugene. Track & Field fans will then want to pop over to check out Hayward Field on the U of O campus. Also, for a panoramic view of the area, make a quick drive or hike up to the top of Skinner Butte.

PORTLAND, OR

The Rose City also touts the nickname Beervana. As craft beer lovers know, Portland was at the forefront of the craft brewing movement dating back to the 1980s. Although some places have certainly caught up to the area in terms of production and the number of breweries, it is still regarded as one of the prime destinations for those looking for local suds. We've been lucky to visit the city many times and love it. I also became a Portland Timbers fan during our time living in Eugene, and the game-day atmosphere there is incredible. But in terms of visiting for beer, you'll be happy to know many of the top options in the city are fairly centrally located!

We will begin our PDX breakdown in the Pearl District, a neighborhood that bumps up to downtown on the western side of the Willamette River. It may seem odd to begin with a brewery not based here, but **Deschutes Brewery** (from Bend) has been an Oregon staple since opening in 1988. They opened up this additional brewery in 2008 inside a former auto body shop built in 1919. Besides the lovely beer and delicious food, the taproom is a gorgeous design with lots of wood carvings. I also have a soft spot for this brewery, as their *Black Butte Porter* was one of the few craft options on tap at a bar I frequented in college. I will now highlight **Von Ebert Brewing**, although they have since closed their location in the Pearl District that I visited. Have no fear, though; they still have three locations in the Portland area where you can drink their award-winning beers, such as *Nothing Noble IPA*, the GABF bronze medal-winner from 2020. In the adjoining Slabtown neighborhood, you can visit one of the six **Breakside Brewery** locations scattered across the state. The *Mexican Chocolate Stout* and *Riverside IPA* were both very well done.

Taking one of the many bridges over the river to East Portland is where a majority of the action lies. Starting south in the Brooklyn neighborhood, **Ruse Brewing** set up shop in the Iron Fireman Collective Building, built in the 1920s. I enjoyed some live music and the *Audio Aquatic New England IPA* during my stop. Two neighborhoods directly north (Richmond and Hosford-Abernethy) could complete a nice brewery-hopping excursion. In the former is **Little Beast Brewing**, which calls a former psychic house home. The small, cozy interior is complemented by additional outdoor seating in a large tent. I was impressed with *Sylvestris*, a fruited gose with Pinot Noir grapes. Just west in the Hosford-Abernethy neighborhood is **Baerlic Brewing**, which is paired up with Ranch Pizza in their "indoor beer garden." Down the street is **Chuckanut Brewery**'s P-Nut Beer Hall. Based in Bellingham, WA, they make arguably my favorite lagers in the country. All six lagers I tried have won a medal at GABF, and the Kolsch (the best, in my opinion) and Vienna lager have four gold medals each.

The next stop is in the Buckman neighborhood, but sadly, the first place I want to mention closed in 2024. **Cascade Brewing** was founded in 1998, and their **Barrel House** was an absolute must-visit for sour ale fans. They had twenty-five different sours on tap, showcasing an incredible variety of creative and quality choices. Around the corner is an outpost of a well-known Oregon brewery, which thankfully is still open. **Rogue Ales** is based in Newport but also has a brewery here in Portland that was previously the Dragon Bistro & Pub. The taproom features a cool mural that combines Newport and Portland, which is very fitting. Their *Dead Guy Ale*, a Maibock, is quite popular, and they also make spirits, canned cocktails, and CBD seltzers. To the northwest of that pair is **Wayfinder Beer**, another lager-centric spot inside a large brick building that has long hosted a music venue. The *Hell Lagerbier* was my top selection there.

Further north of the downtown area is the next selection of breweries. Right across from the Moda Center in the Leftbank Building is **Upright Brewing**. If Saisons are your thing, this is a place I would recommend getting them. One more exit up I-5 is **StormBreaker Brewing**. You already know I am a fan of cool flight boards, and **StormBreaker's** is shaped like the Fremont Bridge. They also have a second location in the Boise neighborhood and are named for a little-known nickname of Mt. Hood. Get the *Go Fugg Ya Self Coffee Stout* if you can.

It's finally time to highlight one of my favorite breweries, **Great Notion Brewing**. With three locations in the Portland area (and two in Seattle), they have become a recognizable name, producing bold flavored sours, mouthwatering IPAs, tasty stouts, and everything in between. They won my Best Small Brewery in 2018, and their *Blueberry Muffin Sour* won my Best Sour the same year. I visited the taproom in the Alberta neighborhood and dug the Lumberjack-themed spot. A short drive from there is **Old Town Brewing**. Old Town Pizza opened in downtown back in 1974, and they eventually opened a location to the Northeast in 2008 where the brewing would take place. Three of the four beers in my flight won a medal at GABF, including *Paulie's Not Irish Red Ale*.

My Take: Portland is famous for its impact on craft brewing, and to this day, it is still on the shortlist of the best places to take a Beercation. I have always reveled in my time in the city and definitely recommend beer lovers to visit it at least once.

Quick Tip: Book lovers need to visit the iconic Powell's City of Books. Located downtown, it is the world's largest independent bookstore. Taking up an entire city block with multiple levels and color-coded rooms, it is one of my wife's favorite places.

SEATTLE, WA

As I've been saying, I love the Pacific Northwest. We were lucky enough to call the largest city in the region home for a brief time in the Spring of 2022. There's Pike Place Market, the iconic Space Needle, Mt. Rainier in the distance, and lots of delicious beer. I've found in my travels that Seattle doesn't usually get the same attention on a national scale that some other West Coast stalwarts like Portland and San Diego get, but they rank right up there in terms of the excellence of the breweries.

The best place for us to start is the Ballard neighborhood. It's one of the best brewery neighborhoods in the country, both for its quantity and quality of options. The number of high-end breweries that are within walking distance is staggering. Depending on how ambitious you are, there are thirteen to eighteen different breweries that you are able to stroll to. I'm honestly not even sure where to start! One of my favorites was **Urban Family Brewing**, though. Opened in early 2020, this sleek spot is known for its IPAs and sours. *Preservation*, a raspberry and blackberry sour, was a finalist for my Best Sour in 2021. One of the earlier breweries in this neighborhood is right across the street, **Stoup Brewing. Stoup**, meaning drinking vessel, has been around since 2013 and has award-winning beers such as the *Northwest Red Ale*.

Around the corner from that pair is **Reuben's Brews**, which was established in 2012. They opened the Ballard location in 2015 and there's a wall covered with all their medals and awards. The *Triumvirate IPA* and *Gose* were big winners here. A couple blocks southwest is the Renton-based **Bickersons Brewhouse**. This location opened in the Spring of 2022 while we were living there, and they had a large tent with live music. Really good beer all the way around, but I especially enjoyed the *My Boy Milk Stout*. Getting to have a conversation with co-founder Frank was a bonus! While it's technically a bit further away than the other breweries in this area, you are not far from **Cloudburst Brewing**'s Shilshole location. The 2021 Brewery of the Year at GABF, they are well known for their killer IPAs, but also excel at lagers. One of my nominees in the Best IPA category in 2022 was *So Much Fun*. There is another location near Pike Place Market if that is more convenient too.

Back more in the heart of Ballard (actually, just a couple blocks from those first three places I mentioned) is a trio along the same stretch. **Fair Isle Brewing** focuses on mixed-cultured saisons and oak-aged ales, and I was delighted with my visit. *Leila*, a Saison with purple Egyptian barley, took home my award for Best Beer (Other Styles) in 2022. Both that barley and the Pilsner malt come from Washington, and it was fermented with their house blend of wild and feral yeasts and bacteria. Interestingly, their taproom had been used to host a variety of businesses, such as a bulb room for orchids and a machine shop. On the same street is **Bale Breaker Brewing**. They are based in Yakima, where they own their own hop field. It's no surprise they are best known for their IPAs, and my favorite was called *Hazy L*. Yonder Cider is also hosted in their taproom. In between those two breweries and just one street up is **Lucky Envelope Brewing**. The name is part of their way to showcase their Chinese-American heritage! The *Peanut Butter Cream Stout* was quite enjoyable.

Although there are more options in Ballard, we are going to zip east now and pop into the Fremont neighborhood, where **Fremont Brewing** was founded in 2009. One of the largest craft breweries in the state, they are tied to Ballard because they also have an eighty-barrel production facility there. But back at the taproom, there's an outdoor area (most of it covered), and they do great work with barrel-aging as well as their hazy pale ale, *Sky Kraken*. Another brewery named for a neighborhood lies on the other side of I-5, **Ravenna Brewing**. Located in a former mechanic shop, I got to meet the owner, Tommy, during my visit and had a lovely time chatting with him and the rest of the staff. They were actually my 900th brewery visit, and I took a liking to all the beers they offered, especially the *Sequin Camo Hazy IPA*.

Not far from there, along a rail trail that bears the same name, **Burke-Gilman Brewing** offers nineteen tap lines of beer. I had a refreshing *Norwegian Pale Ale* there, and as a bonus, they are dog-friendly. Then, easing our way toward downtown, **Holy Mountain Brewing** has been incredibly popular since it opened in 2014. The bright and airy taproom serves amazing beer, such as the *Demonteller Foudre-aged Saison*.

If you are stuck around downtown, and specifically Pike Place, there are a couple of options for craft beer. I already mentioned **Cloudburst** has a location near there, but for the best brewery view in the city, head to **Old Stove Brewing**. Part of **Pike Place Market**, you get to take in sweeping views of Elliot Bay from inside or outside the taproom. There's also a large food menu if you are hungry. A quick walk from there is Pike Brewing, which has been around since 1989. Not only are you visiting a brewpub there, but also the Microbrewery Museum! Beer memorabilia is everywhere across both levels; it is a feast for your eyes.

There are some other places I'd like to highlight from the southern side of the city. The big name is **Georgetown Brewing**. As some of the others in Seattle, they share a name with the neighborhood they are located in. Until 2017, they were draft-only and were the largest draft-only brewery in the country. Now they are in the Top 50 largest craft breweries and make a multitude of beers across many different styles. Nearby, **Lowercase Brewing** has a GABF-winning brown ale and several excellent lagers, and if you need a gluten-free option, **Ghostfish Brewing** is one of the best I've been to in that category. If you are attending a Mariners or Seahawks game, **Seapine Brewing** and **Fast Fashion Brewing** are your two best bets.

I also need to shout out the suburb of Renton. My good friend Matt Holt (who is my go-to for anything fresh-hop IPA-related and was also a podcast guest) lives there, and I was able to pop down and check out some delicious beers. I already mentioned **Bickerson Brewhouse** is from there, but two other spots are worth mentioning. The best lagers I had in the area were at **Four Generals Brewing**, which won Small Brewery of the Year at the Washington Beer Awards in 2022. Around the corner is **Dubtown Brewing**, where the friendly, inviting environment was complimented by a vanilla porter called *G Money*.

My Take: I love the city of Seattle, even if traffic can be brutal. It's a beautiful area with a vibrant beer scene. Obviously, basing yourself in the Ballard neighborhood is the best call, but as I discussed, there are quality breweries all around the area.

Quick Tip: It may seem cliche to visit Starbucks, and while going to the original location at Pike Place Market is more of a wait than it's worth, I would recommend visiting the Reserve Roastery. It's a gorgeous facility and there you can get a flight of their coffees before going out for flights of beer.

ANCHORAGE, AK

I may have taken the nickname "The Last Frontier" a bit literally, as Alaska was the last state I visited a brewery when I made my trip there in the summer of 2024. My parents were able to come along for this trip, meaning that my dad was there with me for this major milestone. Similar to Hawaii, there are plenty of challenges for breweries that set up shop in a state far removed from the rest of the country. But that has not prevented them from churning out spectacular beer and serving them in stunning settings! Anchorage is the one true major city in Alaska, with nearly 40 percent of the state's population calling it home. Because of this, it should be no surprise that it is also home to the state's most robust craft beer scene, with a healthy helping of options scattered throughout.

We will start downtown, which just so happens to be where my first Alaskan brewery visit took place. **49th State Brewing** has one of the best facilities you will find just about anywhere in terms of experience. You have the choice of three different levels: a more traditional space on the main level with the brewery and kitchen, the second level that is split between indoor and outdoor seating, and the third level rooftop bar area. No matter where you go, you are treated to views of the Cook Inlet, but up top is where you get a 360-degree perspective that also includes the downtown skyline and plenty of mountains. This space was originally built in 1917 as the Elks Lodge, and it should be noted that while the primary brewing facility is here in Anchorage (actually, right down the hill), **49th State** was originally founded near Denali. I was treated to a wonderful tour by Andrew, the marketing director, and thoroughly enjoyed several beers during our visit. In particular, *Smok*, their award-winning smoked lager, was incredible, and the food was excellent as well. Speaking of food, you can find more of it just a couple blocks away at **Glacier Brewhouse**. Established in 1996, they are one of the oldest breweries in the state and have a very cool woodsy-feeling space. We ate brunch there, and I was a fan of the Alaska Seafood Scramble.

Downtown is on the northern end of the city, and so we begin working our way south to find the rest of the breweries. The first stop in this direction is **Onsite Brewing**, which is "climber-owned." Four of the seven beers on tap when I visited were IPAs, but if they are all as good as *Roar of the Ruth* (a hazy IPA), then I can't blame them for cranking them out! **Cynosure Brewing** is up next. Located in an old furniture store, they opened in 2016. The taproom space leads you into the brewery, and there's also a cool mountain mural on one wall. All the beers here were well done, but if I were to recommend a specific one, it would be *Leyland*, the American Lager. Close by is the trendy **Brewerks** inside a warehouse building. The laid-back taproom is open to the brewery and has an upper loft area. The tap list rotates a decent amount, but for what it's worth, my favorite was a gose called *All Along the Briny*.

One of the biggest surprises of my trip was at **Turnagain Brewing**, where I was very impressed with all the beers! Owner Ted Rosenzweig is a surgeon but got hooked on craft beer and actually won homebrewer of the year prior to opening up the brewery. They took over the former **King Street Brewing** location, and I enjoyed learning that the wood for the tables came from old-growth redwood that was originally brought to Alaska in the 1930s to build water tanks. *Framb Was*, a framboise-style raspberry sour, and *Mexi*, a German lager, were my two top picks here, but you can't go wrong with any of them. Just about due east is another of the original Alaska breweries: **Midnight Sun Brewing**. Founded in 1995, they are the oldest in the city. Their taproom is on the second level of the building, referred to as "The Loft." They are probably best known for barleywines and barrel-aged stouts. In the same neighborhood is **Magnetic North Brewing**, which offers brewing classes! You can sign up for a class, learn how to brew, and you get to keep the beer once it's finished. Another fun fact: they had a Kentucky Common on tap, which you rarely see anywhere.

These last two breweries in Anchorage that I will discuss are on the same block and comprise arguably the best one-two punch you could ask for. I already mentioned one of them: **King Street Brewing**. Opened in 2011, they are a staple of the local beer scene and have the awards to back it up. They would move down the street in 2018 to this larger facility, which includes a three-story taproom that showcases the mountains to the east. The *Grapefruit Squeeze Kettle Sour* was so good, but be sure to try their flagship *Hefeweizen* and flagship *Stout*, too.

Across the street is my favorite in Alaska and one of the best breweries I have visited: **Anchorage Brewing**. They have become well-known for their use of barrels and foeders and often push the envelope on ABV with certain styles. But on my visit, I was able to witness that they knock it out of the park across just about every style. *All Seeing*, their blueberry sour with handpicked Alaskan blueberries, is one of the best sours I've ever tried. *Time For a Change*, a Czech Pilsner, was one of the best lighter-style lagers I had in 2024. *The Nectar*, a Brett Saison with honey, was a nominee for my Best Beer (Other Styles). My dad was head-over-heels for *We Are All Replaceable*, a bourbon barrel-aged Imperial stout with vanilla that clocks in at a massive 18.9% ABV. It was slightly too boozy for my personal taste, but I could tell it was one of the most immaculate barrel-aged stouts I've ever had. Oh, and they have a great space! Inside is like a small forest of foeders, and outside features several custom fire pits and a rooftop balcony looking out at the mountains. This place is an absolute must-visit.

Before wrapping up, I want to mention a pair of breweries outside of Anchorage but in the general area. The first, to the south, is **Girdwood Brewing**, located in the town with the same name. Located forty to fifty minutes to the south along Turnagain Arm, this is an impressive spot. Nestled into the mountains, the ski theme fits well, and the beer is sure to keep you coming back for more. *Down the Chute Kolsch* and *Funk Berry Pie Pastry Sour* were both beers I would have enjoyed getting full pours of. In another direction from the city (northeast), **Odd Man Rush Brewing** is located in Eagle River, en route to the Mat-Su Valley. The hockey-themed spot has a massive old scoreboard hanging above the two-level taproom, and I had a nice oak-aged sour Belgian brown farmhouse ale called *Amplification*.

I should note that there are some strange and restrictive laws and regulations in Alaska that visitors need to know. Breweries can only stay open until 9 pm, cannot have televisions for entertainment purposes, can only host four live events a year, and can only serve each customer thirty-six ounces on any given day. If you are brewery hopping, that last one doesn't matter much, but if you want to belly up to the bar at a particular spot, it's something to keep in mind. Maybe by the time you are reading this these laws have been changed, but the most recent adaptation was passed in 2024.

My Take: If you are planning a pure Beercation in Alaska, Anchorage is the best place to start. It is the easiest to get to, has the most breweries, and on top of that, there is a lot to do in and around the city.

Quick Tip: Although there are multiple National Parks within driving distance of Anchorage that are worthy of a visit, one place my whole family enjoyed was the area around the Eagle River Nature Center in Chugach State Park. There are some great shorter trails with gorgeous viewpoints, along with more strenuous options for the more seasoned hiker.

JUNEAU, AK

The state capital of Alaska is intriguing, as you must take a plane or boat to arrive. Nestled between the Coast Mountain Range and Gastineau Channel, the picturesque small city is a popular tourist stop, particularly for cruise ships going up and down the Alaskan panhandle. The city is split into a few sections, and interestingly, downtown is not in the center. In fact, where the state capitol, touristy shops, and most of the museums are located is actually on the southern end of the city. The largest population center, Mendenhall Valley, is about ten miles north of there, where you will find the airport and the famous Mendenhall Glacier. There are other smaller neighborhoods scattered along the coast, such as Douglas, Auke Bay, and Thane.

The best place to start is with the brewery that people in the lower 48 have probably heard the most about. **Alaskan Brewing** was founded in 1986 and became the first brewery in Juneau since prohibition. Since then, they have grown immensely and are the only brewery from Alaska that is widely distributed across much of the country. Best known for their *Alaskan Amber*, I was surprised that my favorite beer from my visit was actually a tropical offering, *Island Ale* (which is packed with passionfruit, tangerine, and guava). Their main facility and taproom are located in the Lemon Creek neighborhood, which is part way between downtown and Mendenhall Valley. But if you are getting off a cruise ship, they also have their Public House right downtown by the docks. It offers great views of the channel and Douglas Island (assuming one of the ships isn't parked directly in front of it).

It should not be a shocker that a majority of the breweries set up shop downtown, where there is plenty of heavy foot traffic. I should note that when I say "majority," it is quite literally referring to three breweries (including **Alaskan**'s Public House). The other two are both within walking distance, which can make for a fun brewery crawl even if you do not have your own transportation. The first one you'll run into working your way north into downtown is **Barnaby Brewing**, named for founder and brewer Matt Barnaby. Opened in 2017, the simple space was formerly home to the Juneau Arts & Humanities Council. One of my favorite Alaskan beers came from here, *The Goods From The Woods*, a delicious spruce tip pale ale that tastes of the wilderness. About a block away is **Devil's Club Brewing**, named for the local plant that, while dangerous, is also used for a variety of medicinal purposes. They have two separate spaces (upstairs and downstairs) and make plenty of solid beers like *Silt Milk Stout*.

The final stop is back up north, in Auke Bay. Here, you will find one of the best brewery views anywhere at **Forbidden Peak Brewing**. A spacious covered patio in the front of the building provides panoramic views of the harbor, bay, and surrounding islands. An interesting tidbit about the building: it used to be the bookstore for the neighboring University of Alaska Southeast. If you are hungry, Red Spruce, a global street food eatery, is located inside the taproom as well. But if you are like me and are here for the beer, I highly recommend *Forbidden 7's*, a *SMASH IPA*, and *Red Spruce Ale*, a red ale with spruce tips. In other words, come for the view, but stay for the beer.

My Take: Juneau is a beautiful city that is a fantastic place to visit. While they may not boast a high number of breweries, I enjoyed beers at each of my stops here. That, and the convenience of downtown for most of them makes it a nice stop for cruisers and regular tourists alike.

Quick Tip: If you need to escape the hullabaloo of downtown (it can get very hectic depending on the number of cruise ships), take a trip a bit up north to Eagle Beach to explore the natural beauty of the area.

HAWAII

Do you know how some children's books have buttons or flaps that allow music to play? I wish I could have "Over the

Rainbow" by Israel Kamakawiwo'ole reverberate off these pages as you start this section. If you have been to Hawaii, you know it is one of the most unique, stunning, and simply magical places not just in the United States, but the entire world. My family had the chance to go on an inter-island cruise in 2024, which allowed us to explore the four major islands in the chain. Each one had its own distinctive feel and provided remarkable experiences. In terms of brewing, Hawaii has a rich and interesting history. I highly recommend my friend Paul Kan's book *Hawaii Beer: A History of Brewing in Paradise*. It outlines the history of brewing on the islands, has profiles on many of the breweries, features interviews with beer people around the state, and plenty of information on the challenges of brewing in the middle of the ocean. Below, I've broken down my own experience by island:

OAHU

Honolulu is far and away the population hub of the state. It is the state capital and home to many attractions, such as Diamond Head State Monument and Pearl Harbor National Memorial. It also has by far the most breweries of anywhere in the state. The highest concentration is in the Kaka'ako neighborhood, just south of downtown and a little north of the Waikiki area. My favorite brewery here was **Hana Koa Brewing**. They took over a former Coca-Cola factory and transformed it into a sleek, modern, two-level taproom. There is a full food menu, a full bar, and a very intriguing tap list. *Sunny Showers IPA* was one of the many awesome hoppy options, but I also tried a black lager, a gose with orange and tangerine, and a red ale brewed with cacao, ginger, and dragon fruit powder. Definitely a must-stop in Honolulu.

Close by is another worthwhile place to visit, **Howzit Brewing**. They are one of the newer kids on the block, opening in 2023. The brewer came from **Burke-Gilman Brewing**, which you just read about in the Seattle section. It's a more basic setup here, but the beer certainly stands out. This includes *586 Was My Number*, a creditable West Coast IPA, and I was very impressed with the slightly "out there" *Churro Cream Ale*. There are several other options within walking distance as well: **Honolulu Beerworks**, **Aloha Beer Company**, along with the Village Bottle Shop & Tasting Room.

A short jaunt to the Northwest takes us to the other two breweries I visited in Honolulu. **Beer Lab HI** has three locations in the area, but I visited the Beretania one. They first opened in 2016, and this particular taproom is fully outside. There is coverage, don't worry, but you'll be getting plenty of the pleasant Hawaiian breeze. Even the brewing system is just behind some chain link fence with a roof above it. I loved all the murals, too. They had cool options like *Everybody's Somebody's Mule* (a sour ale with ginger and key lime) and *Annie Mango* (a golden ale with li hing and mango). Speaking of fun ingredients, I loved a beer called *Calamansi Crush*, which was a sour ale with Calamansi lemons. This beer was found at **Lokahi Brewing**, where they are brewing plenty of sours (along with some other stuff, of course). By the way, Lokahi means "the essence of unity, harmony, connection, and embracing diversity."

MAUI

The island of Maui is a well-known tourist destination. With Haleakalā National Park, the Road to Hana, and the numerous beaches around its edges, there is no doubting why people flock here. There are some quality breweries though as well! We'll start with the big dog, **Maui Brewing**. They opened in 2005 and now have five locations, with a majority of them on this island. The main brewery and restaurant in Kihei is a massive and modern space with an expansive outdoor area. Solar panels cover the roof, they send spent grain to local farms, and also participate in grassroots eco-activities. You may have also heard of them from their purchase of trendy

California-based **Modern Times**. But in terms of their own beer, I enjoyed everything I sampled, especially *Prickly Dilemma*, a Lilikoi and prickly pear sour.

At a little higher altitude toward the national park, you will find **Mahalo Aleworks** in Pukalani. There are not many breweries with a better view. Their two-level taproom provides a sweeping perspective of the island as it looks out at the ocean and some towns down at sea level. They are also a very sustainable brewery, as they are fully solar powered, use reclaimed water, and also send spent grains to nearby farms. The *Chasin Chickens Kolsch* was very refreshing.

HAWAII

The Big Island was the only island we had two separate ports: Hilo and Kailua-Kona. Some highlights here include Hawaii Volcanoes National Park, Rainbow Falls, and simply strolling around Kailua-Kona to browse the shops and enjoy the beach. I'll also shout out Panaewa Rainforest Zoo and Gardens, as my wife and kids all loved our stop there. Not far from the zoo, in the town of Kea'au, is **Wailuku Brew Works**. Opened in July of 2023, they are named for a local river near the owner's home. It's a smaller, cozy taproom, but it does offer a nice variety of beer. The *Steineken Pilsner* was my favorite. Back in the island's largest city, Hilo, is the properly named **Hilo Brewing**. Their slogan, "Little Brewery, Big Island," fits perfectly. Established in 2018, they are located in a former Pepsi plant and have a simple, industrial taproom open to the brewery. While they only had two of their own beers on tap (*Mauna Kea Red Ale* and *Volcano Red Ale*), I thought both were very solid.

On the opposite side of the island in Kailua-Kona is the Hawaiian brewery most people are familiar with, **Kona Brewing**. As you are reading this, they have been around for over three decades, and although some may have frowned when they were bought out by "Big Beer" and shipped most of the production to the mainland, they have continued to grow and are one of the largest craft brewers in the US. One of the best parts of visiting their brewpub on the edge of downtown is that the beer there is actually made on-site, so you can enjoy classics like *Longboard Island Lager* and *Hanalei Island IPA* while also trying some experimental beers.

A short walk from there is **Ola Brewing**. They were my 1,300th brewery, and I proudly wear their t-shirt often. Opened in 2017, they focus on sustainability and supporting local agriculture. Not only that, they are also both employee and community-owned. There's a second location in Hilo, too, if that is where you are visiting. But here at their original location, you can view the brewhouse through some windows and drink delicious beers like the *Lilikoi Lime Milkshake IPA* and the *Kiawe Brown Ale*. I also want to mention **Big Island Brewhaus** in Waimea. I was told by several people it is one of the local favorites, but sadly it was too far away from our ports for us to get to. Would have loved to have tried *Graham's Pilsner* or *Overboard IPA*.

KAUAI

Our final stop will be the island of Kauai. In terms of natural beauty, it was probably my favorite of the four islands we visited. Waimea Canyon State Park, in particular, is jaw-dropping, but places like Kīlauea Lighthouse and 'Opaeka'a Falls are also gorgeous. You've probably watched a movie shot here, such as *Jurassic Park*, *Pirates of the Caribbean*, *Avatar*, or *The Descendants*. Even the animated Disney movie *Lilo & Stitch* was inspired by the town of Hanapepe! Close to Hanapepe in Port Allen is the United States' westernmost brewery, **Kauai Island Brewing**. They also have a second location in Koloa Town, and both serve food, but at this location, they are located right down the street from the ocean. It has a sports bar feel with jerseys and TVs everywhere and an upstairs area with pinball machines.

We were docked in Lihue during our two days on the

island, and downtown you will be able to visit **Kauai Beer Company**, which has been around since 2013. They took over a building that dates back to 1930, and their theme leans heavily into the abundance of the wild local chickens found all over Hawaii, but particularly on Kauai. The logo, the plethora of merch options, and even some of the beers (such as *Austrian Chicken*, a Vienna lager) all fall under the concept. Of course, I bought a chicken shirt. I did enjoy that Vienna lager, but the *Tropical Armadillo Pale Ale* was probably my favorite. Another brewery on the island is **Napali Brewing**. Named for the famed Napali Coast, they provide a very Hawaiian experience. Plants are everywhere in the taproom, the Pupu food menu features local ingredients, and the logo itself feels very Hawaiian. The beers, such as the *Local Boy Lager*, are more traditional and straightforward, but they pair well with the food.

My Take: Before my trip, I had mostly been under the impression that the Hawaiian beer scene was underwhelming (at least according to some of the people I talked to). But in reality, I found some very good beers on every island I visited. Outside of Honolulu there may not be super dense brewery growth, but I was overall quite pleased with the breweries I visited and know that more openings are on the way.

Quick Tip: If you do the inter-island cruise, I highly recommend just renting a car in each port. It enables you to make your own itinerary, go at your own pace (faster or slower), and be adaptable, and it is much cheaper. In most ports, there are rentals within walking distance.

OTHER CITIES AND AREAS

Bakersfield, CA: My one-night stop in Bakersfield included a trio of breweries, although one has since closed. In terms of beers, my favorite was **Dionysus Brewing**. Housed in a garage-like space, the sours here were the star of the show. **Lengthwise Brewing** seemed like a smart spot to go if you have kids, as several families were enjoying the arcade games and food.

Joshua Tree National Park (CA): The final National Park area I'll be highlighting, this unique ecosystem is an incredibly interesting place to visit. After a day of hiking around the desert, you may want to grab a cold beer! I went to a pair of places, **Coachella Valley Brewing** in Thousand Palms and **La Quinta Brewing** (not affiliated with the hotel) in Palm Springs. At the time of my visit in 2018, those were the only two in the area, but there are now several more in the nearby towns that compose the Coachella Valley.

Bay Area (CA): This is one area that I would love to dive deeper into, as I have only been to a handful scattered throughout this region. **Barebottle Brewing**, in San Francisco's Bernal Heights neighborhood, was founded by three beer judges and offers homebrewing classes. Their blonde Ale w/coffee and vanilla beans was delectable, as well as a spiced porter called *Tough Cookies*. Across the bay is the delightful **Roses' Taproom** inside an old knife shop in Oakland's Temescal neighborhood. A light and airy taproom features an array of plants and great beers such as *Hay Day Cream Ale*. **Headlands Brewing** in Lafayette is a spot that has a generous outdoor area with a walk-up bar if that's your sort of thing, and if you are flying in or out of SFO, **Drake's Brewery** has a taproom in Harvey Milk Terminal 1. Also, shoutout to **Mare Island Brewing's Ferry Taproom** in Vallejo for having great views of the Napa River as it heads out to San Pablo Bay.

Chico, CA: I mentioned **Sierra Nevada Brewing** in my Asheville section, but this is one brewery that needs more attention. Ken Grossman spearheaded the growth of one of the nation's most well-known and beloved breweries, starting back in 1980. Their flagship *Pale Ale* was a staple in my dad's fridge when I was growing up in the 1990s, and you could say because of that, it is part of the reason why I got into craft beer. I took the tour in Chico and had a blast learning the history, smelling different hops, and, of course, sampling beers. During that visit, my favorite was *Hazy Little Thing IPA* but I've had many enjoyable beers produced by them.

Bend, OR: I sadly visited Bend before my true "Brewery Travels" days, meaning my solo stop was at **10 Barrel Brewing**'s brewpub, where we enjoyed pizza and I loved getting to try *Raspberry Crush* (which was a variation of the first sour I tried it at Growler Guys in Eugene) from the source. Also, my time there was predominantly due to Bend Brewfest, which was the first beer festival I ever went to. Whenever I get back, places like **Crux Fermentation Project**, **Boneyard Beer**, and **The Ale Apothecary** will be on my agenda.

Tacoma, WA: Located on the southern end of Puget Sound, Tacoma may get overshadowed by Seattle to the north, but there's some quality beer being made here. And that starts with **SiG Brewing**, where a cornucopia of sours and IPAs are served up in a sleek, modern taproom. Oh, and there's brick oven pizza and local art for sale. **E9 Brewing** was the city's first brewery back in 1995, but it has evolved over time and now has such delights as a barrel-blended wild ale with cherries. My other stop in town was **Odd Otter Brewing**. Located right downtown, the building has had many lives, including as a print shop, WW2 barracks, and an International Harvester manufacturer.

Mt. Vernon, WA: The primary reason we took the jaunt up to Mt. Vernon was for the colorful Skagit Valley Tulip Festival, and while the acres of beautiful flowers are wonderful, visitors also have some beer options. Downtown has a pair of breweries, **District Brewing** inside a former antique shop, and the women-owned **Temperate Habits Brewing**, where I had their Mac & Cheese Burger. My favorite in terms of beer was to the north at **Farmstrong Brewing**. If you visit the former Sears appliance showroom, I would get the *Stackin Hay IPA*.

Spokane, WA: The Lilac City is the hub of Eastern Washington. We loved walking around downtown and Riverfront Park, and I also walked away impressed by the beer scene. For lagers, head to **Whistle Punk Brewing** inside the historic Pacific States Electric Building. IPA fanatics will want to check out **Lumberbeard Brewing**, although they do offer a nice variety as well. **For the Love of God Brewing** is the most unique experience, as the cozy, woodsy taproom serves up some incredibly interesting beers (I had a sour ale with raspberry, blackberry, waffle cone, pretzel, vanilla bean, cream cheese, and milk sugar when I visited)! The busiest spot I visited was **Brick West Brewing**, and the 120-year-old Watts Automotive building provides a spacious taproom.

Mat-Su Valley (AK): Located to the north of Anchorage, this is the area that many travelers traverse through on their way north to Denali. But there are plenty of interesting places worth stopping at in this area, such as the Iditarod Headquarters in Wasilla! And after meeting the sled dogs you can visit **Last Frontier Brewing** and **Bearpaw River Brewing**. We ate at **Last Frontier** and quite enjoyed our meal, while I had a nice milk stout called *Mat Maid* at **Bearpaw River**. Not far away in Palmer, **Bleeding Heart Brewing** is well-known for its *Beet IPA*, brewed with its namesake, Alaskan-grown beets.

We have reached the end of our travels together. Spanning fifty states (and a certain federal district), six different time zones, and well over 100 cities and 1,000 breweries, we have covered a large swath of land. My hope is that throughout these "breakdowns," you were able to understand just how special each beer scene is across the country. From the well-known breweries to the hidden gems, you are bound to find well-crafted beer just about everywhere. While I always try to showcase the good in every brewery, some tend to stick out as my favorites—which is what you will read about next.

Award Winners

"What's your favorite brewery?" I get asked that question and other variations of it quite often. Below is the closest you will get to an answer from me. Each year, I publish an Annual Review that includes twenty "awards." Each award has five nominees and one winner, with only breweries I visited that year (and for the first time) being eligible. I also do not count multiple locations as separate entries for awards, and list the location of the place I visited.

For example, **Sierra Nevada** was eligible for my 2nd Annual Review after I visited the Chico location, but I did not include them again after visiting North Carolina. However, I will still factor secondary visits in for the honorable mentions. Is that a weird rule? Sure, maybe, but that's how I started doing it all those years ago and have stuck by it. After all, these are my fake awards to give out! I have compiled the winners for every award and also included four Honorable Mentions for each one. Some years were stronger than others in certain categories, which is why I wanted to throw in some of the bonus "nominees" to these tables.

This will give you an idea of some of my favorite breweries, beers, and experiences from my travels. It should be noted that for any given category, less than 1 percent of the breweries I have visited are mentioned, meaning many worthy breweries and beers are not on these lists.

LIST OF MY ANNUAL AWARDS

BEST TAPROOM INTERIOR		Location
1st Annual Review	**Magic Hat Brewing**	South Burlington, VT
2nd Annual Review	**Stone Brewing**	Escondido, CA
3rd Annual Review	**St. Joseph Brewery**	Indianapolis, IN
4th Annual Review	**Ministry of Brew**	Baltimore, MD
5th Annual Review	**Mars Theatre Brewing**	Mars Hill, NC
6th Annual Review	**Moontown Brewing**	Whitestown, IN
7th Annual Review	**Beer in the Barn Brewery**	St. Donatus, IA

Honorable Mentions: **Broxton Brewery & Public House** (Los Angeles, CA), **Frey's Brewing** (Mt. Airy, MD), **Great Revivalist Brewery** (Clinton, IA), **Pike Brewing** (Seattle, WA)

BEST TAPROOM LOCATION/VIEW		Location
1st Annual Review	Notch Brewing	Salem, MA
2nd Annual Review	Green Tree Brewery	Le Claire, IA
3rd Annual Review	Flathead Lake Brewing	Bigfork, MT
4th Annual Review	Oasis Texas Brewing	Austin, TX
5th Annual Review	MAP Brewing	Bozeman, MT
6th Annual Review	Leinenkugel's Brewing	Milwaukee, WI
7th Annual Review	Forbidden Peak Brewing	Juneau, AK

Honorable Mentions: **Cabin Creek Brewing** (Georgetown, CO), **Old Stove Brewing** (Seattle, WA), **Hollywood Brewery** (Hollywood Beach, FL), **Mahalo Aleworks** (Pukalani, HI)

BEST FLIGHT BOARD		Location	Design
1st Annual Review	Lone Pine Brewing	Portland, ME	Ski
2nd Annual Review	Amplified Ales	San Diego, CA	Guitar-shaped
3rd Annual Review	Octopi Brewing	Waunakee, WI	Octopus tentacle
4th Annual Review	Crooked Tooth Brewing	Tucson, AZ	Skateboard
5th Annual Review	Mockery Brewing	Denver, CO	Colorado license plate
6th Annual Review	Two Roads Brewing	Stratford, CT	Blue arm with pointing finger
7th Annual Review	CheezHead Brewing	Beloit, WI	Cheesehead

Honorable Mentions: **FlyteCo Brewing** (Denver, CO; airplane-shaped), **Big Sky Brewing** (Missoula, MT cow skull-shaped), **Jailbreak Brewing** (Laurel, MD; key-shaped), **Sockeye Brewing** (Boise, ID; sockeye salmon-shaped)

BEST LOGO		Location
1st Annual Review	Catawba Brewing	Asheville, NC
2nd Annual Review	Joyride Brewing	Edgewater, CO
3rd Annual Review	Thumb Knuckle Brewing	Luxemburg, WI
4th Annual Review	Crooked Crab Brewing	Odenton, MD
5th Annual Review	Ravenna Brewing	Seattle WA
6th Annual Review	Strings Sports Brewery	Jacksonville, FL
7th Annual Review	Kauai Beer Company	Lihue, HI

Honorable Mentions: **Wizard Works Brewing** (Milwaukee, WI), **Torch & Crown Brewing** (Manhattan, NY), **Off Color Brewing** (Chicago, IL), **Deschutes Brewery** (Portland, OR)

BEST TAP HANDLES		Location	Design
1st Annual Review	Tennessee Brew Works	Nashville, TN	Guitar necks
2nd Annual Review	Bare Bones Brewery	Oshkosh, WI	Dog bones
3rd Annual Review	Central Waters Brewing	Amherst, WI	Herons
4th Annual Review	Falling Knife Brewing	Minneapolis, MN	Knives
5th Annual Review	Frog Level Brewing	Waynesville, NC	Frogs sitting on top of levels
6th Annual Review	Chandeleur Island Brewing	Gulfport, MS	Fishing rods
7th Annual Review	Commerce Street Brewery Hotel	Mineral Point, WI	Looks like the building with a dog sitting on top

Honorable Mentions: **Gatlinburg** (Gatlinburg, TN; Bears holding a beer), **Fiction** (Denver, CO; book spines), **Revolution** (Chicago, IL; colorful fists), **Delta Beer Lab** (Madison, WI; science beakers)

BEST BEER CITY (LARGE)	
1st Annual Review	Chicago, IL
2nd Annual Review	San Diego, CA
3rd Annual Review	St. Louis, MO
4th Annual Review	Austin, TX
5th Annual Review	Denver, CO
6th Annual Review	New York, NY
7th Annual Review	Anchorage, AK

Honorable Mentions: Portland (OR), Seattle (WA), Cincinnati (OH), Milwaukee (WI)

BEST BEER CITY (SMALL)	
1st Annual Review	Portland, ME
2nd Annual Review	Madison, WI
3rd Annual Review	Duluth, MN
4th Annual Review	Asheville, NC
5th Annual Review	Longmont, CO
6th Annual Review	Charleston, WV
7th Annual Review	Juneau, AK

Honorable Mentions: Richmond (VA), Grand Rapids (MI), Charleston (SC), Burlington (VT)

BEST BEER EXPERIENCE	
1st Annual Review	Boston Beer Co. tour with my dad
2nd Annual Review	Tour at Sierra Nevada in Chico, CA
3rd Annual Review	500th brewery visit at Central Waters
4th Annual Review	Beercation in Austin, TX with my dad
5th Annual Review	1,000th brewery visit at Bierstadt Lagerhaus
6th Annual Review	Podcast at Butchertown Brewing with David McKinney
7th Annual Review	Alaska trip to hit milestone of visiting a brewery in all 50 states

Honorable Mentions: Great Taste of the Midwest, ABA Museum in Potosi, Great American Beer Festival, First beer festival (Bend Brewfest)

MOST INTERESTING BREWERY		Location
1st Annual Review	Earth Eagle Brewings	Portsmouth, NH
2nd Annual Review	White Labs Brewing	San Diego, CA
3rd Annual Review	Books & Brews	Zionsville, IN
4th Annual Review	Pretentious Beer Co.	Knoxville, TN
5th Annual Review	Pilot Project Brewing	Chicago, IL
6th Annual Review	Carillon Brewing	Dayton, OH
7th Annual Review	Commerce Street Brewery Hotel	Mineral Point, WI

Honorable Mentions: **Mobcraft Brewing** (Milwaukee, WI), **Potosi Brewery** (Potosi, WI), **The Big Texan Brewery** (Amarillo, TX), **Dos Luces Brewing** (Denver, CO)

BEST BEER NAME		Beer Name	Beer Style
1st Annual Review	Southern Swells Brewing: Jacksonville Beach, FL	*Not the Gumdrop Buttons*	Mixed Berry Berliner Weisse
2nd Annual Review	Woods Boss Brewing: Denver, CO	*The Dreams That Stuff Are Made Of*	Saison
3rd Annual Review	Kettlehouse Brewing: Missoula, MT	*Fresh Bongwater*	Hemp Pale Ale
4th Annual Review	Aslin Brewing: Alexandria, VA	*Man-eating Toaster*	Cinnamon Toast Crunch Inspired IPA
5th Annual Review	Off Color Brewing: Chicago, IL	*Chicago Craft Gin Week is a Thing*	American Wild Ale aged in Gin Barrels
6th Annual Review	TLC Brew Works: Holy Cross, IA	*Jan's 401K*	Maple Brown Ale
7th Annual Review	Barnaby Brewing: Juneau, AK	*The Goods From The Woods*	Spruce Tip Pale Ale

Honorable Mentions: **Grand Rapids Brewing**: Grand Rapids, MI (*Sportsball Contest Watching Drink*; American Light Lager), **Servaes Brewing**: Shawnee, KS: (*Like Butterflies: Shark Attack*; Sour Witbier with blue raspberry, cherry, and orange), **Ghost Monkey Brewing**: Mt. Pleasant, SC (*Sparkles For Fluffy Unicorns*; Cotton Candy Sour), **Hourglass Brewing**: Orlando, FL (*Brown Beer Brown Beer What Do You See*; Brown Ale)

BEST LIGHTER STYLE BEER		Beer Name	Beer Style
1st Annual Review	Notch Brewing: Salem, MA	*Land Speed Record*	Session Pale Ale
2nd Annual Review	Latchkey Brewing: San Diego, CA	*San Diego 1915 Lager*	Pale Lager
3rd Annual Review	Castle Danger Brewing: Two Harbors, MN	*Castle Cream Ale*	Cream Ale
4th Annual Review	Bow and Arrow Brewing: Albuquerque, NM	*Denim Tux*	Blue Corn Pilsner
5th Annual Review	Chuckanut Brewery: Portland, OR	*Kolsch*	Kolsch
6th Annual Review	Wild East Brewing: Brooklyn, NY	*Patience & Gratitude 2023*	Foeder-lagered Czech Pilsner
7th Annual Review	Anchorage Brewing: Anchorage, AK	*Time For a Change*	Czech Pilsner

Honorable Mentions: **Bierstadt Lagerhaus**: Denver, CO (*Slow Pour Pils*; Pilsner), **Columbia Craft Brewing**: Columbia, SC (*Carolinian Blonde*; Blonde Ale), **Trve Brewing**: Denver, CO (*Happy Tuesday*; Light Lager with corn grits), **Halfway Crooks Beer**: Atlanta, GA (*Radix*; German Pilsner)

BEST IPA		Beer Name	Beer Style
1st Annual Review	The Alchemist Brewery: Stowe, VT	*The Crusher*	American Double IPA
2nd Annual Review	Mike Hess Brewing: San Diego, CA	*Into the Sunset*	Blood Orange IPA
3rd Annual Review	Lion's Tail Brewing: Neenah, WI	*Juice Cloud*	New England IPA
4th Annual Review	Sapwood Cellars Brewery: Columbia, MD	*Cheater Hops #18*	Double Dry-hopped IPA
5th Annual Review	Baere Brewing: Denver, CO	*C3(i)PA*	West Coast IPA
6th Annual Review	Phase Three Brewing: Lake Zurich, IL	*Pixel Density*	Hazy IPA
7th Annual Review	Hop Butcher For The World: Chicago, IL	*Through the Uprights*	Hazy Double IPA

Honorable Mentions: **Revelry Brewing**: Charleston, SC (*Lefty Lousey*; West Coast IPA), **Daredevil Brewing**: Speedway, IN (*Lift Off*; American IPA), **Lumen Beer Co**: Omaha, NE (*Bounce*; Hazy IPA), **Ex Novo Brewing**: Portland, OR (*Eliot IPA*; Northwest IPA)

BEST SOUR		Beer Name	Beer Style
1st Annual Review	Foam Brewers: Burlington, VT	*Stranger Things*	Smoked Apple Gose
2nd Annual Review	Great Notion Brewing: Portland, OR	*Blueberry Muffin*	Sour Ale with Oregon blueberries
3rd Annual Review	Speciation Artisan Ales: Grand Rapids, MI	*Meiotic Drive*	Foeder-aged Solera Sour with elderberries
4th Annual Review	Salud Cerveceria: Charlotte, NC	*Dairelyerweisse*	Berliner Weisse with cherry, raspberry, strawberry, blackberry, and pomegranate
5th Annual Review	Burns Family Artisan Ales: Denver, CO	*Genie^Logical V11: Blossoms I*	Mixed Culture Sour Ale with Colorado begonia, crabapple, and peony blossoms
6th Annual Review	Grimm Artisanal Ales: Brooklyn, NY	*Super Spruce*	Dry-hopped Gose with spruce tips
7th Annual Review	Anchorage Brewing: Anchorage, AK	*All Seeing*	Sour Ale with Alaskan blueberries

Honorable Mention: **Maplewood Brewery**: Chicago, IL (*Preservation*; Sour Foeder Raspberry), **New Glarus Brewing**: New Glarus, WI (*Raspberry Tart*; Wisconsin Fruit Ale), **Prairie Artisan Ales**: Oklahoma City, OK (*Rainbow Sherbet*; Sour Ale with rainbow sherbet flavors), **Russian River Brewing**: Santa Rosa, CA (*Supplication*; Sour Brown Ale aged in Pinot Noir barrels)

BEST DARK BEER		Beer Name	Beer Style
1st Annual Review	Trillium Brewing: Canton, MA	*Vanilla Pot & Kettle*	Oatmeal Porter with vanilla beans
2nd Annual Review	Bear Roots Brewing: Vista, CA	*Bear Cookie*	Chocolate Peanut Butter Milk Stout
3rd Annual Review	Perennial Artisan Ales: St. Louis, MO	*Intentionally Indulgent*	Imperial Stout with vanilla, coffee, chocolate sauce
4th Annual Review	Peabody Heights Brewing: Baltimore, MD	*Feasts of Trumpets*	Honey Cake Porter
5th Annual Review	Mountains Walking Brewery: Bozeman, MT	*Big Couloir Porter*	American Porter
6th Annual Review	Angry Chair Brewing: Tampa, FL	*Approbation*	Imperial Stout with hazelnut, maple, cinnamon, coffee, and vanilla
7th Annual Review	Firestone Walker Brewing: Marina Del Rey, CA	*Parabolita*	Barrel-aged Imperial Stout blended with Velvet Merlin Milk Stout and infused with Madagascar vanilla beans, cocoa nibs, and sea salt

Honorable Mentions: **Barrel Theory Beer Co**: St. Paul, MN (*Island Fudge*; Imperial Stout with cocao, vanilla, and hazelnut), **Mikerphone Brewing**: Elk Grove Village, IL (*Super Imperial Smells Like Bean Spirit*; Imperial Stout with coffee and maple syrup), **Grist House Craft Brewery**: Pittsburgh, PA (*Good Bird House*; Czech Dark Lager), **Eagle Park Brewing**: Milwaukee, WI (*Booze for Breakfast: French Toast*; Imperial Breakfast Stout with Vermont maple syrup, cascara cinnamon, and Madagascar vanilla)

BEST BEER (OTHER STYLES)		Beer Name	Beer Style
1st Annual Review	Maple Island Brewing: Stillwater, MN	*Maple Island Bock*	Bock with maple syrup
2nd Annual Review	Tannery Bend Beerworks: Napa, CA	*Capps*	Belgian Dubbel with candy cap mushrooms
3rd Annual Review	Blacklist Brewing: Duluth, MN	*Or de Belgique*	Belgian Strong Ale
4th Annual Review	Brink Brewing: Cincinnati, OH	*Hold the Reins*	English Mild
5th Annual Review	Fair Isle Brewing: Seattle, WA	*Leila*	Saison with Egyptian purple barley
6th Annual Review	Trace Brewing: Pittsburgh, PA	*Foeder Saison*	Foeder Saison
7th Annual Review	Barnaby Brewing: Juneau, AK	*The Goods From The Woods*	Spruce Tip Pale Ale

Honorable Mentions: **Vasen Brewing**: Richmond, VA (*Hefeweizen*; Hefeweizen), **Third Space Brewing**: Milwaukee, WI (*Unite the Clans*; Scottish-style Rye Ale), **Comrade Brewing**: Denver, CO (*Redcon*; Red Ale), **Sideward Brewing**: Orlando, FL (*Make it Dangerous*; English Pale Ale fermented on ex-bourbon barrel staves)

MOST SURPRISING BEER		Beer Name	Beer Style
1st Annual Review	Peticolas Brewing: Dallas, TX	*Velvet Hammer*	Imperial Red Ale
2nd Annual Review	Lion Bridge Brewing: Cedar Rapids, IA	*Compensation*	English Mild
3rd Annual Review	Earth Rider Brewing: Superior, WI	*Tap Shack*	Caribbean Lager with lime zest
4th Annual Review	Brightside Aleworks: Altoona, IA	*Enlighten-mint*	Mint Stout
5th Annual Review	Supermoon Beer Co.: Milwaukee, WI	*Wait Until Yesterday*	Red IPA
6th Annual Review	Two Roads Brewing: Stratford, CT	*Roadsmary's Baby*	Pumpkin Ale aged in rum barrels
7th Annual Review	Hilo Brewing: Hilo, HI	*Volcano Red Ale*	Red Ale

Honorable Mentions: **Mayflower Brewing**: Plymouth, MA (*John Barleycorn*; Cream Ale), **Occidental Brewing**: Portland, OR (*Kunstgreep*; Belgian Strong Dark Ale), **Cerebral Brewing**: Denver, CO (*Anomaly Detection*; Barrel-aged Festbier), **Gordon Biersch Brewing**: New Orleans, LA (*Golden Export Lager*; Helles Lager)

MOST SURPRISING BREWERY		Location
1st Annual Review	Right Proper Brewing	Washington DC
2nd Annual Review	Altitude Chophouse & Brewing	Laramie, WY
3rd Annual Review	Blacklist Brewing	Duluth, MN
4th Annual Review	Columbia Craft Brewing	Columbia, SC
5th Annual Review	Gideon's Brewing	Bismarck, ND
6th Annual Review	Georgia Beer Company	Valdosta, GA
7th Annual Review	Turnagain Brewing	Anchorage, AK

Honorable Mentions: **Bias Brewing** (Kalispell, MT), **Lion Bridge Brewing** (Cedar Rapids, IA), **Pint Nine Brewing** (La Vista, NE), **North Pillar Brewing** (Waukesha, WI)

MOST INTERESTING BEER	Beer Name	Beer Style
1st Annual Review	Hidden Cove Brewing: Wells, ME	*Jali*	Tequila Barrel-aged Sour Ale with charred jalapenos, dried apricots, and agave nectar
2nd Annual Review	Stone Brewing: Escondido, CA	*Pineapple Chili Gose*	Pineapple Chili Gose
3rd Annual Review	Lion's Tail Brewing: Neenah, WI	*Summer Slushee*	Smoothie Sour with blackberries and Meyer lemon
4th Annual Review	Boiler Brewing: Lincoln, NE	*Hot Sauce Barrel-aged Chili & Cinnamon Roll Pastry Sour*	Bourbon barrel-aged Sour with maple syrup, hot sauce, cream cheese, vanilla, and cinnamon
5th Annual Review	Dos Luces Brewery: Denver, CO	*Azteca Pulque*	Pulque (traditional Mayan beverage) with three types of chocolate and cayenne pepper
6th Annual Review	Spanish Marie Brewery: Miami, FL	*Cuba Libre*	Sour Ale conditioned with rum and Coke and lime ice cream
7th Annual Review	Herbiery Taproom: Madison, WI	*Under Tree*	Ale with roasted dandelion root, burdock root, sarsaparilla root, licorice root, ginger root, and nutmeg

Honorable Mentions: **Earth Eagle Brewings**: Portsmouth, NH (*Chaga Groove*; Gruit w/chaga and maple syrup), **DSSOLVR**: Asheville, NC (*Wicked Engine*; Pumpkin Spice Cheesecake Sour), **Hopsquad Brewing**: Austin, TX (*Pepito's Pepino*; Cucumber Basil Wheat Ale), **Hysteria Brewing**: Columbia, MD (*Life's a Shrimp, Peel It*; Gose with Cajun spices, shrimp, and lemon)

BEST BREWERY (LARGE)		Location
1st Annual Review	New Glarus Brewing	New Glarus, WI
2nd Annual Review	Stone Brewing	Escondido, CA
3rd Annual Review	Boulevard Brewing	Kansas City, MO
4th Annual Review	Dogfish Head Brewery	Milton, DE
5th Annual Review	Deschutes Brewery	Portland, OR
6th Annual Review	Brooklyn Brewery	Brooklyn, NY
7th Annual Review	Firestone Walker Brewing	Marina del Rey, CA

Honorable Mentions: **Allagash Brewing** (Portland, ME), **Sierra Nevada Brewing** (Chico, CA/Mills River, NC), **Jester King Brewery** (Austin, TX), **Russian River Brewing** (Santa Rosa, CA)

BEST BREWERY (SMALL)		Location
1st Annual Review	Burial Beer Company	Asheville, NC
2nd Annual Review	Great Notion Brewing	Portland, OR
3rd Annual Review	Perennial Artisan Ales	St. Louis, MO
4th Annual Review	Bow & Arrow Brewing	Albuquerque, NM
5th Annual Review	Mountains Walking Brewery	Bozeman, MT
6th Annual Review	Trace Brewing	Pittsburgh, PA
7th Annual Review	Anchorage Brewing	Anchorage, AK

Honorable Mentions: **Brink Brewing** (Cincinnati, OH), **Chuckanut Brewery** (Portland, OR), **Speciation Artisan Ales** (Comstock Park, MI), **Wild East Brewing** (Brooklyn, NY)

Statistics and Maps

FACTS AND FIGURES

- Number of breweries visited: 1,367
- Number of states: 50 (plus DC)
- Number of cities: 511

STATE-BY-STATE BREAKDOWN:

AK: 22	HI: 14	ME: 19	NJ: 27	SD: 3
AL: 7	IA: 45	MI: 14	NM: 6	TN: 38
AR: 3	ID: 4	MN: 72	NV: 7	TX: 33
AZ: 10	IL: 69	MO: 16	NY: 17	UT: 6
CA: 122	IN: 19	MS: 2	OH: 16	VA: 11
CO: 62	KS: 4	MT: 21	OK: 5	VT: 11
CT: 3	KY: 12	NC: 85	OR: 39	WA: 40
DE: 9	LA: 25	ND: 6	PA: 26	WI: 203
FL: 64	MA: 20	NE: 11	RI: 1	WV: 3
GA: 12	MD: 43	NH: 24	SC: 26	WY: 5
				DC: 5

MY MAPS

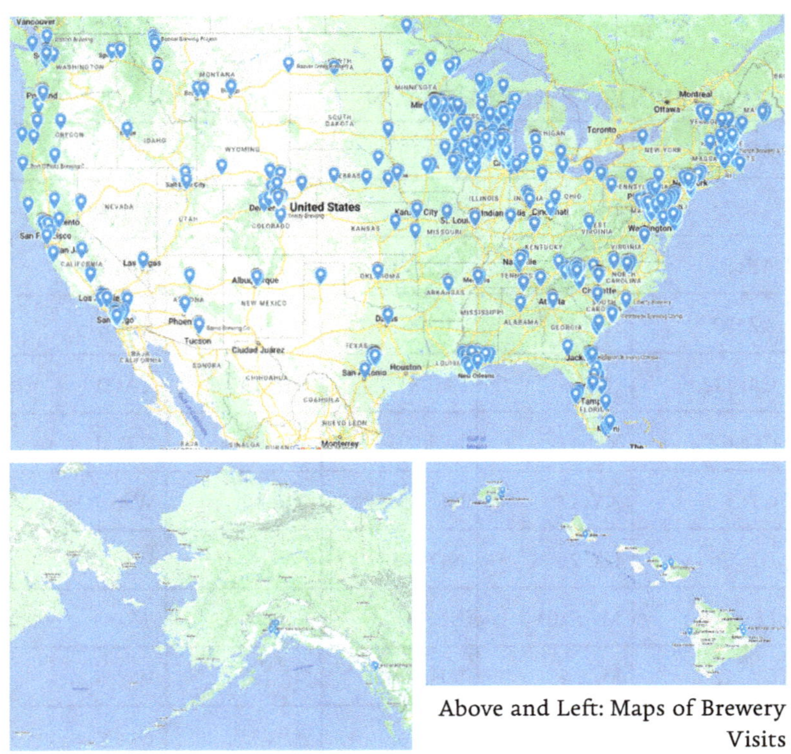

Above and Left: Maps of Brewery
Visits

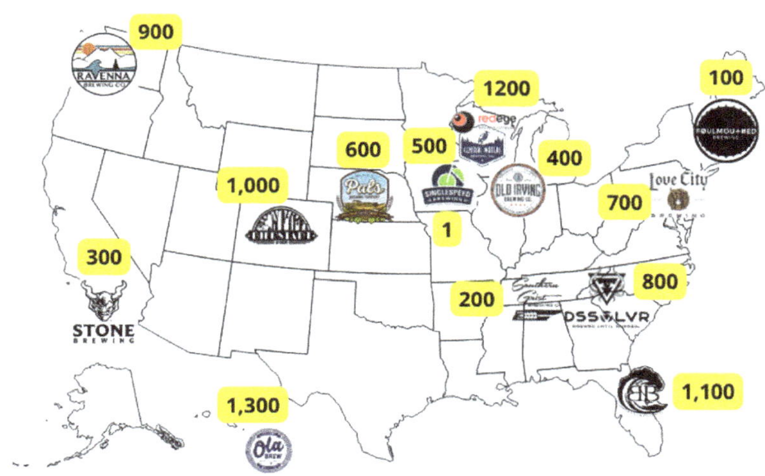

Milestone Brewery Visits

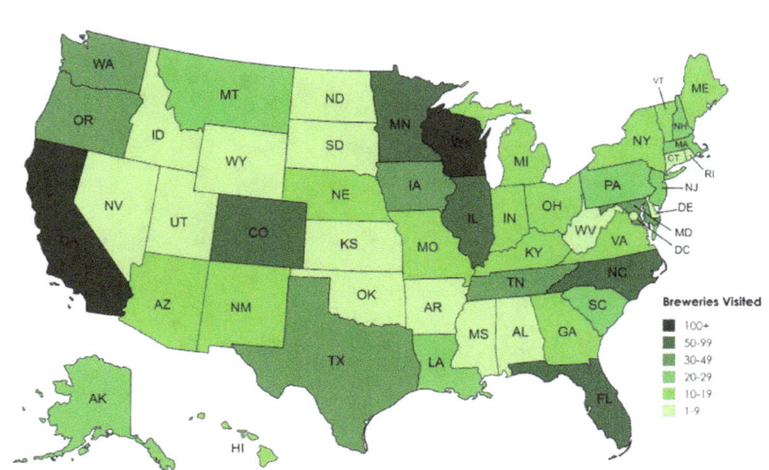

Brewery visits broken down by state

Flights Across America:
The Pictures

Octopi Brewing (Waunakee, WI)

Amorphic Brewing (Milwaukee, WI)

Amplified Aleworks (San Diego, CA)

Anchorage Brewing (Anchorage, AK)

Big Sky Brewing (Missoula, MT)

Blue Springs Brewing (Orange City, FL)

Brink Brewing (Cincinnati, OH)

Bow & Arrow Brewing (Albuquerque, NM)

Burial Beer Co. (Asheville, NC)

Centerpoint Brewing (Indianapolis, IN)

Chuckanut Brewery (Portland, OR)

CheezHead Brewing (Beloit, WI)

Code Beer Co. (Lincoln, NE)

Crooked Tooth Brewing (Tuscon, AZ)

Double Shift Brewing (Kansas City, MO)

Deviant Wolfe Brewing (Sanford, FL)

Ecliptic Brewing (Portland, OR)

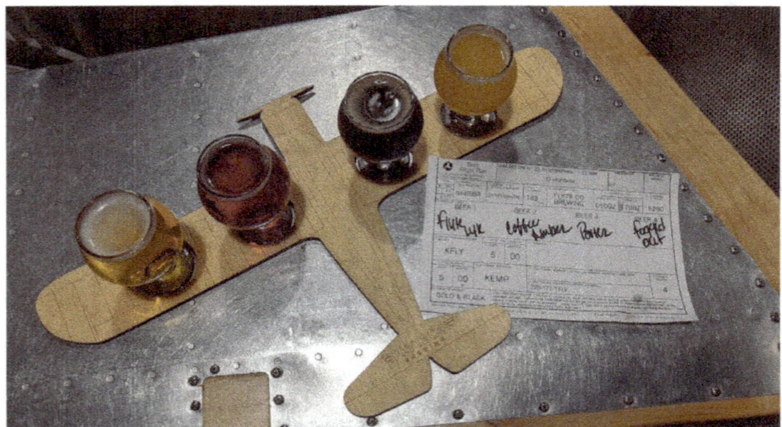

FlyteCo Brewing (Denver, CO)

Fremont Brewing (Seattle, WA)

Forbidden Peak Brewery (Juneau, AK)

Garrison City Beerworks (Dover, NH)

Grimm Artisanal Ales (Brooklyn, NY)

Haymarket Pub & Brewery (Chicago, IL)

HOMES Brewery (Ann Arbor, MI)

Highway 20 Brewing (Elizabeth, IL)

Imagine Nation Brewing (Missoula, MT)

Laughing Sun Brewing (Bismarck, ND)

Jailbreak Brewing (Laurel, MD)

Live Oak Brewing (Del Valle, TX)

Maquoketa Brewing (Maquoketa, IA)

Mikerphone Brewing (Elk Grove Village, IL)

Maui Brewing (Kihei, HI)

Mockery Brewing (Denver, CO)

Olde Hickory Brewery (Hickory, NC)

Port Orleans Brewing (New Orleans, LA)

Orange County Brewers (Orlando, FL)

Prairie Pride Brewing (Grand Island, NE)

Primal Brewery (Belmont, NC)

Rocky Reef Brewing (Woodruff, WI)

Radius Brewing (Emporia, KS)

Sacred Waters Brewing (Kalispell, MT)

Sockeye Brewing (Boise, ID)

Spiral Brewery (Hastings, MN)

Southern Grist Brewing (Nashville, TN)

StormBreaker Brewing (Portland, OR)

Sun King Brewery (Indianapolis, IN)

The Mitten Brewing (Grand Rapids, MI)

The Austin Beer Garden Brewing Company (Austin, TX)

Thumb Knuckle Brewing (Luxemburg, WI)

Two Blokes Brewing (Mt Pleasant, SC)

Two Tides Brewing (Savannah, GA)

Two Roads Brewing (Stratford, CT)

Väsen Brewing (Richmond, VA)

Whistle Hop Brewing (Fairview, NC)

2nd Shift Brewing (St. Louis, MO)

Aeronaut Brewing (Boston, MA)

BarrieHaus Beer Company (Tampa, FL)

BearWaters Brewing (Canton, NC)

BlackStack Brewing (St. Paul, MN)

Broken Bat Brewing (Milwaukee, WI)

Copper State (Green Bay, WI)

Deciduous Brewing (Newmarket, NH)

Eagle Park Brewing (Milwaukee, WI)

Ellipsis Brewing (Orlando, FL)

Eluvium Brewing (Weaverville, NC)

For The Love of God Brewing (Spokane, WA)

Infamous Brewing (Austin, TX)

Lazy Magnolia Brewing (Kiln, MS)

Left Hand Brewing (Longmont, CO)

Little Thistle Brewing (Rochester, MN)

Maine Beer Company (Freeport, ME)

Midwest Coast Brewing (Chicago, IL)

Moto Sonora Brewing (Tuscon, AZ)

Newark Local Beer (Newark, NJ)

Novo Brazil Brewing (Chula Vista, CA)

Other Half Brewing (Manhattan, NY)

Penguin City Brewing (Youngstown, OH)

Portsmouth Brewery (Portsmouth, NH)

Pretentious Beer Company (Knoxville, TN)

Pure Project (San Diego, CA)

Purpose Brewing & Cellars (Fort Collins, CO)

Roundhouse Brewery (Nisswa, MN)

Six Car Pub & Brewery (Amarillo, TX)

Spanish Marie Brewery (Miami, FL)

Switchback Brewing (Burlington, VT)

Tamarack Brewing (Lakeside, MT)

Templin Family Brewing (Salt Lake City, UT)

The Answer Brewpub (Richmond, VA)

The Tank Brewing (Miami, FL)

TLC Brew Works (Holy Cross, IA)

TrimTab Brewing (Birmingham, AL)

Waredaca Brewing (Laytonsville, MD)

Waverly Brewing (Baltimore, MD)

Black Shirt Brewing (Denver, CO)

Central Waters Brewing (Amherst, WI)

Bare Bones Brewery (Oshkosh, WI)

Chandeleur Island Brewing (Gulfport, MS)

Falling Knife Brewing (Minneapolis, MN)

Gatlinburg Brewing (Gatlinburg, TN)

Frog Level Brewing (Waynesville, NC)

Liquid Noise Brewing (Marysville, PA)

Revolution Brewing (Chicago, IL)

Delta Beer Lab (Madison, WI)

Footjoy Farm and Brewing (Cashton, WI)

Masthead Brewing (Cleveland, OH)

Revelry Brewing (Charleston, SC)

Stevens Point Brewery (Stevens Point, WI)

Bierstadt Lagerhaus (Denver, CO)

Carillon Brewing (Dayton, OH)

Broxton Brewery & Public House (Los Angeles, CA)

Foxtown Brewing (Mequon, WI)

Frey's Brewing (Mt Airy, MD)

Ministry of Brew (Baltimore, MD)

Mars Theatre Brewing (Mars Hill, NC)

Moontown Brewing (Whitestown, IN)

The Pike Brewing Company (Seattle, WA)

Trace Brewing (Pittsburgh, PA)

Wandering Leaf Brewing (St. Paul, MN)

Dead Bird Brewing (Milwaukee, WI)

Dees Brothers Brewery (Sanford, FL)

Draught Works (Missoula, MT)

Earthbound Beer (St. Louis, MO)

Great Revivalist Brewery (Clinton, IA)

H.H. Hinder Brewing (Waupaca, WI)

North 20 Brewing (Rosemount, MN)

Raices Brewing (Denver, CO)

Spacecat Brewing (Norwalk, CT)

Steinhardt Brewing (Frederick, MD)

Zony Mash Beer Project (New Orelans, LA)

Wild Air Beerworks (Asbury Park, NJ)

Cabin Creek Brewing (Georgetown, CO)

River Ridge Brewing (Bellevue, IA)

49th State Brewing (Anchorage, AK)

J. Leinenkugel's Barrel Yard (Milwaukee, WI)

Mahalo Aleworks (Makawao, HI)

MAP Brewery (Bozeman, MT)

Oasis Texas Brewing (Austin, TX)

Hollywood Brewery (Hollywood, FL)

Mountain Layers Brewing (Bryson City, NC)

About Atmosphere Press

Founded in 2015, Atmosphere Press was built on the principles of Honesty, Transparency, Professionalism, Kindness, and Making Your Book Awesome. As an ethical and author-friendly hybrid press, we stay true to that founding mission today.

If you're a reader, enter our giveaway for a free book here:

SCAN TO ENTER
BOOK GIVEAWAY

If you're a writer, submit your manuscript for consideration here:

SCAN TO SUBMIT
MANUSCRIPT

And always feel free to visit Atmosphere Press and our authors online at atmospherepress.com. See you there soon!

About the Author

JOEL GEIER has covered the craft beer scene since 2016 via social media, multiple podcasts, his website, and other freelance articles. He resides in Glendale, WI, but has lived in 14 states with his wife Rosa since they were married in 2015. After completing his master's degree in nonprofit management in 2019, he became a stay-at-home dad and is the proud father of Lily and Beau. He loves visiting breweries and sharing his experiences with others, which is culminating with his first book, *Flights Across America*.